MILITARY HISTORY FROM PRIMARY SOURCES

1914-1918
AN EYEWITNESS TO WAR

EDITED BY
BOB CARRUTHERS

Pen & Sword
MILITARY

This edition published in 2012 by
Pen & Sword Military
An imprint of
Pen & Sword Books Ltd
47 Church Street
Barnsley
South Yorkshire
S70 2AS

First published in Great Britain in 2012 in digital format by
Coda Books Ltd.

Copyright © Coda Books Ltd, 2012
Published under licence by Pen & Sword Books Ltd.

ISBN 978 1 78159 151 2

This book includes extracts from 'Over There' by Arnold Bennett originally
published in 1915 by George H. Doran Company, New York, 'Four Weeks in the
Trenches' by Fritz Kreisler originally published in 1915 by Boston and New York,
Houghton Mifflin Company, 'They Shall Not Pass' by Frank H. Simonds originally
published in 1916 by Doubleday, Page & Company, New York, 'An Onlooker in
France 1917-1919' by William Orpen originally published in 1921 by Williams and
Norgate, London.

A CIP catalogue record for this book is
available from the British Library

Printed and bound in Great Britain by
CPI Group (UK) Ltd, Croydon, CR0 4YY

Pen & Sword Books Ltd incorporates the Imprints of Pen & Sword Aviation, Pen &
Sword Family History, Pen & Sword Maritime, Pen & Sword Military, Pen &
Sword Discovery, Pen & Sword Politics, Pen & Sword Atlas, Pen & Sword
Archaeology, Wharncliffe Local History, Wharncliffe True Crime, Wharncliffe
Transport, Pen & Sword Select, Pen & Sword Military Classics, Leo Cooper, The
Praetorian Press, Claymore Press, Remember When, Seaforth Publishing and
Frontline Publishing

For a complete list of Pen & Sword titles please contact
PEN & SWORD BOOKS LIMITED
47 Church Street, Barnsley, South Yorkshire, S70 2AS, England
E-mail: enquiries@pen-and-sword.co.uk

CONTENTS

WAR SCENES ON THE WESTERN FRONT 5
   CHAPTER I: THE ZONE OF PARIS 5
   CHAPTER II: ON THE FRENCH FRONT....................19
   CHAPTER III: RUINS.....................................32
   CHAPTER IV: AT GRIPS.................................46
   CHAPTER V: THE BRITISH LINES 57
   CHAPTER VI: THE UNIQUE CITY 71

FOUR WEEKS IN THE TRENCHES 83
   PREFACE...84
   CHAPTER I 85
   CHAPTER II 97
   CHAPTER III...107

THEY SHALL NOT PASS 119
   CHAPTER I...119
   CHAPTER II 137
   CHAPTER III...151
   CHAPTER IV 161
   CHAPTER V 171

AN ONLOOKER IN FRANCE 183
   PREFACE...183
   CHAPTER I. TO FRANCE (APRIL 1917) 184
   CHAPTER II. THE SOMME (APRIL 1917)................188
   CHAPTER III. AT BRIGADE HEADQUARTERS
      AND ST. POL (MAY-JUNE 1917) 197
   CHAPTER IV. THE YPRES SALIENT
      (JUNE-JULY 1917) 203
   CHAPTER V. THE SOMME IN SUMMER-TIME
      (AUGUST 1917) 209

CHAPTER VI. THE SOMME (SEPTEMBER 1917) 215
CHAPTER VII. WITH THE FLYING CORPS
    (OCTOBER 1917) 224
CHAPTER VIII. CASSEL AND IN HOSPITAL
    (NOVEMBER 1917) 229
CHAPTER IX. WINTER (1917-1918) 236
CHAPTER X. LONDON (MARCH-JUNE 1918) 242
CHAPTER XI. BACK IN FRANCE
    (JULY-SEPTEMBER 1918) 250
CHAPTER XII. AMIENS (OCTOBER 1918) 260
CHAPTER XIII. NEARING THE END
    (OCTOBER 1918) 265
CHAPTER XIV. THE PEACE CONFERENCE............274
CHAPTER XV. PARIS DURING THE PEACE
    CONFERENCE 288
CHAPTER XVI. THE SIGNING OF THE PEACE 293

MORE FROM THE SAME SERIES 298

WAR SCENES ON THE WESTERN FRONT

BY ARNOLD BENNETT

CHAPTER I

THE ZONE OF PARIS

FROM the balcony you look down upon massed and variegated tree-tops as though you were looking down upon a valley forest from a mountain height. Those trees, whose hidden trunks make alleys and squares, are rooted in the history of France. On the dusty gravel of the promenade which runs between the garden and the street a very young man and a girl, tiny figures, are playing with rackets at one of those second-rate ball games beloved by the French petite bourgeoisie. Their jackets and hats are hung on the corner of the fancy wooden case in which an orange-tree is planted. They are certainly perspiring in the heavy heat of the early morning. They are also certainly in love. This lively dalliance is the preliminary to a day's desk-work. It seems ill-chosen, silly, futile. The couple have forgotten, if they ever knew, that they are playing at a terrific and long-drawn moment of crisis in a spot sacred to the finest civilisation.

From the balcony you can see, close by, the Louvre, with its sculptures extending from Jean Goujon to Carpeaux; the Church of St. Clotilde, where Cesar Franck for forty years hid his genius away from popularity; the railway station of the Quai d'Orsay, which first proved that a terminus may excite sensations as fine as those excited by a palace or a temple; the dome of the Invalides; the unique facades, equal to any architecture of modern times, to the north of the Place de la Concorde, where the Ministry of Marine has its home. Nobody who knows Paris, and understands what Paris has meant and still means to humanity, can regard the scene without the most exquisite sentiments of humility, affection, and gratitude. It is impossible to look at the plinths, the mouldings, the carving of the Ministry of Marine and not be thrilled by that supreme expression of national art.

And all this escaped! That is the feeling which one has. All this beauty was menaced with disaster at the hands of beings who comprehended it even less than the simple couple playing ball, beings who have scarcely reached the beginnings of comprehension, and who joined a barbaric ingenuousness to a savage cruelty. It was menaced, but it escaped. Perhaps no city was ever in acuter peril; it escaped by a miracle, but it did escape. It escaped because tens of thousands of soldiers in thousands of taxi-cabs advanced more rapidly than any soldiers could be expected to advance. "The population of Paris has revolted and is hurrying to ask mercy from us!" thought the reconnoitring simpletons in Taubes, when they noted beneath them the incredible processions of taxi-cabs going north. But what they saw was the Sixth Army, whose movement changed the campaign, and perhaps the whole course of history.

"A great misfortune has overtaken us," said a German officer the next day. It was true. Greater than he suspected.

The horror of what might have happened, the splendour of what did happen, mingle in the awed mind as you look over the city from the balcony. The city escaped. And the event seems vaster and more sublime than the mind can bear.

The streets of Paris have now a perpetual aspect of Sunday morning; only the sound of church-bells is lacking. A few of the taxi-cabs have come back; but all the auto-buses without exception are away behind the front. So that the traffic is forced underground, where the railways are manned by women. A horse-bus, dug up out of the past, jogs along the most famous boulevard in the world like a country diligence, with a fat, laughing peasant-woman clinging to its back-step and collecting fare-moneys into the immense pocket of her black apron. Many of the most expensive and unnecessary shops are shut; the others wait with strange meekness for custom.

But the provision shops and all the sturdy cheap shops of the poor go on naturally, without any self-consciousness, just as usual. The pavements show chiefly soldiers in a wild, new variety of uniforms, from pale blue to black, imitated and adapted from all sources, and especially from England—and widows and orphans. The number of young girls and women in mourning, in the heavy mourning affected by the Latin race, is enormous. This crape is the sole casualty list permitted by the French War Office. It suffices. Supreme grief is omnipresent; but it is calm, cheerful, smiling. Widows glance at each other with understanding, like initiates of a secret and powerful society.

Never was Paris so disconcertingly odd. And yet never was it more profoundly itself. Between the slow realisation of a monstrous peril escaped and the equally slow realisation of its power to punish, the French spirit, angered and cold, knows at last what the French spirit is. And to watch and share its mood is positively ennobling to the stranger. Paris is revealed under an enchantment, On the surface of the enchantment the pettinesses of daily existence persist queerly.

Two small rooms and a kitchen on a sixth floor. You could put the kitchen, of which the cooking apparatus consists of two gas-rings, in the roots of the orange-tree in the Tuileries gardens. Everything is plain, and stringently tidy; everything is a special item, separately acquired, treasured. I see again a water-colour that I did years ago and had forgotten; it lives, protected by a glazed frame and by the pride of possession. The solitary mistress of this immaculate home is a spinster sempstress in the thirties. She earns three francs a day, and is rich because she does not spend it all, and has never spent it all. Inexpressibly neat, smiling, philosophic, helpful, she has within her a contentious and formidable tiger which two contingencies, and two only, will arouse. The first contingency springs from any threat of marriage. You must not seek a husband for her; she is alone in the world, and she wants to be. The second springs from any attempt to alter her habits, which in her sight are as sacredly immutable as the ritual of an Asiatic pagoda.

Last summer she went to a small town, to which is attached a very large military camp, to help her sister-in-law in the running of a cafe.

The excursion was to be partly in the nature of a holiday; but, indefatigable on a chair with a needle, she could not stand for hours

7

on her feet, ministering to a sex of which she knew almost nothing.

She had the nostalgia of the Parisian garret. She must go home to her neglected habits. The war was waging. She delayed, from a sense of duty. But at last her habits were irresistible. Officers had said lightly that there was no danger, that the Germans could not possibly reach that small town. Nevertheless, the train that the spinster-sempstress took was the last train to leave. And as the spinster-sempstress departed by the train, so the sister-in-law departed in a pony-cart, with a son and a grandmother in the pony-cart, together with such goods as the cart would hold; and, through staggering adventures, reached safety at Troyes.

"And how did you yourself get on?" I asked the spinster-sempstress.

She answered:

"It was terrible. Ordinarily it is a journey of three or four hours. But that time it lasted three days and two nights. The train was crammed with refugees and with wounded. One was obliged to stand up. One could not move."

"But where did you sleep?"

"I did not sleep. Do I not tell you one was obliged to stand up? I stood up all the first night. The floor was thirty centimetres deep in filth. The second night one had settled down somewhat. I could sit."

"But about eating?"

"I had a little food that I brought with me."

"And drinking?"

"Nothing, till the second day. One could not move. But in the end we arrived. I was broken with fatigue. I was very ill. But I was home. The Boches drank everything in the cafe, everything; but the building was spared—it stood away from the firing. How long do you think the war will last?"

"I'm beginning to think it will last a long time."

"So they say," she murmured, glancing through the window at the prospect of roofs and chimney-cowls. "Provided that it finishes well..."

Except by the look in her eyes, and by the destruction of her once good complexion, it was impossible to divine that this woman's habits had ever been disturbed in the slightest detail. But the gaze and the complexion told the tale.

Next: the Boulevard St. Germain. A majestic flat, heavily and sombrely furnished. The great drawing-room is shut and sheeted with holland. It has been shut for twenty years. The mistress of this home is an aged widow of inflexible will and astounding activity. She gets up at five a.m., and no cook has ever yet satisfied her. The master is her son, a bachelor of fifty. He is paralysed, and always perfectly dressed in the English taste, he passes his life in a wheeled chair. The home is centred in his study, full of books, engravings, a large safe, telephone, theatrophone, newspapers, cigarettes, easy-chairs. When I go in, an old friend, a stockbroker, is there, and "thees" and "thous" abound in the conversation, which runs on investments, the new English loan, banking accounts in London, the rent moratorium in Paris, and the war. It is said that every German is a critic of war. But so is every Frenchman a critic of war. The criticism I now hear is the best spoken criticism, utterly impartial, that I have heard.

"In sum," says the grey-headed stockbroker, "there disengages itself from the totality of the facts an impression, tolerably clear, that all goes very well on the West front."

Which is reassuring. But the old lady, invincible after seven-and-a-half decades spent in the hard acquirement of wisdom, will not be reassured. She is not alarmed, but she will not be reassured. She treats the two men with affectionate malice as children. She knows that "those birds"—that is to say, the Germans—will never be beaten, because they are for ever capable of inventing some new trick.

She will not sit still. A bit of talk, and she runs off with the agility of a girl to survey her household; then returns and cuts into the discussion.

"If you are coming to lunch, Bennett," she says, "come before Monday, because on Monday my cook takes herself away, and as for the new one, I should dare to say nothing. . . . You don't know, Bennett, you don't know, that at a given moment it was impossible to buy salt. I mean, they sold it to you unwillingly, in little screws of paper. It was impossible to get enough. Figure that to yourself, you from London! As for chicory for the morning cafe-au-lait, it existed not. Gold could not buy it."

And again she said, speaking of the fearful days in September 1914:

"What would you? We waited. My little coco is nailed there. He cannot move without a furniture-van filled with things essential to his existence. I did not wish to move. We waited, quite simply. We waited for them to come. They did not come. So much the better That is all."

I have never encountered anything more radically French than the temperament of this aged woman.

Next: the luxury quarter—the establishment of one of those fashionable dressmakers whom you patronise, and whose bills startle all save the most hardened. She is a very handsome woman.

She has a husband and two little boys. They are all there. The husband is a retired professional soldier. He has a small and easy post in a civil administration, but his real work is to keep his wife's books. In August he was re-engaged, and ready to lead soldiers under fire in the fortified camp which Gallieni has evolved out of the environs of Paris; but the need passed, and the uniform was laid aside. The two little boys are combed and dressed as only French and American children are combed and dressed, and with a more economical ingenuity than American children. Each has a beautiful purple silk necktie and a beautiful silk handkerchief to match. You may notice that the purple silk is exactly the same purple silk as the lining of their mother's rich mantle hanging over a chair back.

"I had to dismiss my last few work-girls on Saturday," said the dressmaker. It was no longer possible to keep them. "I had seventy, you know. Now—not one. For a time we made considerably less than the rent. Now we make nothing. Nevertheless, some American clients have been very kind."

Her glance went round the empty white salons with their mirrors in sculptured frames. Naught of her stock was left except one or two fragile blouses and a few original drawings.

Said the husband:

"We are eating our resources. I will tell you what this war means to us. It means that we shall have to work seven or eight years longer than we had the intention to work. What would you?"

He lifted his arms and lowered the corners of his mouth. Then he

French Calvary going to the front, Paris

turned again to the military aspect of things, elaborating it.

The soldier in him finished:

"It is necessary, all the same, to admire these cursed Germans."

"Admire them!" said his wife sharply. "I do not appreciate the necessity. When I think of that day and that night we spent at home!" They live in the eastern suburbs of the city. "When I think of that day and that night! The cannon thundering at a distance of ten kilometres!"

"Thirty kilometres, almost thirty, my friend," the husband corrected.

"Ten kilometres. I am sure it was not more than ten kilometres, my friend."

"But see, my little one. It was at Meaux. Forty kilometres to Meaux. We are at thirteen. That makes twenty-seven, at least."

"It sounded like ten."

"That is true."

"It sounded like ten, my dear Arnold. All day, and all night. We could not go to bed. Had one any desire to go to bed? It was anguish.

11

The mere souvenir is anguish."

She kissed her youngest boy, who had long hair.

"Come, come!" the soldier calmed her.

Lastly: an interior dans le monde; a home illustrious in Paris for the richness of its collections—bric-a-brac, fans, porcelain, furniture, modern pictures; the walls frescoed by Pierre Bonnard and his compeers; a black marble balcony with an incomparable view in the very middle of the city. Here several worlds encountered each other: authors, painters, musicians, dilettanti, administrators. The hostess had good-naturedly invited a high official of the Foreign Office, whom I had not seen for many years; she did not say so, but her aim therein was to expedite the arrangements for my pilgrimages in the war-zone. Sundry of my old friends were present. It was wonderful how many had escaped active service, either because they were necessary to central administration, or because they were neutrals, or because they were too old, or because they had been declined on account of physical unfitness, reformes. One or two who might have come failed to do so because they had perished.

Amid the abounding, dazzling confusion of objects which it was a duty to admire, people talked cautiously of the war. With tranquillity and exactness and finality the high official, clad in pale alpaca and yellow boots, explained the secret significance of Yellow Books, White Books, Orange Books, Blue Books. The ultimate issues were never touched. New, yet unprinted, music was played; Schumann, though German enough, was played. Then literature came to the top. A novelist wanted to know what I thought of a book called "The Way of All Flesh," which he had just read. It is singular how that ruthless book makes its way across all frontiers. He also wanted to know about Gissing, a name new to him. And then a voice from the obscurity of the balcony came startlingly to me in the music-room:

"Tell me! Sincerely—do they hate the Germans in England? Do they hate them, veritably? Tell me. I doubt it. I doubt strongly."

I laughed, rather awkwardly, as any Englishman would.

The transient episode was very detrimental to literary talk.

Negotiations for a private visit to the front languished. The thing was arranged right enough, but it seemed impossible to fix a day actually starting. So I went to Meaux. Meaux had stuck in my ears. Meaux was in history and in romances; it is in Dumas. It was burnt by the Normans in the tenth century, and terrific massacres occurred outside its walls in the fourteenth century, massacres in which the English aristocracy took their full share of the killing. Also, in the seventeenth century, Bossuet was Bishop of Meaux. Finally, in the twentieth century, the Germans just got to Meaux, and they got no further. It was, so far as I can make out, the nearest point to Paris which they soiled.

I could not go even to Meaux without formalities, but the formalities were simple. The dilatory train took seventy minutes, dawdling along the banks of the notorious Marne. In an automobile one could have done the journey in half the time. An automobile, however, would have seriously complicated the formalities. Meaux contains about fourteen thousand inhabitants. Yet it seems, when you are in it, to' consist chiefly of cathedral. When you are at a little distance away from it, it seems to consist of nothing but cathedral. In this it resembles Chartres, and many another city in France.

We obtained a respectable carriage, with a melancholy, resigned old driver, who said:

"For fifteen francs, plus always the pourboire, I will take you to Barcy, which was bombarded and burnt. I will show you all the battlefield."

With those few words he thrilled me.

The road rose slowly from the canal of the Ourcq; it was lined with the most beautiful acacia trees, and through the screen of the acacias one had glimpses of the town, diminishing, and of the cathedral, growing larger and larger. The driver talked to us in faint murmurs over his shoulder, indicating the positions of various villages such as Penchard, Poincy, Crecy, Monthyon, Chambry, Varreddes, all of which will be found, in the future detailed histories of the great locust-advance.

"Did you yourself see any Germans?"

"Yes."

"Where?"

"At Meaux."

"How many?"

He smiled. "About a dozen." He underestimated the number, and the length of the stay, but no matter. "They were scouts. They came into the town for a few hours — and left it. The Germans were deceived. They might have got to Paris if they had liked. But they were deceived."

"How were they deceived?"

"They thought there were more English in front of them than actually there were. The head-quarters of the English were over there, at La Ferte-sous-Jouarre. The English blew up our bridge, as a measure of precaution."

We drove on.

"The first tomb," said the driver, nonchalantly, in his weak voice, lifting an elbow.

There it was, close by the roadside, and a little higher than ourselves. The grave was marked by four short, rough posts on which was strung barbed wire; a white flag; a white cross of painted wood, very simply but neatly made; a faded wreath. We could distinguish a few words of an inscription. "Comrades, 66th Territorials..." Soldiers were buried where they fell, and this was the tomb of him who fell nearest to Paris. It marked the last homicidal effort of the Germans before their advance in this region curved eastwards into a retreat. This tomb was a very impressive thing. The driver had thrilled me again.

We drove on. We were now in a large rolling plain that sloped gradually behind us southwards towards the Marne. It had many little woods and spinneys, and no watercourses. To the civilian it appeared an ideal theatre for a glorious sanguinary battle in which thousands of fathers, sons, and brothers should die violently because some hierarchy in a distant capital was suffering from an acute attack of swelled head. A few trenches here and there could still be descried, but the whole land was in an advanced state of cultivation. Wheat and oats and flaming poppies had now conquered the land, had overrun and possessed it as no Germans could ever do. The raw earth of the trenches struggled vainly against the tide of germination. The harvest was going to be good.

This plain, with its little woods and little villages, glittered with a careless and vast satisfaction in the sheets of sunshine that fell out of a blue too intense for the gaze.

We saw a few more tombs, and a great general monument or cenotaph to the dead, constructed at cross-roads by military engineers. The driver pointed to the village of Penchard, which had been pillaged and burnt by the enemy. It was only about a mile off, but in the strong, dazzling light we could distinguish not the least sign of damage. Then we came to a farm-house by the roadside. It was empty; it was a shell, and its roof was damaged. The Germans had gutted it. They had taken away its furniture as booty. (What they intended to do with furniture out of a perfectly mediocre farm-house, hundreds of miles from home, it is difficult to imagine.) Articles which it did not suit them to carry off they destroyed. Wine-casks of which they could not drink the wine, they stove in. ... And then they retreated.

This farm-house was somebody's house, just as your home is yours, and mine mine. To some woman or other every object in it was familiar. She glanced at the canister on the mantelpiece and said to herself: "I really must clean that canister to-morrow." There the house stood, with holes in its roof, empty. And if there are half a million similarly tragic houses in Europe to-day, as probably there are, such frequency does not in the slightest degree diminish the forlorn tragedy of that particular house which I have beheld.

At last Barcy came into view—the pierced remains of its church tower over the brow of a rise in the plain. Barcy is our driver's show-place. Barcy was in the middle of things. The fighting round Barcy lasted a night and a day, and Barcy was taken and retaken twice.

"You see the new red roofs," said the driver as we approached. "By those new red roofs you are in a state to judge a little what the damage was."

Some of the newly made roofs, however, were of tarred paper.

The street by which we entered had a small-pox of shrapnel and bullet-marks. The post office had particularly suffered: its bones were laid bare. It had not been restored, but it was ready to do any business that fell to be done, though closed on that afternoon. We turned a corner, and came upon the church. The work on the church was well up to the reported Teutonic average. Of its roof only the rafters were

15

French soldiers laying in personal trenches, c1915

left. The windows were all smashed, and their lead fantastically twisted. The west door was entirely gone; a rough grille of strips of wood served in its stead. Through this grille one could see the nave and altar, in a miraculous and horrible confusion. It was as if house-breakers had spent days in doing their best to produce a professional effect. The oak pews were almost unharmed. Immediately behind the grille lay a great bronze bell, about three feet high, covered with beautifully incised inscriptions; it was unhurt.

Apparently nothing had been accomplished, in ten months, towards the restoration of the church. But something was contemplated, perhaps already started. A polished steel saw lay on one of the pews, but there was no workman attached to it.

While I was writing some notes in the porch three little boys came up and diligently stared at me.

"What dost thou want?" I said sharply to the tallest.

"Nothing," he replied.

Then three widows came up, one young, one young and beautiful, one middle-aged.

We got back into the carriage.

"The village seems very deserted," I said to the driver.

"What would you?" he answered. "Many went. They had no home. Few have returned."

All around were houses of which nothing remained but the stone walls.

The Germans had shown great prowess here, and the French still greater. It was a village upon which rival commanders could gaze with pride. It will remember the fourth and the fifth of September 1914.

We made towards Chambry. Chambry is a village which, like Meaux, lies below the plain. Chambry escaped glory; but between it and Barcy, on the intervening slope through which a good road runs, a battle was fought. You know what kind of a battle it was by the tombs. These tombs were very like the others—an oblong of barbed wire, a white flag, a white cross, sometimes a name, more often only a number, rarely a wreath. You see first one, then another, then two, then a sprinkling; and gradually you perceive that the whole plain is dotted with gleams of white flags and white crosses, so that graves seem to extend right away to the horizon marked by lines of trees. Then you see a huge general grave. Much glory about that spot!

And then a tomb with a black cross. Very disconcerting, that black cross! It is different not only in colour, but in shape, from the other crosses. Sinister! You need not to be told that the body of a German lies beneath it. The whole devilishness of the Prussian ideal is expressed in that black cross. Then, as the road curves, you see more black crosses, many black crosses, very many. No flags, no names, no wreaths on these tombs. Just a white stencilled number in the centre of each cross. Women in Germany are still lying awake at nights and wondering what those tombs look like.

Watching over all the tombs, white and black without distinction, are notices: "Respect the Tombs." But the wheat and the oats are not respecting the tombs. Everywhere the crops have encroached on them, half-hiding them, smothering them, climbing right over them.

In one place wheat is ripening out of the very body of a German soldier.

Such is the nearest battlefield to Paris. Corporate excursions to it are forbidden, and wisely. For the attraction of the place, were it given play, would completely demoralise Meaux and the entire district.

In half an hour we were back at an utterly matter-of-fact railway station, in whose cafe an utterly matter-of-fact and capable Frenchwoman gave us tea. And when we reached Paris we had the news that a Staff Captain of the French Army had been detailed to escort us to the front and to show us all that could safely be seen.

Nevertheless, whatever I may experience, I shall not experience again the thrill which I had when the weak and melancholy old driver pointed out the first tomb. That which we had just seen was the front once.

CHAPTER II

ON THE FRENCH FRONT

W E were met at a poste de commandement by the officers in charge, who were waiting for us. And later we found that we were always thus met. The highest officer present—General, Colonel, or Commandant—was at every place at our disposition to explain things—and to explain them with that clarity of which the French alone have the secret and of which a superlative example exists in the official report of the earlier phases of the war, offered to the Anglo-Saxon public through Reuter. Automobiles and chauffeurs abounded for our small party of four. Never once at any moment of the day, whether driving furiously along somewhat deteriorated roads in the car, or walking about the land, did I lack a Staff officer who produced in me the illusion that he was living solely in order to be of use to me. All details of the excursions were elaborately organised; never once did the organisation break down. No pre-Lusitania American correspondent could have been more spoiled by Germans desperately anxious for his goodwill than I was spoiled by these French who could not gain my goodwill because they had the whole of it already. After the rites of greeting, we walked up to the high terrace of a considerable chateau close by, and France lay before us in a shimmering vast semicircle. In the distance, a low range of hills, irregularly wooded; then a river; then woods and spinneys; then vineyards—boundless vineyards which climbed in varying slopes out of the valley almost to our feet. Far to the left was a town with lofty factory chimneys, smokeless.

Peasant women were stooping in the vineyards; the whole of the earth seemed to be cultivated and to be yielding bounteously. It was a magnificent summer afternoon. The sun was high and a few huge purple shadows moved with august deliberation across the brilliant greens. An impression of peace, majesty, grandeur; and of the mild, splendid richness of the soil of France.

"You see that white line on the hills opposite," said an officer, opening a large-scale map.

I guessed it was a level road.

"That is the German trenches," said he. "They are five miles away. Their gun-positions are in the woods. Our own trenches are invisible from here."

It constituted a great moment, this first vision of the German trenches. With the thrill came the lancinating thought: "All of France that lies beyond that line, land just like the land on which I am standing, inhabited by people just like the people who are talking to me, is under the insulting tyranny of the invader." And I also thought, as the sense of distance quickened my imagination to realise that these trenches stretched from Ostend to Switzerland, and that the creators of them were prosecuting similar enterprises as far north-east as Riga, and as far southeast as the confines of Roumania: "The brigands are mad, but they are mad in the grand manner."

We were at the front.

We had driven for twenty miles along a very busy road which was closed to civilians, and along which even Staff officers could not travel without murmuring the password to placate the hostile vigilance of sentries. The civil life of the district was in abeyance, proceeding precariously from meal to meal. Aeroplanes woke the sleep. No letter could leave a post office without a precautionary delay of three days. Telegrams were suspect. To get into a railway station was almost as difficult as to get into paradise. A passport or a safe-conduct was the sine qua non of even the restricted liberty which had survived.

And yet nowhere did I see a frown nor hear a complaint. Everybody comprehended that the exigencies of the terrific military machine were necessary exigencies. Everybody waited, waited, in confidence and with tranquil smiles. Also it is misleading to say that civil life was in abeyance. For the elemental basis of its prosperity and its amenities continued just as though the lunatic bullies of Potsdam had never dictated to Vienna the ultimatum for Serbia. The earth was yielding, fabulously. It was yielding up to within a mile and a half of the German wire entanglements. The peasants would not neglect the earth. Officers remonstrated with them upon their perilous rashness. They replied:

"The land must be tilled."

When the German artillery begins to fire, the blue-clad women sink out of sight amid the foliage. Half an hour after it has ceased they cautiously emerge, and resume. One peasant put up an umbrella, but he was a man.

We were veritably at the front. There was, however, not a whisper of war, nor anything visible except the thin, pale line like a striation on the distant hills. Then a far-off sound of thunder is heard. It is a gun.

A faint puff of smoke is pointed out to us. Neither the rumble nor the transient cloudlet makes any apparent impression on the placid and wide dignity of the scene. Nevertheless, this is war. And war seems a very vague, casual, and negligible thing. We are led about fifty feet to the left, where in a previous phase a shell has indented a huge hole in the earth. The sight of this hole renders war rather less vague and rather less negligible.

"There are eighty thousand men in front of us," says an officer, indicating the benign shimmering, empty landscape.

"But where?"

"Interred—in the trenches."

It is incredible.

"And the other interred—the dead?"

I ask.

"We never speak of them. But we think of them a good deal."

Still a little closer to war. The parc du genie—engineers park. We inspected hills of coils, formidable barbed wire, far surpassing that of farmers, well contrived to tear to pieces any human being who, having got into its entanglement, should try to get out again.

One thought that nothing but steam-chisels would be capable of cutting it. Also stacks of timber for shoring up mines which sappers would dig beneath the enemy trenches. Also sacks to be filled with earth for improvised entrenching. Also the four-pointed contraptions called chevaux de frise, which—however you throw them—will always stick a fatal point upwards, to impale the horse or man who cannot or will not look where he is going. Even tarred paper, for keeping the weather out of trenches or anything else. And all these things in unimagined quantities.

Close by, a few German prisoners performing sanitary duties under a guard. They were men in God's image, and they went about on the assumption that all the rest of the war lay before them and that there was a lot of it. A General told us that he had mentioned to them the possibility of an exchange of prisoners, whereupon they had gloomily and pathetically protested. They very sincerely did not want to go back whence they had come, preferring captivity, humiliation, and the basest tasks to a share in the great glory of German arms. To me they had a brutalised air, no doubt one minor consequence of military ambition in high places.

Not many minutes away was a hospital—what the French call an ambulance de premiere ligne, contrived out of a factory. This was the hospital nearest to the trenches in that region, and the wounded come to it direct from the dressing-stations which lie immediately behind the trenches. When a man falls, or men fall, the automobile is telephoned for, and it arrives at the appointed rendezvous generally before the stretcher-bearers, who may have to walk for twenty or thirty minutes over rough ground. A wounded man may be, and has been, operated upon in this hospital within an hour of his wounding. It is organised on a permanent basis, for cases too serious for removal have, of course, to remain there. Nevertheless, these establishments are, as regards their staff, patients, and material, highly mobile.

One hospital of two hundred beds was once entirely evacuated within sixty minutes upon a sudden order. We walked through small ward after small ward, store-room after store-room, aseptic operating-room and septic operating-room, all odorous with ether, and saw little but resignation, and not much of that, for patients happened to be few. Yet the worn face of the doctor in charge showed that vast labours must have been accomplished in those sombre chambers.

In the very large courtyard a tent operating-hospital was established. The white attendants were waiting within in the pallid obscurity, among tables, glass jars, and instruments. The surgeon's wagon, with hot-water and sterilising apparatus, was waiting without.

The canvas organism was a real hospital, and the point about it was that it could move off complete at twenty-five minutes' notice and set

A line up of Nieuport aircraft on a snow-covered airfield in France.

itself up again in any other ordained location in another twenty-five minutes.

Another short ride, and we were in an aviation park, likewise tented, in the midst of an immense wheatfield on the lofty side of a hill.

There were six hangars of canvas, each containing an aeroplane and serving as a dormitory; and for each aeroplane a carriage and a motor—for sometimes aeroplanes are wounded and have to travel by road; it takes ninety minutes to dismount an aeroplane. Each corps of an army has one of these escadrilles or teams of aeroplanes, and the army as a whole has an extra one, so that, if an army consists of eight corps, it possesses fifty-four aeroplanes. I am speaking now of the particular type of aeroplane employed for regulating artillery fire. It was a young non-commissioned officer with a marked Southern accent who explained to us the secret nature of things. He was wearing both the Military Medal and the Legion of Honour, for he had done wondrous feats in the way of shooting the occupants of Taubes in mid-air. He got out one of the machines, and exhibited its tricks and its wireless apparatus, and invited us to sit in the seat of the flier. The weather was quite unsuitable for flying, but, setting four men to hold the machine in place, he started the Gnome motor and ran it up to two thousand revolutions a minute, creating a draught which bowed the fluttered wheat for many yards behind and blew hats off. And in the middle of this pother he continued to offer lucid and surprising explanations to deafened ears until his superior officer, excessively smart and looking like a cross between a cavalryman and a yachtsman, arrived on the scene swinging a cane.

It was natural that after this we should visit some auto-cannons expressly constructed for bringing down aeroplanes. In front of these marvels it was suggested to us that we should neither take photographs nor write down exact descriptions. As regards the latter, the Staff officers had reason to be reassured. No living journalist could have reproduced the scientific account of the sighting arrangements given to us in an esoteric yet quite comprehensible language by the high priest of these guns, who was a middle-aged artillery Captain. It lasted about twenty minutes. It was complete, final, unchallengeable. At intervals the artillery Captain himself admitted that such-and-such a part of the device was tres beau. It was. There was only one word of which I could not grasp the significance in that connection. It recurred. Several times I determined to ask the Captain what he meant us to understand by that word; but I lacked moral courage. I doubt whether in all the lethal apparatus that I saw in France I saw anything quite equal to the demoniac ingenuity of these massive guns. The proof of guns is in the shooting. These guns do not merely aim at Taubes: they hit them.

I will not, however, derogate from the importance of the illustrious "seventy-five." We saw one of these on an afternoon of much marching up and down hills and among woods, gazing at horses and hot-water douches, baths, and barbers' shops, and deep dug-outs called "Tipperary," and guns of various calibre, including the "seventy-five." The "seventy-five" is a very sympathetic creature, in blue-grey with metallic glints. He is perfectly easy to see when you approach him from behind, but get twenty yards in front of him and he is absolutely undiscoverable. Viewed from the sky, he is part of the forest. Viewed from behind, he is perceived to be in a wooden hut with rafters, in which you can just stand upright. We beheld the working of the gun, by two men, and we beheld the different sorts of shell in their delved compartments. But this was not enough for us.

We ventured to suggest that it would be proper to try to kill a few Germans for our amusement. The request was instantly granted.

"Time for 4,300 metres," said the Lieutenant quickly and sternly, and a soldier manipulated the obus.

It was done. It was done with disconcerting rapidity. The shell was put into its place. A soldier pulled a string. Bang! A neat, clean, not too loud bang! The messenger had gone invisibly forth. The prettiest part of the affair was the recoil and automatic swinging back of the gun. Lest the first shell should have failed in its mission, the Commandant ordered a second one to be sent, and this time the two artillerymen sat in seats attached on either side to the gun itself.

The "seventy-five" was enthusiastically praised by every officer present. He is beloved like a favourite sporting dog, and with cause.

At the side of the village street there was a bit of sharply sloping ground, with a ladder thrown on it to make descent easier. "This way," said one of the officers.

We followed him, and in an instant were in the communication trench. The change was magical in its quickness. At one moment we were on the earth; at the next we were in it. The trench was so narrow that I had to hold my stick in front of me, as there was no room to swing the arms; the chalky sides left traces on the elbows.

The floor was for the most part quite dry, but at intervals there were muddy pools nearly ankle-deep. The top of the trench was about level with the top of my head, and long grasses or chance cereals, bending down, continually brushed the face. An officer was uplifted for the rest of the day by finding a four-leaved clover at the edge of the trench. The day was warm, and the trench was still warmer. Its direction never ceased to change, generally in curves, but now and then by a sharp corner. We walked what seemed to be an immense distance, and then came out on to a road, which we were instructed to cross two by two, as, like the whole of the region, it was subject to German artillery. Far down this road we could see the outlying village for which we were bound. . . .

A new descent into the earth. We proceed a few yards, and the trench suddenly divides into three. We do not know which to take.

An officer following us does not know which to take. The guiding officer is perhaps thirty yards in front! We call. No answer. We climb out of the trench on to the surface desolation; we can see nothing, nothing whatever, but land that is running horribly to waste. Our friends are as invisible as moles. There is not a trace even of their track. This is a fine object-lesson in the efficacy of trenches. At length an officer returns and saves us. We have to take the trench on the extreme right. Much more hot walking, and a complete loss of the notion of direction.

Then we come out on to another portion of the same road at the point where a main line of railway crosses it. We are told to run to shelter. In the near distance a German captive balloon sticks up moveless against the sky. The main line of railway is a sorrowful sight. Its signal-wires hang in festoons. Its rails are rusting. The abandonment of a main line in a civilised country is a thing unknown, a thing contrary to sense, an impossible thing, so that one wonders whether one is not visiting the remains of a civilisation dead and definitely closed. Very strange thoughts pass through the mind. That portion of the main line cannot be used by the Germans because it is within the French positions, and it cannot be used by the French because it is utterly exposed to German artillery. Thus, perhaps ten kilometres of it are left forlorn to illustrate the imbecile brutality of an invasion. There is a good deal more trench before we reach the village which forms the head of a salient in the French line. This village is knocked all to pieces. It is a fearful spectacle. We see a Teddy-bear left on what remains of a flight of stairs, a bedstead buried to the knobs in debris, skeletons of birds in a cage hanging under an eave. The entire place is in the zone of fire, and it has been tremendously bombarded throughout the war.

Nevertheless, some houses still stand, and seventeen civilians— seven men and ten women—insist on remaining there. I talked to one fat old woman, who contended that there was no danger. A few minutes later a shell fell within a hundred yards of her, and it might just as well have fallen on the top of her coiffe, to prove finally to her the noble reasonableness of war and the reality of the German necessity for expansion.

The village church was laid low. In the roof two thin arches of the groining remain, marvellously. One remembers this freak of balance — and a few poor flowers on the altar. Mass is celebrated in that church every Sunday morning. We spoke with the cure, an extremely emaciated priest of middle age; he wore the Legion of Honour. We took to the trenches again, having in the interval been protected by several acres of ruined masonry. About this point geography seemed to end for me. I was in a maze of burrowing, from which the hot sun could be felt but not seen. I saw stencilled signs, such as "Tranchee de repli," and signs containing numbers. I saw a sign over a door: "Guetteur de jour et de nuit" — watcher by day and by night.

"Anybody in there?"

"Certainly."

The door was opened. In the gloom a pale man stood rather like a ghost, almost as disconcerting as a ghost, watching. He ignored us, and kept on watching.

Then through a hole I had a glimpse of an abandoned road, where no man might live, and beyond it a vast wire entanglement. Then we curved, and I was in an open place, a sort of redoubt contrived out of little homes and cattle-stables. I heard irregular rifle-fire close by, but I could not see who was firing I was shown the machine-gun chamber, and the blind which hides the aperture for the muzzle was lifted, but only momentarily. I was shown, too, the deep underground refuges to which every body takes in case of a heavy bombardment. Then we were in the men's quarters, in houses very well protected by advance walls to the north, and at length we saw some groups of men.

"Bonjour, les poilus!"

This from the Commandant himself, with jollity. The Commandant had a wonderful smile, which showed bright teeth, and his gestures were almost as quick as those of his Lieutenant, whom the regiment had christened "The Electric Man."

The soldiers saluted. This salute was so proud, so eager, that it might have brought tears to the eyes. The soldiers stood up very straight, but not at all stiffly. I noticed one man, because I could not notice them all. He threw his head back, and slightly to one side, and his brown beard stuck out. His eyes sparkled. Every muscle was taut. He seemed to be saying, "My Commandant, I know my worth; I am utterly yours—you won't get anything better." A young officer said to me that these men had in them a wild beast and an angel. It was a good saying, and I wished I had thought of it myself.

This regiment had been in this village since the autumn. It had declined to be relieved. It seemed absolutely fresh.

One hears that individual valour is about the same in all armies— everywhere very high. Events appear to have justified the assertion.

German valour is astounding. I have not seen any German regiment, but I do not believe that there are in any German regiment any men equal to these men. After all, ideas must count, and these men know that they are defending an outraged country, while the finest German soldier knows that he is outraging it.

The regiment was relatively very comfortable. It had plenty of room.

It had made a little garden, with little terra-cotta statues. It possessed also a gymnasium ground, where we witnessed some excellent high jumping; and—more surprising—a theatre, with stage, dressing-room, and women's costumes.

The summit of our excitement was attained when we were led into the first-line trench.

"Is this really the first-line trench?"

"It is."

Well, the first-line trench, very remarkably swept and dusted and spotless—as were all the trenches beyond the communication trench— was not much like a trench. It was like a long wooden gallery. Its sides were of wood, its ceiling was of wood, its floor was of wood. The carpentry, though not expert, was quite neat; and we were told that not a single engineer had ever been in the position, which, nevertheless, is reckoned to be one of the most ingenious on the whole front. The gallery is rather dark, because it is lighted only by the loop-holes. These loop-holes are about eight inches square, and more than eight inches deep, because they must, of course, penetrate the outer earthwork. A couple of inches from the bottom a strong wire is fixed across them. At night the soldier puts his gun under this wire, so that he may not fire too high.

The loop-holes are probably less than a yard apart, allowing enough space in front of each for a man to move comfortably. Beneath the loop-holes runs a wooden platform for the men to stand on. Behind the loop-holes, in the ceiling, are large hooks to hang guns on.

Many of the loop-holes are labelled with men's names, written in a good engrossing hand; and between the loop-holes, and level with them, are pinned coloured postcards and photographs of women, girls, and children. Tucked conveniently away in zinc cases underground are found zinc receptacles for stores of cartridges, powders to be used against gas, grenades, and matches.

One gazes through a loop-hole. Occasional firing can be heard, but it is not in the immediate vicinity. Indeed, all the men we can see have stepped down from the platform in order to allow us to pass freely along it and inspect. Through the loop-hole can be distinguished a barbed-wire entanglement, then a little waste ground, then more barbed-wire entanglement (German), and then the German trenches, which are less than half a mile away, and which stretch round behind us in a semicircle.

"Do not look too long. They have very good glasses."

The hint is taken. It is singular to reflect that just as we are gazing privily at the Germans, so the Germans are gazing privily at us. A mere strip of level earth separates them from us, but that strip is impassable, save at night, when the Frenchmen often creep up to the German wire. There is a terrible air of permanency about the whole affair. Not only the passage of time produces this effect; the telephone-wire running along miles of communication-trench, the elaborateness of the fighting trenches, the established routine and regularity of existence—all these also contribute to it. But the air of permanency is fallacious. The Germans are in France.

Every day of slow preparation brings nearer the day when the Germans will not be in France. That is certain. An immense expectancy hangs over the land, enchanting it.

We leave the first-line trench, with regret. But we have been in it!

In the quarters of the Commandant, a farm-house at the back end of the village, champagne was served, admirable champagne. We stood round a long table, waiting till the dilatory should have arrived.

The party had somehow grown. For example, the cure came, amid acclamations. He related how a Lieutenant had accosted him in front of some altar and asked whether he might be allowed to celebrate the Mass. "That depends," said the cure. "You cannot celebrate if you are not a priest. If you are, you can." "I am a priest," said the Lieutenant. And he celebrated the Mass. Also the Intendant came, a grey-haired, dour, kind-faced man. The Intendant has charge of supplies, and he is cherished accordingly. And in addition to the Commandant, and the Electric Man, and our Staff Captains, there were sundry non-commissioned officers, and even privates.

We were all equal. The French Army is by far the most democratic institution I have ever seen. On our journeys the Staff Captains and ourselves habitually ate with a sergeant and a corporal. The corporal was the son of a General. The sergeant was a man of business and a writer. His first words when he met me were in English: "Monsieur Bennett, I have read your books." One of our chauffeurs was a well-known printer who employs three hundred and fifty men — when there is peace. The relations between officers and men are simply unique. I never saw a greeting that was not exquisite. The officers w ere full of knowledge, decision, and appreciative kindliness. The men were bursting with eager devotion.

This must count, perhaps even more than big guns.

The Commandant, of course, presided at the vin d'honneur. His glance and his smile, his latent energy, would have inspired devotion in a wooden block. Every glass touched every glass, an operation which entailed some threescore clinkings. And while we were drinking, one of the Staff Captains — the one whose English was the less perfect of the two — began to tell me of the career of the Commandant, in Algeria and elsewhere. Among other things, he had carried his wounded men on his own shoulders under fire from the field of battle to a place of safety. He was certainly under forty; he might have been under thirty-five.

Said the Staff Captain, ingenuously translating in his mind from French to English, and speaking with slow caution, as though picking his way among the chevaux de frise of the English language:

"There are—very beautiful pages—in his—military life."

He meant: "Il y a de tres belles pages dans sa carriere militaire." Which is subtly not quite the same thing.

As we left the farm-house to regain the communication trench there was a fierce, loud noise like this: ZZZZZ ssss ZZZZ sss ZZZZ. And then an explosion. The observer in the captive balloon had noticed unaccustomed activity in our village, and the consequences were coming. We saw yellow smoke rising just beyond the wall of the farmyard, about two hundred yards away. We received instructions to hurry to the trench. We had not gone fifty yards in the trench when there was another celestial confusion of S's and Z's. Imitating the officers, we bent low in the trench. The explosion followed.

"One, two, three, four, five," said a Captain. "One should not rise till one has counted five, because all the bits have not fallen. If it is a big shell, count ten."

We tiptoed and glanced over the edge of the trench. Yellow smoke was rising at a distance of about three lawn-tennis courts.

"With some of their big shells," said the Captain, "you can hear nothing until it is too late, for the reason that the shell travels more quickly than the sound of it. The sounds reach your ears in inverse order—if you are alive."

A moment later a third shell dropped in the same plot of ground.

And even a mile and a half off, at the other end of the communication trench, when the automobiles emerged from their shelter into the view of the captive balloon, the officers feared for the automobiles, and we fled very swiftly.

We had been to the very front of the front, and it was the most cheerful, confident, high-spirited place I had seen in France, or in England either.

CHAPTER III

RUINS

WHEN you go into Rheims by the Epernay road, the life of the street seems to be proceeding as usual, except that octroi formalities have been abolished. Women, some young and beautiful, stare nonchalantly as the car passes. Children are playing and shrieking in the sunshine; the little cafes and shops keep open door; the baker is busy; middle-aged persons go their ways in meditation upon existence.

It is true there are soldiers; but there are soldiers in every important French town at all seasons of the year in peace-time.

In short, the spectacle is just that ordinarily presented to the poorer exterior thoroughfares leading towards the centre of a city.

And yet, in two minutes, in less than two minutes, you may be in a quarter where no life is left. This considerable quarter is not seriously damaged—it is destroyed. Not many houses, but every house in it will have to be rebuilt from the cellars. This quarter is desolation. Large shops, large houses, small shops, and small houses have all been treated alike. The facade may stand, the roof may have fallen in entirely or only partially, floors may have disappeared altogether or may still be clinging at odd angles to the walls—the middle of every building is the same: a vast heap of what once was the material of a home or a business, and what now is foul rubbish. In many instances the shells have revealed the functioning of the home at its most intimate, and that is seen which none should see. Indignation rises out of the heart. Amid stacks of refuse you may distinguish a bath, a magnificent fragment of mirror, a piece of tapestry, a saucepan. In a funeral shop wreaths still hang on their hooks for sale. Telephone and telegraph wires depend in a loose tangle from the poles. The clock of the Protestant church has stopped at a quarter to six. The shells have been freakish. In one building a shell harmlessly made a hole in the courtyard large enough to bury every commander of a German army; another shell—a 210 mm.—went through an inner wall and opened up the cellars by destroying 150 square feet of ground-floor: ten people were in the cellars, and none was hurt. Uninjured signs of cafes and shops, such as "The Good Hope," "The Success of the Day," meet your gaze with sardonic calm.

The inhabitants of this quarter, and of other quarters in Rheims, have gone. Some are dead. Others are picnicking in Epernay, Paris, elsewhere. They have left everything behind them, and yet they have left nothing. Each knows his lot in the immense tragedy.

Nobody can realise the whole of the tragedy. It defies the mind; and, moreover, the horror of it is allayed somewhat by the beautiful forms which ruin—even the ruin of modern ugly architecture— occasionally takes. The effect of the pallor of a bedroom wall-paper against smoke-blackened masonry, where some corner of a house sticks up like a tall, serrated column out of the confusion, remains obstinately in the memory, symbolising, somehow, the grand German deed.

For do not forget that this quarter accurately represents what the Germans came out of Germany into France deliberately to do. This material devastation, this annihilation of effort, hope, and love, this substitution of sorrow for joy—is just what plans and guns were laid for, what the worshipped leaders of the Fatherland prepared with the most wanton and scientific solicitude. It is desperately cruel. But it is far worse than cruel—it is idiotic in its immense futility. The perfect idiocy of the thing overwhelms you. And to your reason it is monstrous that one population should overrun another with murder and destruction from political covetousness as that two populations should go to war concerning a religious creed. Indeed, it is more monstrous. It is an obscene survival, a phenomenon that has strayed through some negligence of fate, into the wrong century.

Strange, in an adjoining quarter, partly but not utterly destroyed, a man is coming home in a cab with luggage from the station, and the servant-girl waits for him at the house-door. And I heard of a case where a property-owner who had begun to build a house just before the war has lately resumed building operations. In the Esplanade Ceres the fountain is playing amid all the ravage; and the German trenches, in that direction, are not more than two miles away.

It is quite impossible for any sane man to examine the geography of the region of destruction which I have so summarily described without being convinced that the Germans, in shelling it, were simply aiming at the Cathedral. Tracing the streets affected, one can follow distinctly the process of their searching for the precise range of the Cathedral. Practically the whole of the damage is concentrated on the line of the Cathedral.

But the Cathedral stands.

Its parvis is grass-grown; the hotels on the parvis are heavily battered, and if they are not destroyed it is because the Cathedral sheltered them; the Archbishop's palace lies in fragments; all around is complete ruin. But the Cathedral stands, high above the level of disaster, a unique target, and a target successfully defiant.

The outer roof is quite gone; much masonry is smashed; some of the calcined statues have exactly the appearance of tortured human flesh. But in its essence, and in its splendid outlines, the building remains—apparently unconquerable. The towers are particularly serene and impressive. The deterioration is, of course, tremendously severe. Scores, if not hundreds, of statues, each of which was a masterpiece, are spoilt; great quantities of carving are defaced; quite half the glass is irremediably broken; the whole of the interior non-structural decoration is destroyed. But the massiveness of the Cathedral has withstood German shrapnel. The place will never be the same again, or nearly the same.

Nevertheless, Rheims Cathedral triumphantly exists.

The Germans use it as a vent for their irritation. When things go wrong for them at other parts of the front, they shell Rheims Cathedral. It has absolutely no military interest, but it is beloved by civilised mankind, and therefore is a means of offence. The French tried to remove some of the glass, utilising an old scaffolding. At once the German shells came. Nothing was to be saved that shrapnel could destroy. Shrapnel is futile against the body of the Cathedral, as is proved by the fact that 3,000 shells have fallen on or near it in a day and a night. If the Germans used high-explosive, one might believe that they had some deep religious aim necessitating the non-existence of the Cathedral. But they do not use high-explosive here. Shrapnel

"A" Company of the 4th Battalion, Royal Fusiliers (9th Brigade, 3rd Division) on 22 August, 1914, resting in the square at Mons, Belgium, the day before the Battle of Mons. Minutes after this photo was taken the company moved into position at Nimy on the bank of the Mons-Condé Canal.

merely and uselessly torments.

When I first saw the Cathedral I was told that there had been calm for several days. I know that German agents in neutral countries constantly deny that the Cathedral is now shelled. When I saw the Cathedral again the next morning, five shells had just been aimed at it. I inspected the hole excavated by a 155-mm. shell at the foot of the eastern extremity, close to the walls. This hole was certainly not there when I made the circuit of the Cathedral on the previous evening. It came into existence at 6.40 a.m., and I inspected it at 8.20 a.m., and a newspaper boy offered me that morning's paper on the very edge of it. A fragment of shell, picked up warm by the architect in charge of the Cathedral and given to me, is now in my pocket.

We had a luncheon party at Rheims, in a certain hotel. This hotel had been closed for a time, but the landlady had taken heart again.

The personnel appeared to consist solely of the landlady and a relative. Both women were in mourning. They served us themselves, and the meal was excellent, though one could get neither soda-water nor cigars. Shells had greeted the city a few hours earlier, but their effect had been only material; they are entirely ignored by the steadfast inhabitants, who do their primitive business in the desolated, paralysed organism with an indifference which is as resigned as it is stoic. Those ladies might well have been blown to bits as they crossed the courtyard bearing a dish of cherries or a bottle of wine. The sun shone steadily on the rich foliage of the street, and dogs and children rollicked mildly beneath the branches. Several officers were with us, including two Staff officers. These officers, not belonging to the same unit, had a great deal to tell each other and us: so much, that the luncheon lasted nearly two hours. Some of them had been in the retreat, in the battles of the Marne and of the Aisne, and in the subsequent trench fighting; none had got a scratch. Of an unsurpassed urbanity and austerity themselves, forming part of the finest civilisation which this world has yet seen, thoroughly appreciative of the subtle and powerful qualities of the race to which they belong, they exhibited a chill and restrained surprise at the manners of the invaders. One had seen two thousand champagne bottles strewn around a chateau from which the invaders had decamped, and the old butler of the house going carefully through the grounds and picking up the bottles which by chance had not been opened. The method of opening champagne, by the way, was a stroke of the sabre on the neck of the bottle. The German manner was also to lay the lighted cigar on the finest table-linen, so that by the burnt holes the proprietors might count their guests. Another officer had seen a whole countryside of villages littered with orchestrions and absinthe-bottles, groundwork of an interrupted musical and bacchic fete whose details must be imagined, like many other revolting and scabrous details, which no compositor would consent to set up in type, but which, nevertheless, are known and form a striking part of the unwritten history of the attack on civilisation. You may have read hints of these things again and again, but no amount of previous preparation will soften for you the shock of getting them first-hand from eyewitnesses whose absolute reliability it would be fatuous to question.

What these men with their vivid gestures, bright eyes, and perfect phrasing most delight in is personal heroism. And be it remembered that, though they do tell a funny story about German scouts who, in order to do their work, painted themselves the green of trees—and then, to complete the illusion, when they saw a Frenchman began to tremble like leaves—they give full value to the courage of the invaders. But, of course, it is the courage of Frenchmen that inspires their narrations. I was ever so faintly surprised by their candid and enthusiastic appreciation of the heroism of the auxiliary services. They were lyrical about engine-drivers, telephone-repairers, stretcher-bearers, and so on. The story which had the most success concerned a soldier (a schoolmaster) who in an engagement got left between the opposing lines, a quite defenceless mark for German rifles. When a bullet hit him, he cried, "Vive la France!" When he was missed he kept silent. He was hit again and again, and at each wound he cried, "Vive la France!" He could not be killed. At last they turned a machine-gun on him and raked him from head to foot. "Vive la———"

It was a long, windy, dusty drive to Arras. The straight, worn roads of flinty chalk passed for many miles through country where there was no unmilitary activity save that of the crops pushing themselves up. Everything was dedicated to the war. Only at one dirty little industrial town did we see a large crowd of men waiting after lunch to go into a factory. These male civilians had a very odd appearance; it was as though they had been left out of the war by accident, or by some surprising benevolence. One thought first, "There must be some mistake here." But there was probably no mistake. These men were doubtless in the immense machine.

After we had traversed a more attractive agricultural town, with a town hall whose architecture showed that Flanders was not very far off, the soil changed and the country grew more sylvan and delectable. And the sun shone hotly. Camps alternated with orchards, and cows roamed in the camps and also in the orchards.

And among the trees could be seen the blue draperies of women at work. Then the wires of the field-telephones and telegraphs on their elegantly slim bamboos were running alongside us. And once or twice, roughly painted on a bit of bare wood, we saw the sign: "Vers le Front." Why any sign should be necessary for such a destination I could not imagine. But perhaps humour had entered into the matter.

At length we perceived Arras in the distance, and at a few

kilometres it looked rather like itself: it might have been a living city.

When, however, you actually reach Arras you cannot be deceived for an instant as to what has happened to the place. It offers none of the transient illusion of Rheims. The first street you see is a desolation, empty and sinister. Grimy curtains bulge out at smashed windows. Everywhere the damage of shells is visible. The roadway and the pavements are littered with bits of homes. Grass flourishes among the bits. You proceed a little further to a large, circular place, once imposing. Every house in it presents the same blighted aspect. There is no urban stir. But in the brief intervals of the deafening cannonade can be heard one sound—blinds and curtains fluttering against empty window-frames and perhaps the idle, faint banging of a loose shutter. Not even a cat walks. We are alone, we and the small group of Staff officers who are acting as our hosts.

We feel like thieves, like desecrators, impiously prying. At the other side of the place a shell has dropped before a house and sliced away all its front. On the ground floor is the drawing-room. Above that is the bedroom, with the bed made and the white linen smoothly showing. The marvel is that the bed, with all the other furniture, does not slide down the sloping floor into the street. But everything remains moveless and placid. The bedroom is like a show. It might be the bedroom of some famous man exposed to worshipping tourists at sixpence a head. A few chairs have fallen out of the house, and they lie topsy-turvy in the street amid the debris; no one has thought to touch them. In all directions thoroughfares branch forth, silent, grass-grown, and ruined.

"You see the strong fortress I have!" says the Commanding Officer with genial sarcasm. "You notice its high military value. It is open at every end. You can walk into it as easily as into a windmill. And yet they bombard it. Yesterday they fired twenty projectiles a minute for an hour into the town. A performance absolutely useless! Simple destruction! But they are like that!"

So we went forward further into the city, and saw sights still stranger.

Of one house nothing but the roof was left, the roof made a triumphal arch. Everywhere potted plants, boxed against walls or suspended from window-frames, were freshly blooming. All the streets were covered with powdered glass. In many streets telegraph and telephone wires hung in thick festoons like abandoned webs of spiders, or curled themselves round the feet; continually one had to be extricating oneself from them. Continually came the hollow sound of things falling and slipping within the smashed interiors behind the facades. And then came the sound of a baby crying. For this city is not, after all, uninhabited. We saw a woman coming out of her house and carefully locking the door behind her. Was she locking it against shells, or against burglars? Observe those pipes rising through gratings in the pavement, and blue smoke issuing therefrom. Those pipes are the outward sign that such inhabitants as remain have transformed their cellars into drawing-rooms and bedrooms. We descended into one such home.

The real drawing-room, on the ground-floor, had been invaded by a shell. In that apartment richly-carved furniture was mixed up with pieces of wall and pieces of curtain under a thick layer of white dust.

But this underground home, with its arched roof and aspect of extreme solidity, was tidy and very snugly complete in all its arrangements, and the dark entrance to it well protected against the hazards of bombardment.

"Nevertheless," said the master of the home, "a 210-mm shell would penetrate everything. It would be the end."

He threw up his hands with a nonchalant gesture. He was a fatalist worthy of his city, which is now being besieged and ruined not for the first time. The Vandals (I mean the original Vandals) laid waste Arras again and again. Then the Franks took it. Then, in the ninth century, the Normans ravaged it; and then Charles the Simple; and then Lothair; and then Hugh Capet. In the fifteenth century Charles VI. besieged it for seven weeks, and did not take it. Under Louis XI.

it was atrociously outraged. It revolted, and was retaken by assault, its walls razed, its citizens expatriated, and its name changed.

Useless! The name returned, and the citizens. At the end of the fifteenth century it fell under Spanish rule, and had no kind of peace whatever until after another siege by a large French army, it was regained by France in 1640. Fourteen years later the House of Austria had yet another try for it, and the Archduke Leopold laid siege to the city. He lost 7,000 men, 64 guns, 3,000 horses, and all his transport, and fled. (Last August was the first August in two hundred and sixty years which has not witnessed a municipal fete in celebration of this affair.) Since then Arras has had a tolerably quiet time, except during the Revolution. It suffered nothing in 1870. It now suffers. And apparently those inhabitants who have stood fast have not forgotten how to suffer; history must be in their veins.

In the street where we first noticed the stove-pipes sprouting from the pavement, we saw a postman in the regulation costume of the French postman, with the regulation black, shiny wallet-box hanging over his stomach, and the regulation pen behind his ear, smartly delivering letters from house to house. He did not knock at the doors; he just stuck the letters through the empty window-frames.

He was a truly remarkable sight.

Then we arrived by a curved street at the Cathedral of St. Vaast. St. Vaast, who preached Christianity after it had been forgotten in Arras, is all over the district in the nomenclature of places. Nobody among the dilettanti has a good word to say for the Cathedral, which was built in the latter half of the eighteenth and the first half of the nineteenth centuries, and which exhibits a kind of simple baroque style, with Corinthian pillars in two storeys. But Arras Cathedral is the most majestic and striking ruin at the Front. It is superlatively well placed on an eminence by itself, and its dimensions are tremendous. It towers over the city far more imposingly than Chartres Cathedral towers over Chartres. The pale simplicity of its enormous lines and surfaces renders it better suited for the martyrdom of bombardment than any Gothic building could possibly be. The wounds are clearly visible on its flat facades, uncomplicated by much carving and statuary. They are terrible wounds, yet they do not appreciably impair the ensemble of the fane. Photographs and pictures of Arras Cathedral ought to be cherished by German commanders, for they have accomplished nothing more austerely picturesque, more religiously impressive, more idiotically sacrilegious, more exquisitely futile than their achievement here.

And they are adding to it weekly. As a spectacle, the Cathedral of

Rheims cannot compare with the Cathedral of Arras.

In the north transept a 325-mm. shell has knocked a clean hole through which a mastodon might wriggle. Just opposite this transept, amid universal wreckage, a cafe is miraculously preserved. Its glass, mugs, counters, chairs, and ornaments are all there, covered with white dust, exactly as they were left one night.

You could put your hand through a window aperture and pick up a glass. Close by, the lovely rafter-work of an old house is exposed, and, within, a beam has fallen from the roof to the ground. This beam is burning. The flames are industriously eating away at it, like a tiger gnawing in tranquil content at its prey which it has dragged to a place of concealment. There are other fires in Arras, and have been for some days. But what are you to do? A step further on is a greengrocer's shop, open and doing business.

We gradually circled round the Cathedral until we arrived at the Town Hall, built in the sixteenth century, very carefully restored in the nineteenth, and knocked to pieces in the twentieth. We approached it from the back, and could not immediately perceive what had happened to it, for later erections have clustered round it, and some of these still existed in their main outlines. In a great courtyard stood an automobile, which certainly had not moved for months. It was a wreck, overgrown with rust and pustules. This automobile well symbolised the desolation, open and concealed, by which it was surrounded. A touchingly forlorn thing, dead and deaf to the never-ceasing, ever-reverberating chorus of the guns!

To the right of the Town Hall, looking at it from the rear, we saw a curving double row of mounds of brick, stone, and refuse.

Understand: these had no resemblance to houses; they had no resemblance to anything whatever except mounds of brick, stone, and refuse. The sight of them acutely tickled my curiosity. "What is this?"

"It is the principal street in Arras." The mind could picture it at once— one of those narrow, winding streets which in ancient cities perpetuate the most ancient habits of the citizens, maintaining their commercial pre-eminence in the face of all town-planning; a street leading to the Town Hall; a dark street full of jewellers' shops and ornamented women and correctness and the triumph of correctness; a street of the "best" shops, of high rents, of famous names, of picturesque signs; a street where the wheels of traffic were continually interlocking, but a street which would not, under any consideration, have widened itself by a single foot, because its narrowness was part of its prestige. Well, German gunnery has brought that street to an end past all resuscitation. It may be rebuilt— it will never be the same street.

"What's the name of the street?" I asked.

None of the officers in the party could recall the name of the principal business street in Arras, and there was no citizen within hail. The very name had gone, like the forms of the houses. I have since searched for it in guides, encyclopaedias, and plans; but it has escaped me—withdrawn and lost, for me, in the depths of history.

The street had suffered, not at all on its own account, but because it happened to be in the line of fire of the Town Hall. It merely received some portion of the blessings which were intended for the Town Hall, but which overshot their mark. The Town Hall (like the Cathedrals here and at Rheims) had no military interest or value, but it was the finest thing in Arras, the most loved thing, an irreplaceable thing; and therefore the Germans made a set at it, as they made a set at the Cathedrals. It is just as if, having got an aim on a soldier's baby, they had started to pick off its hands and feet, saying to the soldier: "Yield, or we will finish your baby." Either the military ratiocination is thus, or the deed is simple lunacy.

When we had walked round to the front of the Town Hall we were able to judge to what extent the beautiful building had monopolised the interest of the Germans. The Town Hall stands at the head of a magnificent and enormous arcaded square, uniform in architecture, and no doubt dating from the Spanish occupation. Seeing this square, and its scarcely smaller sister a little further on, you realise that indeed you are in a noble city. The square had hardly been touched by the bombardment. There had been no shells to waste on the square while the more precious Town Hall had one stone left upon another. From the lower end of the square, sheltered from the rain by the arcade, I made a rough sketch of what remains of the Town Hall. Comparing this sketch with an engraved view taken from exactly the same spot, one can see graphically what had occurred.

A few arches of the ground-floor colonnade had survived in outline.

Of the upper part of the facade nothing was left save a fragment of wall showing two window-holes. The rest of the facade, and the whole of the roof, was abolished. The later building attached to the left of the facade had completely disappeared. The carved masonry of the earlier building to the right of the facade had survived in a state of severe mutilation. The belfry which, rising immediately behind the Town Hall, was once the highest belfry in France (nearly 250 feet), had vanished. The stump of it, jagged like the stump of a broken tooth, obstinately persisted, sticking itself up to a level a few feet higher than the former level of the crest of the roof. The vast ruin was heaped about with refuse.

Arras is not in Germany. It is in France. I mention this fact because it is notorious that Germany is engaged in a defensive war, and in a war for the upholding of the highest civilisation. The Germans came all the way across Belgium, and thus far into France, in order to defend themselves against attack. They defaced and destroyed all the beauties of Arras, and transformed it into a scene of desolation unsurpassed in France, so that the highest civilisation might remain secure and their own hearths intact. One wonders what the Germans would have done had they been fighting, not a war of defence and civilisation, but a war of conquest and barbarism. The conjecture may, perhaps, legitimately occupy the brains of citizens.

In any case, the French Government would do well to invite to such places as Arras, Soissons, and Senlis groups of Mayors of the cities of all countries, so that these august magistrates may behold for themselves and realise in their souls what defensive war and the highest civilisation actually do mean when they come to the point.

Personally, I am against a policy of reprisals, and yet I do not see how Germany can truly appreciate what she has done unless an object-lesson is created for her out of one of her own cities. And she emphatically ought to appreciate what she has done. One city would suffice. If, at the end of the war, Cologne were left as Arras was when I visited it, a definite process of education would have been accomplished in the Teutonic mind. The event would be hard on

Cologne, but not harder than the other event has been on Arras.

Moreover, it is held, I believe, that the misfortunes of war bring out all that is finest in the character of a nation, and that therefore war, with its sweet accompaniments, is a good and a necessary thing. I am against a policy of reprisals, and yet—such is human nature— having seen Arras, I would honestly give a year's income to see Cologne in the same condition. And to the end of my life I shall feel cheated if Cologne or some similar German town is not in fact ultimately reduced to the same condition. This state of mind comes of seeing things with your own eyes.

Proceeding, we walked through a mile or two of streets in which not one house was inhabited nor undamaged. Some of these streets had been swept, so that at the first glance they seemed to be streets where all the citizens were indoors, reflecting behind drawn blinds and closed shutters upon some incredible happening. But there was nobody indoors. There was nobody in the whole quarter— only ourselves; and we were very unhappy and unquiet in the solitude. Almost every window was broken; every wall was chipped; chunks had been knocked out of walls, and at intervals there was no wall. One house showed the different paperings of six rooms all completely exposed to the gaze. The proprietor evidently had a passion for anthracite stoves; in each of the six fireplaces was an anthracite stove, and none had fallen. The post office was shattered.

Then the railway station of Arras! A comparatively new railway station, built by the Compagnie du Nord in 1898. A rather impressive railway station. The great paved place in front of it was pitted with shell-holes of various sizes. A shell had just grazed the elaborate facade, shaving ornaments and mouldings off it. Every pane of glass in it was smashed. All the ironwork had a rich brown rust. The indications for passengers were plainly visible. Here you must take your ticket; here you must register your baggage; here you must wait. We could look through the station as through the ribs of a skeleton. The stillness of it under the rain and under the echoes of the tireless artillery was horrible. It was the most unnatural, ghostly, ghastly railway station one could imagine. As within the station, so on the platforms. All the glass of the shelters for passengers was broken to little bits; the ironwork thickly encrusted.

The signals were unutterably forlorn in their ruin. And on the lines themselves rampant vegetation had grown four feet high—a conquering jungle. The defence of German soil is a mighty and a far-reaching affair. This was on July 7th, 1915.

CHAPTER IV

AT GRIPS

I HAVE before referred to the apparent vagueness and casualness of war on its present scarcely conceivable scale. When you are with a Staff officer, you see almost everything. I doubt not that certain matters are hidden from you; but, broadly speaking, you do see all that is to be seen. Into the mind of the General, which conceals the strategy that is to make history, of course you cannot peer. The General is full of interesting talk about the past and about the present, but about the future he breathes no word. If he is near the centre of the front he will tell you blandly, in answer to your question, that a great movement may not improbably be expected at the wings. If he is at either of the wings he will tell you blandly that a great movement may not improbably be expected at the centre. You are not disappointed at his attitude, because you feel when putting them that such questions as yours deserve such answers as his.

But you are assuredly disappointed at not being able to comprehend even the present—what is going on around you, under your eyes, deafening your ears.

For example, I hear the sound of guns. I do not mean the general sound of guns, which is practically continuous round the horizon, but the particular sound of some specific group of guns. I ask about them. Sometimes even Staff officers may hesitate before deciding whether they are enemy guns or French guns. As a rule, the civilian distinguishes an enemy shot by the sizzling, affrighting sound of the projectile as it rushes through the air towards him; whereas the French projectile, rushing away from him, is out of hearing before the noise of the gun's explosion has left his ears. But I may be almost equidistant between a group of German and a group of French guns.

When I have learnt what the guns are and their calibre, and, perhaps, even their approximate situation on the large-scale Staff map, I am not much nearer the realisation of them. Actually to find them might be half a day's work, and when I have found them I have simply found several pieces of mechanism each hidden in a kind of hut, functioning quite privately and disconnectedly by the aid of a few perspiring men. The affair is not like shooting at anything. A polished missile is shoved into the gun. A horrid bang—the missile has disappeared, has simply gone. Where it has gone, what it has done, nobody in the hut seems to care. There is a telephone close by, but only numbers and formulae—and perhaps an occasional rebuke—come out of the telephone, in response to which the perspiring men make minute adjustments in the gun or in the next missile.

Of the target I am absolutely ignorant, and so are the perspiring men. I am free to go forth and look for the target. It is pointed out to me. It may be a building or a group of buildings; it may be something else. At best, it is nothing but a distant spot on a highly complex countryside. I see a faint puff of smoke, seemingly as harmless as a feather momentarily floating. And I think: Can any reasonable person expect that those men with that noisy contrivance in the enclosed hut away back shall plant a mass of metal into that far-off tiny red patch of masonry lost in the vast landscape? And, even if by chance they do, for what reason has that particular patch been selected? What influence could its destruction have on the mighty course of the struggle? . . . Thus it is that war seems vague and casual, because a mere fragment of it defeats the imagination, and the bits of even the fragment cannot be fitted together. Why, I have stood in the first-line trench itself and heard a fusillade all round me, and yet have seen nothing and understood nothing of the action!

It is the same with the movements of troops. For example, I slept in a town behind the front, and I was wakened up—not, as often, by an aeroplane—but by a tremendous shaking and throbbing of the hotel. This went on for a long time, from just after dawn till about six o'clock, when it stopped, only to recommence after a few minutes. I got up, and found that, in addition to the hotel, the whole town was shaking and throbbing. A regiment was passing through it in auto-buses. Each auto-bus held about thirty men, and the vehicles rattled after one another at a distance of at most thirty yards. The auto-buses were painted the colour of battleships, and were absolutely uniform except that some had permanent and some only temporary roofs, and some had mica windows and some only holes in the sides. All carried the same number of soldiers, and in all the rifles were stacked in precisely the same fashion. When one auto-bus stopped, all stopped, and the soldiers waved and smiled to girls at windows and in the street. The entire town had begun its day. No matter how early you arise in these towns, the town has always begun its day.

The soldiers in their pale-blue uniforms were young, lively, high-spirited, and very dusty; their moustaches, hair, and ears were noticeably coated with dust. Evidently they had been travelling for hours. The auto-buses kept appearing out of the sun-shot dust-cloud at the end of the town, and disappearing round the curve by the Town Hall. Occasionally an officer's automobile, or a car with a couple of nurses, would intervene momentarily; and then more and more and more auto-buses, and still more. The impression given is that the entire French Army is passing through the town. The rattle and the throbbing and the shaking get on my nerves. At last come two breakdown-vans, and the procession is finished. I cannot believe that it is really finished, but it is; and the silence is incredible.

Well, I have seen only a couple of regiments go by. Out of the hundreds of regiments in the French Army, just two! But whence they had come, what they had done, whither they were travelling, what they were intended to do—nobody could tell me. They had an air as casual and vague and aimless as a flight of birds across a landscape.

There were more picturesque pilgrimages than that. One of the most picturesque and touching spectacles I saw at the front was the march of a regiment of the line into another little country town on a very fine summer morning. First came the regimental band. The brass instruments were tarnished; the musicians had all sorts of paper packages tied to their knapsacks. Besides being musicians they were real soldiers, in war-stained uniforms. They marched with an air of fatigue. But the tune they played was bright enough.

Followed some cyclists, keeping pace with the marchers. Then an officer on a horse. Then companies of the regiment. The stocks of many of the rifles were wrapped in dirty rags. Every man carried all that was his in the campaign, including a pair of field-glasses. Every man was piled up with impedimenta—broken, torn, soiled and cobbled impedimenta. And every man was very, very tired.

A young officer on foot could scarcely walk. He moved in a kind of trance, and each step was difficult. He may have been half asleep.

At intervals a triangular sign was borne aloft—red, blue, or some other tint. These signs indicated the positions of the different companies in the trenches. (Needless to say that the regiment had come during the night from a long spell of the trenches—but what trenches?) Then came the gorgeous regimental colours, and every soldier in the street saluted them, and every civilian raised his hat.

I noticed more and more that the men were exhausted, were at the limit of their endurance. Then passed a group which was quite fresh.

A Red Cross detachment! No doubt they had had very little to do.

After them a few horses, grey and white; and then field-kitchens and equipment-carts. And then a machine-gun on a horse's back; others in carts; pack-mules with ammunition-boxes; several more machine-gun sections. And then more field-kitchens. In one of these the next meal was actually preparing, and steam rose from under a great iron lid. On every cart was a spare wheel for emergencies; the hub of every wheel was plaited round with straw; the harness was partly of leather and partly of rope ending in iron hooks. Later came a long Red Cross van, and after it another field-kitchen encumbered with bags and raw meat and strange oddments, and through the interstices of the pile, creeping among bags and raw meat, steam gently mounted, for a meal was maturing in that perambulating kitchen also. Lastly, came a cart full of stretchers and field-hospital apparatus. The regiment, its music still faintly audible, had gone by—self-contained, self-supporting. There was no showiness of a review, but the normal functioning, the actual dailiness, of a line regiment as it lives strenuously in the midst of war.

My desire was that the young officer in a trance should find a good bed instantly. The whole thing was fine; it was pathetic; and, above all, it was mysterious. What was the part of that regiment in the gigantic tactics of Joffre?

However, after a short experience at the front one realises that though the conduct of the campaign may be mysterious, it is neither vague nor casual. I remember penetrating through a large factory into a small village which constituted one of the latest French conquests. An officer who had seen the spot just after it was taken, and before it was "organised," described to me the appearance of the men with their sunken eyes and blackened skins on the day of victory. They were all very cheerful when I saw them; but how alert, how apprehensive, how watchful! I felt that I was in a place where anything might happen at any moment. The village and the factory were a maze of trenches, redoubts, caves, stairs up and stairs down, machine-guns, barbed wire, enfilading devices were all ready.

When we climbed to an attic-floor to look at the German positions, which were not fifty yards away, the Commandant was in a fever till we came down again, lest the Germans might spy us and shell his soldiers. He did not so much mind them shelling us, but he objected to them shelling his men. We came down the damaged stairs in safety.

A way had been knocked longitudinally through a whole row of cottages. We went along this—it was a lane of watchful figures—and then it was whispered to us not to talk, for the Germans might hear! And we peered into mines and burrowed and crawled. We disappeared into long subterranean passages and emerged among a lot of soldiers gaily eating as they stood. Close by were a group of men practising with hand-grenades made harmless for the occasion. I followed the Commandant round a corner, and we gazed at I forget what. "Don't stay here," said the Commandant. I moved away. A second after I had moved a bullet struck the wall where I had been standing. The entire atmosphere of the place, with its imminent sense of danger from an invisible enemy and fierce expectation of damaging that enemy, brought home to me the grand essential truth of the front, namely, that the antagonists are continually at grips, like wrestlers, and straining every muscle to obtain the slightest advantage. ''Casual'' would be the very last adjective to apply to those activities.

Once, after a roundabout tour on foot, one of the Staff Captains ordered an automobile to meet us at the end of a certain road. Part of this road was exposed to German artillery four or five miles off.

No sooner had the car come down the road than we heard the fearsome sizzling of an approaching shell. We saw the shell burst before the sound of the sizzling had ceased. Then came the roar of the explosion. The shell was a 77-mm. high-explosive. It fell out of nowhere on the road. The German artillery methodically searched the exposed portion of the road for about half an hour. The shells dropped on it or close by it at intervals of two minutes, and they were planted at even distances of about a hundred yards up and down the slope. I watched the operation from a dug-out close by. It was an exact and a rather terrifying operation. It showed that the invisible Germans were letting nothing whatever go by; but it did seem to me to be a fine waste of ammunition, and a very stupid application of a scientific ideal; for while shelling it the Germans must have noticed that there was nothing at all on the road. We naturally decided not to go up that road in the car, but to skulk through a wood and meet the car in a place of safety. The car had, sooner or later, to go up the road, because there was not another road. The Commandant who was with us was a very seasoned officer, and he regarded all military duties as absolute duties. The car must return along that road. Therefore, let it go. The fact that it was a car serving solely for the convenience of civilians did not influence him. It was a military car, driven by a soldier.

"You may as well go at once," he said to the chauffeur. "We will assist at your agony. What do you say?" he laughingly questioned a subordinate.

"Ah! My Commandant," said the junior officer cautiously, "when it is a question of the service — — —"

We should naturally have protested against the chauffeur adventuring upon the shell-swept road for our convenience; but he was diplomatic enough to postpone the journey. After a time the shelling ceased, and he passed in safety. He told us when we met him later for the drive home that there were five large holes in the road.

On another occasion, when we were tramping through interminable communication-trenches on a slope, a single rash exposure of two of our figures above the parapet of the trench drew down upon us a bombardment of high-explosive. For myself, I was completely exhausted by the excursion, which was nearing its end, and also I was faint from hunger. But immediately the horrible sizzling sound overhead and an explosion just in front made it plain to me that we were to suffer for a moment's indiscretion, I felt neither fatigue nor hunger. The searching shells fell nearer to us. We ran in couples, with a fair distance between each couple, according to instructions, along the rough, sinuous inequalities of the deep trench. After each visitation we had to lie still and count five till all the fragments of shell had come to rest. At last a shell seemed to drop right upon me.

The earth shook under me. My eyes and nose were affected by the fumes of the explosion. But the shell had not dropped right upon me. It had dropped a few yards to the left. A trench is a wonderful contrivance. Immediately afterwards, a friend picked up in the trench one of the warm shots of the charge. It was a many-facetted ball, beautifully made, and calculated to produce the maximum wound.

This was the last shell to fall. We were safe. But we realised once again, and more profoundly, that there is nothing casual in the conduct of war.

At no place was the continuously intense character of the struggle—like that of two leviathan wrestlers ever straining their hardest at grips—more effectually brought home to me than in the region known now familiarly to the whole world as Notre Dame de Lorette, from the little chapel that stood on one part of it. An exceedingly ugly little chapel it was, according to the picture postcards. There are thousands of widows and orphans wearing black and regretting the past and trembling about the future to-day simply because the invaders had to be made to give up that religious edifice which they had turned to other uses.

The high, thickly wooded land behind the front was very elaborately organised for living either above ground or underground, according to the circumstances of the day. To describe the organisation would be impolitic. But it included every dodge. And the stores, entombed in safety, comprised all things. I remember, for example, stacks of hundreds of lamp-chimneys. Naught lacked to the completeness of the scene of war. There were even prisoners. I saw two young Germans under guard in a cabin. They said that they had got lost in the labyrinth of trenches, and taken a wrong turning. And I believe they had. One was a Red Cross man—probably a medical student before, with wine and song and boastings, he joined his Gott, his Kaiser, and his comrades in the great mission of civilisation across

Belgium. He was dusty and tired, and he looked gloomily at the earthen floor of the cabin. Nevertheless, he had a good carriage and a passably intelligent face, and he was rather handsome. I sympathised with this youth, and I do not think that he was glad to be a prisoner. Some people can go and stare at prisoners, and wreak an idle curiosity upon them. I cannot. A glance, rather surreptitious, and I must walk away. Their humiliation humiliates me, even be they Prussians of the most offensive variety.

A little later we saw another prisoner being brought in—a miserable, tuberculous youth with a nervous trick of the face, thin, very dirty, enfeebled, worn out; his uniform torn, stained, bullet-pierced, and threadbare. Somebody had given him a large hunk of bread, which he had put within the lining of his tunic; it bulged out in front like a paunch. An officer stopped to question him, and while the cross-examination was proceeding a curio-hunting soldier came up behind and cut a button off the tunic. We learnt that the lad was twenty-one years of age, and that he had been called up in December 1914.

Before assisting in the conquest of France he was employed in a paper factory. He tried to exhibit gloom, but it was impossible for him quite to conceal his satisfaction in the fact that for him the fighting was over. The wretched boy had had just about enough of world-dominion, and he was ready to let the Hohenzollerns and Junkers finish up the enterprise as best they could without his aid. No doubt, some woman was his mother. It appeared to me that he could not live long, and that the woman in question might never see him again. But every ideal must have its victims; and bereavement, which counts chief among the well-known advantageous moral disciplines of war, is, of course, good for a woman's soul. Besides, that woman would be convinced that her son died gloriously in defence of an attacked Fatherland.

When we had got clear of prisoners and of the innumerable minor tools of war, we came to something essential—namely, a map. This map, which was shown to us rather casually in the middle of a wood, was a very big map, and by means of different coloured chalks it displayed the ground taken from the Germans month by month. The yellow line showed the advance up to May; the blue line showed the further advance up to June; and fresh marks in red showed graphically a further wresting which had occurred only in the previous night. The blue line was like the mark of a tide on a chart; in certain places it had nearly surrounded a German position, and shortly the Germans would have to retire from that position or be cut off. Famous names abounded on that map—such as Souchez, Ablain St. Nazaire, St. Eloi, Fonds de Buval. Being on a very large scale, the map covered a comparatively small section of the front; but, so far as it went, it was a map to be gazed upon with legitimate pride.

The officers regarded it proudly. Eagerly they indicated where the main pressures were, and where new pressures would come later.

Their very muscles seemed to be strained in the ardour of their terrific intention to push out and destroy the invader. While admitting, as all the officers I met admitted, the great military qualities of the enemy, they held towards him a more definitely contemptuous attitude than I could discover elsewhere. "When the Boches attack us," said one of them, "we drive them back to their trench, and we take that trench. Thus we advance." But, for them, there was Boche and Boche. It was the Bavarians whom they most respected. They deemed the Prussians markedly inferior as fighters to the Bavarians. The Prussians would not hold firm when seriously menaced. The Prussians, in a word, would not "stick it." Such was the unanimous verdict here.

Out beyond the wood, on the hillside, in the communication-trenches and other trenches, we were enabled to comprehend the true significance of that phrase uttered so carelessly by newspaper-readers—Notre Dame de Lorette. The whole of the ground was in heaps. There was no spot, literally, on which a shell had not burst.

Vegetation was quite at an end. The shells seemed to have sterilised the earth. There was not a tree, not a bush, not a blade of any sort, not a root. Even the rankest weeds refused to sprout in the perfect desolation. And this was the incomparable soil of France.

The trenches meandered for miles through the pitted brown slopes, and nothing could be seen from them but vast encumbrances of barbed wire. Knotted metal heaped on the unyielding earth!

The solitude of the communication-trenches was appalling, and the continuous roar of the French seventy-fives over our heads did not alleviate it. In the other trenches, however, was much humanity, some of it sleeping in deep, obscure retreats, but most of it acutely alive and interested in everything. A Captain with a shabby uniform and a strong Southern accent told us how on March 9th he and his men defended their trench in water up to the waist and lumps of ice in it knocking against their bodies.

"I was summoned to surrender," he laughed. "I did not surrender.

We had twenty killed and twenty-four with frostbitten feet as a result of that affair. Yes—March 9th."

March 9th, 1915, obviously divided that officer's life into two parts, and not unnaturally!

A little further on we might hear an officer speaking somewhat ardently into a telephone:

"What are they doing with that gun? They are shooting all over the shop. Tell them exactly———"

Still a little further on, and another officer would lead us to a spot where we could get glimpses of the plain. What a plain! Pit-heads, superb vegetation, and ruined villages—tragic villages illustrating the glories and the transcendent common-sense of war and invasion.

That place over there is Souchez—familiar in all mouths from Arkansas to Moscow for six months past. What an object! Look at St. Eloi! Look at Angres! Look at Neuville St. Vaast! And look at Ablain St. Nazaire, the nearest of all! The village of Ablain St.

Nazaire seems to consist now chiefly of exposed and blackened rafters; what is left of the church sticks up precisely like a little bleached bone. A vision horrible and incredible in the immense luxuriance of the plain! The French have got Ablain St. Nazaire. We may go to Ablain St. Nazaire ourselves if we will accept the risks of shelling. Soldiers were seriously wounded there on that very day, for we saw them being carried therefrom on stretchers towards the motor-ambulance and the hospital.

After more walking of a very circuitous nature, I noticed a few bricks in the monotonous expanse of dwarf earth-mounds made by shells.

"Hello!" I said. "Was there a cottage here?"

No! What I had discovered was the illustrious chapel of Notre

Dame de Lorette.

Then we were in a German trench which the French had taken and transformed into one of their own trenches by turning its face. It had a more massive air than the average French trench, and its cellarage, if I may use this civilian word, was deeper than that of any French trench. The officers said that often a German trench was taken before the men resting in those profound sleeping-holes could get to the surface, and that therefore they only emerged in order to be killed or captured.

After more heavy trudging we came to trenches abandoned by the Germans and not employed by the French, as the front had moved far beyond them. The sides were dilapidated. Old shirts, bits of uniform, ends of straps, damaged field-glass cases, broken rifles, useless grenades lay all about. Here and there was a puddle of greenish water. Millions of flies, many of a sinister bright burnished green, were busily swarming. The forlornness of these trenches was heartrending. It was the most dreadful thing that I saw at the front, surpassing the forlornness of any destroyed village whatsoever.

And at intervals in the ghastly residue of war arose a smell unlike any other smell. ... A leg could be seen sticking out of the side of the trench. We smelt a number of these smells, and saw a number of these legs. Each leg was a fine leg, well-clad, and superbly shod in almost new boots with nail-protected soles. Each leg was a human leg attached to a human body, and at the other end of the body was presumably a face crushed in the earth. Two strokes with a pick, and the corpses might have been excavated and decently interred.

But not one had been touched. Buried in frenzied haste by amateur, imperilled grave-diggers with a military purpose, these dead men decayed at leisure amid the scrap-heap, the cess-pit, the infernal squalor which once had been a neat, clean, scientific German earthwork, and which still earlier had been part of a fair countryside.

The French had more urgent jobs on hand than the sepulture of these victims of a caste and an ambition. So they liquefied into corruption in their everlasting boots, proving that there is nothing like leather. They were a symbol. With alacrity we left them to get forward to the alert, straining life of war.

CHAPTER V

THE BRITISH LINES

YOU should imagine a large plain, but not an empty plain, nor a plain entirely without hills. There are a few hills, including at least one very fine eminence (an agreeable old town on the top), with excellent views of the expanse. The expanse is considerably diversified. In the first place it is very well wooded; in the second place it is very well cultivated; and in the third place it is by no means uninhabited.

Villages abound in it; and small market towns are not far off each other. These places are connected by plenty of roads (often paved) and canals, and by quite an average mileage of railways. See the plain from above, and the chief effect is one of trees. The rounded tops of trees everywhere obscure the view, and out of them church-towers stick up; other architecture is only glimpsed. The general tints are green and grey, and the sky as a rule is grey to match.

Finally, the difference between Northern France and Southern Belgium is marked only by the language of shop and cafe signs; in most respects the two sections of the Front resemble each other with extraordinary exactitude.

The British occupation—which is marked of course by high and impressive cordiality—is at once superficially striking and subtly profound.

"What do you call your dog?" I asked a ragamuffin who was playing with a nice little terrier in a village street where we ate an at fresco meal of jam-sandwiches with a motor-car for a buffet.

He answered shyly, but with pride:

"Tommy."

The whole countryside is criss-crossed with field telegraph and telephone wires. Still more spectacular, everywhere there are traffic directions. And these directions are very large and very curt. "Motor-lorries dead slow," you see in immense characters in the midst of the foreign scene. And at all the awkward street corners in the towns a soldier directs the traffic. Not merely in the towns, but in many and many a rural road you come across a rival of the Strand.

For the traffic is tremendous, and it is almost all mechanical transport. You cannot go far without encountering, not one or two, but dozens and scores of motor-lorries, which, after the leviathan manner of motor-lorries, occupy as much of the road as they can.

When a string of these gets mixed up with motor-cars, a few despatch-riders on motor-cycles, a peasant's cart, and a company on the march, the result easily surpasses Piccadilly Circus just before the curtains are rising in West End theatres. Blocks may and do occur at any moment. Out of a peaceful rustic solitude you may run round a curve straight into a block. The motor-lorries constitute the difficulty, not always because they are a size too large for the country, but sometimes because of the human nature of Tommies.

The rule is that on each motor-lorry two Tommies shall ride in front and one behind. The solitary one behind is cut off from mankind, and accordingly his gregarious instinct not infrequently makes him nip on to the front seat in search of companionship. When he is established there impatient traffic in the rear may screech and roar in vain for a pathway; nothing is so deaf as a motor-lorry. The situation has no disadvantage for the trio in front of the motor-lorry until a Staff officer's car happens to be inconvenienced. Then, when the Staff officer does get level, there is a short, sharp scene, a dead silence, and the offender creeps back, a stricken sinner, to his proper post.

The encumbered and busy roads, and the towns crammed with vehicles and vibrating with military activity, produce upon you such an overwhelming impression of a vast and complex organisation that your thought rushes instantly to the supreme controller of that organisation, the man ultimately responsible for all of it. He does not make himself invisible. It becomes known that he will see you at a certain hour. You arrive a few minutes before that hour. The building is spacious, and its Gallic aspect is intensified by the pure Anglo-Saxonism of its terrific inhabitants. In a large outer office you are presented to the various brains of the Expeditionary Force, all members of the General Staff—famous names among them, celebrities, specialists, illustrious with long renown. They walk in and out, and they sit smoking and chatting, as if none of them was anybody in particular. And as a fact, you find it a little difficult to appreciate them at their lawful worth, because you are aware that in the next room, behind those double doors, is he at whose nod the greatest among them tremble.

"The Commander-in-Chief will see you." You go forward, and I defy you not to be daunted.

The inner chamber has been a drawing-room. It still is partially a drawing-room. The silk panels on the walls have remained, and in one corner a grand piano lingers. In the middle is a plain table bearing a map on a huge scale. There he is, the legendary figure.

You at last have proof that he exists. He comes towards the door to meet you. A thick-set man, not tall, with small hands and feet, and finger-nails full of character. He has a short white moustache, and very light-coloured eyes set in a ruddy complexion. His chin is noticeable. He is not a bit dandiacal. He speaks quietly and grimly and reflectively. He is a preoccupied man. He walks a little to and fro, pausing between his short, sparse sentences. When he talks of the Germans he has a way of settling his head and neck with a slight defiant shake well between his shoulders. I have seen the gesture in experienced boxers and in men of business when openly or implicitly challenged. It is just as if he had said: "Wait a bit! I shall get even with that lot—and let no one imagine the contrary!" From the personality of the man there emanates all the time a pugnacious and fierce doggedness. After he has formally welcomed you into the meshes of his intimidating organisation, and made a few general observations, he says, in a new tone: "Well———," and you depart. And as you pass out of the building the thought in your mind is:

"I have seen him!" After the Commander-in-Chief there are two other outstanding and separately existing notabilities in connection with the General Staff. One is the Quartermaster-General, who superintends the supply of all material; and the other is the Adjutant-General, who superintends the supply of men. With the latter is that formidable instrument of authority, the Grand Provost Marshal, who superintends behaviour and has the power of life and death. Each of these has his Staff, and each is housed similarly to the Commander-in-Chief. Then each Army (for there is more than one army functioning as a distinct entity)—each Army has its Commander with his Staff. And each Corps of each Army has its Commander with his Staff. And each Division of each Corps of each Army has its Commander with his Staff. And each Brigade of each Division of each Corps of each Army has its Commander with his Staff; but though I met several Brigadier-Generals, I never saw one at his head-quarters with his Staff. I somehow could not penetrate lower than the entity of a Division. I lunched, had tea, and dined at the headquarters of various of these Staffs, with a General as host.

They were all admirably housed, and their outward circumstances showed a marked similarity. The most memorable thing about them was their unending industry.

"You have a beautiful garden," I said to one General.

"Yes," he said. "I have never been into it."

He told me that he rose at six and went to bed at midnight.

As soon as coffee is over after dinner, and before cigars are over, the General will say:

"I don't wish to seem inhospitable, but———"

And a few minutes later you may see a large lighted limousine moving off into the night, bearing Staff officers to their offices for the evening seance of work which ends at twelve o'clock or thereabouts.

The complexity and volume of work which goes on at even a Divisional Headquarters, having dominion over about twenty thousand full-grown males, may be imagined; and that the bulk of such work is of a business nature, including much tiresome routine, is certain. Of the strictly military labours of Headquarters, that which most agreeably strikes the civilian is the photography and the map-work. I saw thousands of maps. I inspected thick files of maps all showing the same square of country under different military conditions at different dates. And I learnt that special maps are regularly circulated among all field officers.

The fitting-out and repairing sheds of the Royal Flying Corps were superb and complete constructions, at once practical and very elegant. I visited them in the midst of a storm. The equipment was prodigious; the output was prodigious; the organisation was scientific; and the staff was both congenial and impressive. When one sees these birdcages full of birds and comprehends the spirit of flight, one is less surprised at the unimaginable feats which are daily performed over there in the sky northwards and eastwards. I saw a man who flew over Ghent twice a week with the regularity of a train.

He had never been seriously hit. These airmen have a curious physical advantage. The noise of their own engine, it is said, prevents them from hearing the explosions of the shrapnel aimed at them.

The British soldier in France and Flanders is not a self-supporting body.

He needs support, and a great deal of support. I once saw his day's rations set forth on a tray, and it seemed to me that I could not have consumed them in a week of good appetite. The round of meat is flanked by plenteous bacon, jam, cheese, and bread. In addition there are vegetables, tea, sugar, salt, and condiments, with occasional butter; and once a week come two ounces of tobacco and a box of matches for each ounce. But the formidable item is the meat. And then the British soldier wants more than food; he wants, for instance, fuel, letters, cleanliness; he wants clothing, and all the innumerable instruments and implements of war. He wants regularly, and all the time.

Hence you have to imagine wide steady streams of all manner of things converging upon Northern France not only from Britain but from round about the globe. The force of an imperative demand draws them powerfully in, night and day, as a magnet might. It is impossible to trace exactly either the direction or the separate constituents of these great streams of necessaries. But it is possible to catch them, or at any rate one of them, at the most interesting point of its course: the point at which the stream, made up of many converging streams, divides suddenly and becomes many streams again.

That point is the rail-head.

Now, a military rail-head is merely an ordinary average little railway station, with a spacious yard. There is nothing superficially romantic about it. It does not even mark the end of a line of railway. I have in mind one which served as the Head-quarters of a Divisional Supply Column. The organism served just one division—out of the very many divisions in France and Flanders. It was under the command of a Major. This Major, though of course in khaki and employing the same language and general code as a regimental Major, was not a bit like a regimental Major. He was no more like a regimental Major than I am myself. He had a different mentality, outlook, preoccupation. He was a man in business. He received orders—I use the word in the business sense—from the Brigades of the Division; and those orders, ever varying, had to be executed and delivered within thirty-six hours. Quite probably he had never seen a trench; I should be neither surprised nor pained to learn that he could only hit a haystack with a revolver by throwing the revolver at the haystack. His subordinates resembled him. Strategy, artillery-mathematics, the dash of infantry charges—these matters were not a bit in their line. Nevertheless, when you read in a despatch that during a prolonged action supplies went regularly up to the Front under heavy fire, you may guess that fortitude and courage are considerably in their line. These officers think about their arriving trains, and about emptying them in the shortest space of time; and they think about their motor-lorries and the condition thereof; and they pass their lives in checking lists and in giving receipts for things and taking receipts for things. Their honour may be in a receipt. And all this is the very basis of war.

My Major handled everything required for his division except water and ammunition. He would have a train full of multifarious provender, and another train full of miscellanies—from field-guns to field-kitchens—with letters from wives and sweethearts in between.

And all these things came to him up the line of railway out of the sea simply because he asked for them and was ready to give a receipt for them. He was not concerned with the magic underlying their appearance at his little rail-head; he only cared about the train being on time, and the lorries being in first-class running order. He sprayed out in beneficent streams from his rail-head tons of stuff every day. Every day he sent out two hundred and eighty bags of postal matter to the men beyond. The polish on the metallic portions of his numerous motor-lorries was uncanny. You might lift a bonnet and see the bright parts of the engine glittering like the brass of a yacht. Dandyism of the Army Service Corps!

An important part of the organism of the rail-head is the Railway Construction Section Train. Lines may have to be doubled. The Railway Construction Section Train doubles them; it will make new railways at the rate of several miles a day; it is self-contained, being simultaneously a depot, a workshop, and a barracks.

Driving along a road you are liable to see rough signs nailed to trees, with such words on them as "Forage," "Groceries," "Meat," "Bread," etc. Wait a little, and you may watch the Divisional Supply at a further stage. A stream of motor-lorries—one of the streams sprayed out from the rail-head—will halt at those trees and unload, and the stuff which they unload will disappear like a dream and an illusion. One moment the meat and the bread and all the succulences are there by the roadside, each by its proper tree, and the next they are gone, spirited away to camps and billets and trenches. Proceed further, and you may have the luck to see the mutton which was frozen in New Zealand sizzling in an earth-oven in a field christened by the soldiers with some such name as Hampstead Heath. The roasted mutton is a very fine and a very appetising sight. But what quantities of it! And what an antique way of cooking!

As regards the non-edible supplies, the engineer's park will stir your imagination. You can discern every device in connection with warfare. (To describe them might be indiscreet—it would assuredly be too lengthy.) . . . Telephones such as certainly you have never seen! And helmets such as you have never seen! Indeed, everything that a soldier in full work can require, except ammunition.

The ammunition-train in process of being unloaded is a fearsome affair. You may see all conceivable ammunition, from rifle cartridges to a shell whose weight is liable to break through the floors of lorries, all on one train. And not merely ammunition, but a thousand pyrotechnical and other devices; and varied bombs. An officer unscrews a cap on a metal contraption, and throws it down, and it begins to fizz away in the most disconcerting manner. And you feel that all these shells, all these other devices, are simply straining to go off. They are like things secretly and terribly alive, waiting the tiny gesture which will set them free. Officers, handling destruction with the nonchalance of a woman handling a hat, may say what they like—the ammunition train is to my mind an unsafe neighbour. And the thought of all the sheer brain-power which has gone to the invention and perfecting of those propulsive and explosive machines causes you to wonder whether you yourself possess a brain at all.

You can find everything in the British lines except the British Army.

The same is to be said of the French lines; but the in discoverability of the British Army is relatively much more striking, by reason of the greater richness and complexity of the British auxiliary services. You see soldiers—you see soldiers everywhere; but the immense majority of them are obviously engaged in attending to the material needs of other soldiers, which other soldiers, the fighters, you do not see—or see only in tiny detachments or in single units.

Thus I went for a very long walk, up such hills and down such dales as the country can show, tramping with a General through exhausting communication-trenches, in order to discover two soldiers, an officer and his man; and even they were not actual fighters. The officer lived in a dug-out with a very fine telescope for sole companion. I was told that none but the General commanding had the right to take me to that dug-out. It contained the officer's bed, the day's newspapers, the telescope, a few oddments hung on pegs pushed into the earthen walls, and, of equal importance with the telescope, a telephone. Occasionally the telephone faintly buzzed, and a very faint, indistinguishable murmur came out of it.

But the orderly ignored this symptom, explaining that it only meant that somebody else was talking to somebody else. I had the impression of a mysterious underground life going on all around me.

The officer's telescopic business was to keep an eye on a particular section of the German front, and report everything. The section of front comprised sundry features extremely well known by reputation to British newspaper readers. I must say that the reality of them was disappointing. The inevitable thought was: "Is it possible that so much killing has been done for such trifling specks of earth?"

The officer made clear all details to us; he described minutely the habits of the Germans as he knew them. But about his own habits not a word was said. He was not a human being—he was an observer, eternally spying through a small slit in the wall of the dug-out. What he thought about when he was not observing, whether his bed was hard, how he got his meals, whether he was bored, whether his letters came regularly, what his moods were, what was his real opinion of that dug-out as a regular home—these very interesting matters were not even approached by us. He was a short, mild officer, with a quiet voice. Still, after we had shaken hands on parting, the General, who had gone first, turned his bent head under the concealing leafage, and nodded and smiled with a quite particular cordial friendliness. "Good-afternoon, Blank," said the General to the officer, and the warm tone of his voice said: "You know—don't you, Blank?—how much I appreciate you." It was a transient revelation. As, swallowed up in trenches, I trudged away from the lonely officer, the General, resuming his ordinary worldly tone, began to talk about London music-halls and Wish Wynne and other artistes.

Then on another occasion I actually saw at least twenty fighting men! They were not fighting, but they were pretending, under dangerous conditions, to fight. They had to practise the bombing of a German trench—with real bombs. The young officer in charge explained to us the different kinds of bombs. "It's all quite safe," he said casually, "until I take this pin out." And he took the pin out. We saw the little procession of men that were to do the bombing. We saw the trench, with its traverses, and we were shown just how it would be bombed, traverse by traverse. We saw also a "crater" which was to be bombed and stormed. And that was about all we did see. The rest was chiefly hearing, because we had to take shelter behind such slight eminences as a piece of ordinary waste ground can offer. Common wayfarers were kept out of harm by sentries. We were instructed to duck. We ducked. Bang! Bang! Bang! Bang! Bang!—Bang! Then the mosquito-like whine of bits of projectile above our heads! Then we ventured to look over, and amid wisps of smoke the bombers were rushing a traverse. Strange to say, none of them was killed, or even wounded.

On still another occasion I saw a whole brigade, five or six thousand men, with their first-line transport, and two Generals with implacable eyes watching them for faults. It was a fine, very picturesque display of Imperial militancy, but too marvellously spick-and-span to produce any illusion of war. So far as I was concerned, its chief use was to furnish a real conception of numbers. I calculated that if the whole British Army passed before my eyes at the same brisk rate as that solitary and splendid brigade, I should have to stare at it night and day for about three weeks, without surcease for meals. This calculation only increased my astonishment at the obstinate in-discoverability of the Army.

Once I did get the sensation of fighting men existing in bulk. It was at the baths of a new division—the New Army. I will mention in passing that the real enthusiasm of Generals concerning the qualities of the New Army was most moving—and enheartening.

The baths establishment was very British—much more British than any of those operating it perhaps imagined. Such a phenomenon could probably be seen on no other front. It had been contrived out of a fairly large factory. It was in charge of a quite young subaltern, no doubt anxious to go and fight, but condemned indefinitely to the functions of baths-keeper. In addition to being a baths-keeper this young subaltern was a laundry-manager; for when bathing the soldiers left their underclothing and took fresh. The laundry was very large; it employed numerous local women and girls at four francs a day. It had huge hot drying-rooms where the women and girls moved as though the temperature was sixty degrees instead of being over a hundred. All these women and girls were beautiful, all had charm, all were more or less ravishing—simply because for days we had been living in a harsh masculine world—a world of motor-lorries, razors, trousers, hob-nailed boots, maps, discipline, pure reason, and excessively few mirrors. An interesting item of the laundry was a glass-covered museum of lousy shirts, product of prolonged trench-life in the earlier part of the war, and held by experts to surpass all records of the kind!

The baths themselves were huge and simple—a series of gigantic steaming vats in which possibly a dozen men lathered themselves at once. Here was fighting humanity; you could see it in every gesture. The bathers, indeed, appeared to be more numerous than they in fact were. Two hundred and fifty could undress, bathe, and re-clothe themselves in an hour, and twelve hundred in a morning.

Each man of course would be free to take as many unofficial baths, in tin receptacles and so on, as he could privately arrange for and as he felt inclined for. Companies of dirty men marching to the baths, and companies of conceitedly clean men marching from the baths, helped to strengthen the ever-growing suspicion that a great Army must be hidden somewhere in the neighbourhood.

Nevertheless, I still saw not the ultimate destination of all those streams of supply which I have described.

I had, however, noted a stream in the contrary direction—that is, westwards and southwards towards the Channel and England. You can first trace the beginnings of this stream under the sound of the guns (which you never see). A stretcher brought to a temporary shelter by men whose other profession is to play regimental music; a group of men bending over a form in the shelter; a glimpse of dressings and the appliances necessary for tying up an artery or some other absolutely urgent job. That shelter is called the Aid Post.

From it the horizontal form goes to (2) the Advanced Dressing Station, where more attention is given to it; and thence to (3) the Field Ambulance proper, where the case is really diagnosed and provisionally classed. By this time motor-ambulances have been much used; and the stream, which was a trickle at the Aid Post, has grown wider. The next point (4) is the Casualty Clearing Station.

Casualty Clearing Stations are imposing affairs. Not until the horizontal form reaches them can an operation in the full sense of the word be performed upon it. The Clearing Station that I saw could accommodate seven hundred cases, and had held nearer eight hundred. It was housed in an extensive public building. It employed seven surgeons, and I forget how many dressers. It had an abdominal ward, where cases were kept until they could take solid food; and a head ward; and an officers' ward; immense stores; a Church of England chapel; and a shoot down which mattresses with patients thereon could be slid in case of fire.

Nearly seven hundred operations had been performed in it during the war. Nevertheless, as the young Colonel in charge said to me: "The function of a Clearing Station is to clear. We keep the majority of the

A French Red Cross train bearing sick and wounded soldiers to Paris after passing through a field hospital. One of the nurses is making a tour of the train, distributing coffee to the slightly wounded and sick men.

cases only a few hours." Thence the horizontal forms pass into (5) Ambulance Trains. But besides Ambulance trains there are Ambulance barges, grand vessels flying the Union Jack and the Red Cross, with lifts, electric light, and an operating-table. They are towed by a tug to the coast through convenient canals.

You may catch the stream once more, and at its fullest, in (6) the splendid hospitals at Boulogne. At Boulogne the hospital laundry work is such that it has overpowered the town and has to be sent to England. But even at Boulogne, where the most solid architecture, expensively transformed, gives an air of utter permanency to the hospitals, the watchword is still to clear, to pass the cases on. The next stage (7) is the Hospital Ship, specially fitted out, waiting in the harbour for its complement. When the horizontal forms leave the ship they are in England; they are among us, and the great stream divides into many streams, just as at the rail-head at the other end the great stream of supply divides into many streams, and is lost.

Nor are men the only beings cared for. One of the strangest things I saw at Boulogne was a horse-hospital, consisting of a meadow of many acres. Those who imagine that horses are not used in modern war should see the thousands of horses tethered in that meadow. Many if not most of them were suffering from shell wounds, and the sufferers were rather human. I saw a horse operated on under chloroform. He refused to come to after the operation was over, and as I left he was being encouraged to do so by movements of the limbs to induce respiration. Impossible, after that, to think of him as a mere horse!

But before I left the British lines I did manage to glimpse the British Army, the mysterious sea into which fell and were swallowed up, and from which trickled the hundreds of small runlets of wounded that converged into the mighty stream of pain at Boulogne. I passed by a number of wooden causeways over water-logged ground, and each causeway had the name of some London street, and at last I was stopped by a complicated wall of sandbags with many curves and involutions. To "dig in" on this particular landscape is impracticable, and hence the "trenches" are above ground and sandbags are their walls. I looked through a periscope and saw barbed wire and the German positions. I was told not to stand in such-and-such a place because it was exposed. A long line of men moved about at various jobs behind the rampart of sandbags; they were cheerfully ready to shoot, but very few of them were actually in the posture of shooting. A little further behind gay young men seemed to be preparing food. Here and there were little reposing places.

A mere line, almost matching the sand-bags in colour! All the tremendous organisation in the rear had been brought into being solely for the material sustenance, the direction, and the protection of this line! The guns roared solely in its aid. For this line existed the clearing stations and hospitals in France and in Britain. I dare say I saw about a quarter of a mile of it. The Major in command of what I saw accompanied me some distance along the causeways into comparative safety. As we were parting he said:

"Well, what do you think of our 'trenches'?"

In my preoccupied taciturnity I had failed to realise that, interesting as his "trenches" were to me, they must be far more interesting to him, and that they ought to have formed the subject of conversation.

"Fine!" I said.

And I hope my monosyllabic sincerity satisfied him.

We shook hands, and he turned silently away to the everlasting peril of his post. His retreating figure was rather pathetic to me. Looking at it, I understood for the first time what war in truth is. But I soon began to wonder anxiously whether our automobile would get safely past a certain exposed spot on the high road.

CHAPTER VI
THE UNIQUE CITY

WHEN we drew near Ypres we met a civilian wagon laden with furniture of a lower middle-class house, and also with lengths of gilt picture frame-moulding. There was quite a lot of gilt in the wagon. A strong, warm wind was blowing, and the dust on the road and from the railway track was very unpleasant. The noise of artillery persisted. As a fact, the wagon was hurrying away with furniture and picture-frame mouldings under fire. Several times we were told not to linger here and not to linger there, and the automobiles, emptied of us, received very precise instructions where to hide during our absence. We saw a place where a shell had dropped on to waste ground at one side of the road, and thrown up a mass of earth and stones on to the roof of an asylum on the other side of the road. The building was unharmed; the well-paved surface of the road was perfect—it had received no hurt; but on the roof lay the earth and stones. Still, we had almost no feeling of danger. The chances were a thousand to one that the picture-frame maker would get safely away with his goods; and he did. But it seemed odd—to an absurdly sensitive, non-Teutonic mind it seemed somehow to lack justice— that the picture-framer, after having been ruined, must risk his life in order to snatch from the catastrophe the debris of his career.

Further on, within the city itself, but near the edge of it, two men were removing uninjured planks from the upper floor of a house; the planks were all there was in the house to salve. I saw no other attempt to make the best of a bad job, and, after I had inspected the bad job, these two attempts appeared heroic to the point of mere folly.

I had not been in Ypres for nearly twenty years, and when I was last there the work of restoring the historic buildings of the city was not started. (These restorations, especially to the Cloth Hall and the Cathedral of St. Martin, were just about finished in time for the opening of hostilities, and they give yet another proof of the German contention that Belgium, in conspiracy with Britain, had deliberately prepared for the war—and, indeed, wanted it!) he Grande Place was quite recognisable. It is among the largest public squares in Europe, and one of the very few into which you could put a medium-sized Atlantic liner. There is no square in London or (I think) New York into which you could put a 10,000-ton boat. A 15,000-ton affair, such as even the Arabic, could be arranged diagonally in the Grande Place at Ypres.

This Grande Place has seen history. In the middle of the thirteenth century, whence its chief edifices date, it was the centre of one of the largest and busiest towns in Europe, and a population of 200,000 weavers was apt to be uproarious in it. Within three centuries a lack of comprehension of home politics and the simple brigandage of foreign politics had reduced Ypres to a population of 5,000. In the seventeenth century Ypres fell four times. At the beginning of the nineteenth century it ceased to be a bishopric. In the middle of the nineteenth century it ceased to be fortified; and in the second decade of the twentieth century it ceased to be inhabited. Possessing 200,000 inhabitants in the thirteenth century, 5,000 inhabitants in the sixteenth century, 17400 inhabitants at the end of the nineteenth century, it now possesses 0 inhabitants. It is uninhabited. It cannot be inhabited. Scarcely two months before I saw it, the city—I was told—had been full of life; in the long period of calm which followed the bombardment of the railway-station quarter in November 1914 the inhabitants had taken courage, and many of those who had fled from the first shells had sidled back again with the most absurd hope in their hearts. As late as the third week in April the Grande Place was the regular scene of commerce, and on market-days it was dotted with stalls upon which were offered for sale such frivolous things as postcards displaying the damage done to the railway-station quarter.

Then came the major bombardment, which is not yet over.

You may obtain a just idea of the effects of the major bombardment by adventuring into the interior of the Cathedral of St. Martin. This Cathedral is chiefly thirteenth-century work. Its tower, like that of the Cathedral at Malines, had never been completed—nor will it ever be, now—but it is still, with the exception of the tower of the Cloth Hall, the highest thing in Ypres. The tower is a skeleton. As for the rest of

The ruins of the Cathedral of St. Martin's Church in Ypres, Belgium.

the building, it may be said that some of the walls alone substantially remain. The choir—the earliest part of the Cathedral—is entirely unroofed, and its south wall has vanished. The apse has been blown clean out. The Early Gothic nave is partly unroofed. The transepts are unroofed, and of the glass of the memorable rose window of the south transept not a trace is left—so far as I can remember.

In the centre of the Cathedral, where the transepts meet, is a vast heap of bricks, stone, and powdery dirt. This heap rises irregularly like a range of hills towards the choir; it overspreads most of the immense interior, occupying an area of, perhaps, from 15,000 to 20,000 square feet. In the choir it rises to a height of six or seven yards. You climb perilously over it as you might cross the Alps. This incredible amorphous mass, made up of millions of defaced architectural fragments of all kinds, is the shattered body of about half the Cathedral. I suppose that the lovely carved choir-stalls are imbedded somewhere within it. The grave of Jansen is certainly at the bottom of it. The aspect of the scene, with the sky above, the jagged walls, the interrupted arches, and the dusty piled mess all around, is intolerably desolate. And it is made the more so by the bright colours of the great altar, two-thirds of which is standing, and the still brighter colours of the organ, which still clings, apparently whole, to the north wall of the

73

choir. In the sacristy are collected gilt candelabra and other altar-furniture, turned yellow by the fumes of picric acid. At a little distance the Cathedral, ruin though it is, seems solid enough; but when you are in it the fear is upon you that the inconstant and fragile remains of it may collapse about you in a gust of wind a little rougher than usual.

You leave the outraged fane with relief. And when you get outside you have an excellent opportunity of estimating the mechanism which brought about this admirable triumph of destruction; for there is a hole made by a 17-inch shell; it is at a moderate estimate fifty feet across, and it has happened to tumble into a graveyard, so that the hole is littered with the white bones of earlier Christians.

The Cloth Hall was a more wonderful thing than the Cathedral of St. Martin, which, after all, was no better than dozens of other cathedrals. There was only one Cloth Hall of the rank of this one. It is not easy to say whether or not the Cloth Hall still exists. Its celebrated three-story facade exists, with a huge hiatus in it to the left of the middle, and, of course, minus all glass. The entire facade seemed to me to be leaning slightly forward; I could not decide whether this was an optical delusion or a fact. The enormous central tower is knocked to pieces, and yet conserves some remnant of its original outlines; bits of scaffolding on the sides of it stick out at a great height like damaged matches. The slim corner towers are scarcely hurt. Everything of artistic value in the structure of the interior has disappeared in a horrible confusion of rubble. The eastern end of the Cloth Hall used to be terminated by a small beautiful Renaissance edifice called the Niewwerk, dating from the seventeenth century. What its use was I never knew; but the Niewwerk has vanished, and the Town Hall next door has also vanished; broken walls, a few bits of arched masonry, and heaps of refuse alone indicate where these buildings stood in April last.

So much for the two principal buildings visible from the Grande Place. The Cloth Hall is in the Grande Place, and the Cathedral adjoins it. The only other fairly large building in the Place is the Hopital de Notre Dame at the north-east end. This white-painted erection, with its ornamental gilt sign, had continued substantially to exist as a structural entity; it was defaced, but not seriously. Every other building in the place was smashed up. To walk right round the Place is to walk nearly half a mile; and along the entire length, with the above exceptions, there was nothing but mounds of rubbish and fragments of upstanding walls. Here and there in your perambulation you may detect an odour with which certain trenches have already familiarised you. Obstinate inhabitants were apt to get buried in the cellars where they had taken refuge. In one place what looked like a colossal sewer had been uncovered. I thought at the time that the sewer was somewhat large for a city of the size of Ypres, and it has since occurred to me that this sewer may have been the ancient bed of the stream Yperlee, which in some past period was arched over.

"I want to make a rough sketch of all this," I said to my companions in the middle of the Grande Place, indicating the Cloth Hall, and the Cathedral, and other grouped ruins. The spectacle was, indeed, majestic in the extreme, and if the British Government has not had it officially photographed in the finest possible manner, it has failed in a very obvious duty; detailed photographs of Ypres ought to be distributed throughout the world.

My companions left me to myself. I sat down on the edge of a small shell-hole some distance in front of the Hospital. I had been advised not to remain too near the building lest it might fall on me. The paved floor of the Place stretched out around me like a tremendous plain, seeming the vaster because my eyes were now so much nearer to the level of it. On a bit of facade to the left the word "CYCLE " stood out in large black letters on a white ground. This word and myself were the sole living things in the Square. In the distance a cloud of smoke up a street showed that a house was burning. The other streets visible from where I sat gave no sign whatever. The wind, strong enough throughout my visit to the Front, was now stronger than ever. All the window-frames and doors in the Hospital were straining and creaking in the wind. The loud sound of guns never ceased. A large British aeroplane hummed and buzzed at a considerable height overhead. Dust drove along.

I said to myself: "A shell might quite well fall here any moment."

I was afraid. But I was less afraid of a shell than of the intense loneliness. Rheims was inhabited; Arras was inhabited. In both cities there were postmen and newspapers, shops, and even cafes.

But in Ypres there was nothing. Every street was a desert; every room in every house was empty. Not a dog roamed in search of food. The weight upon my heart was sickening. To avoid complications I had promised the Staff officer not to move from the Place until he returned; neither of us had any desire to be hunting for each other in the sinister labyrinth of the town's thoroughfares. I was, therefore, a prisoner in the Place, condemned to solitary confinement. I ardently wanted my companions to come back. . . .

Then I heard echoing sounds of voices and footsteps. Two British soldiers appeared round a corner and passed slowly along the Square. In the immensity of the Square they made very small figures. I had a wish to accost them, but Englishmen do not do these things, even in Ypres. They glanced casually at me; I glanced casually at them, carefully pretending that the circumstances of my situation were entirely ordinary.

I felt safer while they were in view; but when they had gone I was afraid again. I was more than afraid; I was inexplicably uneasy. I made the sketch simply because I had said that I would make it.

And as soon as it was done, I jumped up out of the hole and walked about, peering down streets for the reappearance of my friends. I was very depressed, very irritable; and I honestly wished that I had never accepted any invitation to visit the Front. I somehow thought I might never get out of Ypres alive. When at length I caught sight of the Staff officer I felt instantly relieved. My depression, however, remained for hours afterwards.

Perhaps the chief street in Ypres is the wide Rue de Lille, which runs from opposite the Cloth Hall down to the Lille Gate, and over the moat water into the Lille road and on to the German lines. The Rue de Lille was especially famous for its fine old buildings. There was the Hospice Belle, for old female paupers of Ypres, built in the thirteenth century. There was the Museum, formerly the Hotel Merghelynck, not a very striking edifice, but full of antiques of all kinds. There was the Hospital of St. John, interesting, but less interesting than the Hospital of St. John at Bruges. There was the Gothic Maison de Bois, right at the end of the street, with a rather wonderful frontage. And there was the famous fourteenth-century Steenen, which since my previous visit had been turned into the post office. With the exception of this last building, the whole of the Rue de Lille, if my memory is right, lay in ruins. The shattered post office was splendidly upright, and in appearance entire; but, for all I know, its interior may have been destroyed by a shell through the roof. Only the acacia-trees flourished, and the flies, and the weeds between the stones of the paving. The wind took up the dust from the rubbish heaps which had been houses and wreathed it against what bits of walls still maintained the perpendicular. Here, too, was the unforgettable odour, rising through the interstices of the smashed masonry which hid subterranean chambers.

We turned into a side-street of small houses—probably the homes of lace-makers. The street was too humble to be a mark for the guns of the Germans, who, no doubt, trained their artillery by the aid of a very large scale municipal map on which every building was separately indicated. It would seem impossible that a map of less than a foot to a mile could enable them to produce such wonderful results of carefully wanton destruction. And the assumption must be that the map was obtained from the local authorities by some agent masquerading as a citizen. I heard, indeed, that known citizens of all the chief towns returned to their towns or to the vicinity thereof in the uniform and with the pleasing manners of German warriors. The organisation for doing good to Belgium against Belgium's will was an incomparable piece of chicane and pure rascality. Strange— Belgians were long ago convinced that the visitation was inevitably coming, and had fallen into the habit of discussing it placidly over their beer at nights.

To return to the side-street. So far as one could see, it had not received a dent, not a scratch. Even the little windows of the little red houses were by no means all broken. All the front doors stood ajar. I hesitated to walk in, for these houses seemed to be mysteriously protected by influences invisible. But in the end the vulgar, yet perhaps legitimate, curiosity of the sightseer, of the professional reporter, drove me within the doors. The houses were so modest that they had no entrance-halls or lobbies. One passed directly from the street into the parlour. Apparently the parlours were completely furnished. They were in an amazing disorder, but the furniture was there. And the furnishings of all of them were alike, as the furnishings of all the small houses of a street in the Five Towns or in a cheap London suburb. The ambition of these homes had been to resemble one another. What one had all must have. Under ordinary circumstances the powerful common instinct to resemble is pitiable. But here it was absolutely touching.

Everything was in these parlours. The miserable, ugly ornaments, bought and cherished and admired by the simple, were on the mantelpieces. The drawers of the mahogany and oak furniture had been dragged open, but not emptied. The tiled floors were littered with clothes, with a miscellany of odd possessions, with pots and pans out of the kitchen and the scullery, with bags and boxes. The accumulations of lifetimes were displayed before me, and it was almost possible to trace the slow transforming of young girls into brides, and brides into mothers of broods.

Within the darkness of the interiors I could discern the stairs. But I was held back from the stairs. I could get no further than the parlours, though the interest of the upper floors must have been surpassing.

So from house to house. I handled nothing. Were not the military laws against looting of the most drastic character! And at last I came to the end of the little street. There are many such streets in Ypres. In fact, the majority of the streets were like that street. I did not visit them, but I have no doubt that they were in the same condition. I do not say that the inhabitants fled taking naught with them. They must obviously have taken what they could, and what was at once most precious and most portable. But they could have taken very little. They departed breathless without vehicles, and probably most of the adults had children to carry or to lead. At one moment the houses were homes, functioning as such. An alarm, infectious like the cholera, and at the next moment the deserted houses became spiritless, degenerated into intolerable museums for the amazement of a representative of the American and the British Press! Where the scurrying families went to I never even inquired. Useless to inquire. They just lost themselves on the face of the earth, and were henceforth known to mankind by the generic name of "refugees"—such of them as managed to get away alive.

After this the solitude of the suburbs, with their maimed and rusting factories, their stagnant canals, their empty lots, their high, lusty weeds, their abolished railway and tram stations, was a secondary matter leaving practically no impression on the exhausted sensibility.

A few miles on the opposite side of the town were the German artillery positions, with guns well calculated to destroy Cathedrals and Cloth Halls. Around these guns were educated men who had spent years—indeed, most of their lives—in the scientific study of destruction. Under these men were slaves who, solely for the purposes of destruction, had ceased to be the free citizens they once were. These slaves were compelled to carry out any order given to them, under pain of death. They had, indeed, been explicitly told on the highest earthly authority that, if the order came to destroy their fathers and their brothers, they must destroy their fathers and their brothers: the instruction was public and historic.

The whole organism has worked, and worked well, for the destruction of all that was beautiful in Ypres, and for the break-up of an honourable tradition extending over at least eight centuries. The operation was the direct result of an order. The order had been carefully weighed and considered. The successful execution of it brought joy into many hearts, high and low. "Another shell in the Cathedral!" And men shook hands ecstatically around the excellent guns. "A hole in the tower of the Cloth Hall." General rejoicing! "The population has fled, and Ypres is a desert!" Inexpressible enthusiasm among specially educated men, from the highest to the lowest. So it must have been. There was no hazard about the treatment of Ypres. The shells did not come into Ypres out of nowhere. Each was the climax of a long, deliberate effort originating in the brains of the responsible leaders. One is apt to forget all this.

"But," you say, "this is war, after all." After all, it just is.

The future of Ypres exercises the mind. Ypres is only one among many martyrs. But, as matters stand at present it is undoubtedly the chief one. In proportion to their size, scores of villages have suffered as much as Ypres, and some have suffered more. But no city of its mercantile, historical, and artistic importance has, up to now, suffered in the same degree as Ypres. Ypres is entitled to rank as the very symbol of the German achievement in Belgium. It stood upon the path to Calais; but that was not its crime. Even if German guns had not left one brick upon another in Ypres, the path to Calais would not thereby have been made any easier for the well-shod feet of the apostles of might, for Ypres never served as a military stronghold and could not possibly have so served; and had the Germans known how to beat the British Army in front of Ypres, they could have marched through the city as easily as a hyena through a rice-crop. The crime of Ypres was that it lay handy for the extreme irritation of an army which, with three times the men and three times the guns, and thirty times the vainglorious conceit, could not shift the trifling force opposed to it last autumn. Quite naturally the boasters were enraged. In the end, something had to give way. And the Cathedral and Cloth Hall and other defenceless splendours of Ypres gave way, not the trenches. The yearners after Calais did themselves no good by exterminating fine architecture and breaking up innocent homes, but they did experience the relief of smashing something. Therein lies the psychology of the affair of Ypres, and the reason why the Ypres of history has come to a sudden close.

In order to envisage the future of Ypres, it is necessary to get a clear general conception of the damage done to it. Ypres is not destroyed. I should estimate that when I saw it in July at least half the houses in it were standing entire, and, though disfigured, were capable of being rapidly repaired. Thousands of the humble of Ypres could return to their dwellings and resume home-life there with little trouble, provided that the economic situation was fairly favourable — and, of course, sooner or later the economic situation is bound to be favourable, for the simple reason that it must ultimately depend upon the exertions of a people renowned throughout the world for hard and continuous industry.

On the other hand, practically all that was spectacular in the city, all the leading, all the centre round which civic activities had grouped themselves for centuries, is destroyed. Take the Grande Place. If Ypres is to persist in a future at all comparable to its immediate past (to say nothing of its historic past), the privately owned buildings on the Grande Place will, without exception, have to be begun all over again, and before that task can be undertaken the foundations will have to be cleared—a tremendous undertaking in itself. I do not know how many privately owned buildings there were on the Grande Place, but I will guess a hundred and fifty, probably none of which was less than three stories in height. All these buildings belonged to individuals, individuals who intimately possessed them and counted on them as a source of income or well-being, individuals who are now scattered, impoverished, and acutely discouraged. The same is to be said of the Rue de Lille and of other important streets.

Suppose the Germans back again in the land of justice, modesty, and unselfishness; and suppose the property-owners of Ypres collected once more in Ypres. The enterprise of reconstruction facing them will make such a demand of initiative force and mere faith as must daunt the most audacious among them. And capital dragged out of a bankrupt Germany will by no means solve the material problem. For labour will be nearly as scarce as money; the call for labour in every field cannot fail to surpass in its urgency any call in history. The simple contemplation of the gigantic job will be staggering. To begin with, the withered and corrupt dead will have to be excavated from the cellars, and when that day comes those will be present who can say: "This skeleton was So-and-So's child," "That must have been my mother." Terrific hours await Ypres. And when (or if) the buildings have been re-erected, tenants will have to be found for them—and then think of the wholesale refurnishing! The deep human instinct which attaches men and women to a particular spot of the earth's surface is so powerful that almost certainly the second incarnation of Ypres will be initiated, but that it will be carried very far towards completion seems to me to be somewhat doubtful. To my mind the new Ypres cannot be more than a kind of camp amid the dark ruins of the old, and the city must remain for generations, if not for ever, a ghastly sign and illustration of what cupidity and stupidity and vanity can compass together when physical violence is their instrument.

The immediate future of Ypres, after the war, is plain. It will instantly become one of the show-places of the world. Hotels will appear out of the ground, guides and touts will pullulate at the railway station, the tour of the ruins will be mapped out, and the tourists and globe-trotters of the whole planet will follow that tour in batches like staring sheep. Much money will be amassed by a few persons out of the exhibition of misfortune and woe. A sinister fate for a community! Nevertheless, the thing must come to pass, and it is well that it should come to pass. The greater the number of people who see Ypres for themselves, the greater the hope of progress for mankind.

If the facade of the Cloth Hall can be saved, some such inscription as the following ought to be incised along the length of it:

"On July 31st, 1914, The German Minister At Brussels Gave A Positive And Solemn Assurance That Germany Had No Intention Of Violating The Neutrality Of Belgium. Four Days Later The German Army Invaded Belgium. Look Around."

When you are walking through that which was Ypres, nothing arouses a stronger feeling—half contempt, half anger—than the thought of the mean, miserable, silly, childish, and grotesque excuses which the wit of Germany has invented for her deliberately planned crime. And nothing arouses a more grim and sweet satisfaction than the thought that she already has the gravest reason to regret it, and would give her head not to have committed it. Despite all vauntings, all facile chatterings about the alleged co-operation of an unknowable and awful God, all shriekings of unity and power, all bellowings about the perfect assurance of victory, all loud countings of the fruits of victory—the savage leaders of the deluded are shaking in their shoes before the anticipated sequel of an outrage ineffable alike in its barbarism and in its idiocy.

FOUR WEEKS IN THE TRENCHES: THE WAR STORY OF A VIOLINIST

BY FRITZ KREISLER

To My Dear Wife Harriet
The Best Friend And Staunchest Comrade In All Circumstances
Of Life I Dedicate This Little Book In Humble Token Of
Everlasting Gratitude And Devotion

PREFACE

THIS brief record of the fighting on the Eastern front in the great war is the outcome of a fortunate meeting.

The writer chanced to be dining with Mr. Kreisler soon after his arrival in this country, after his dismissal from the hospital where he recovered from his wound. For nearly two hours he listened, thrilled and moved, to the great violinist's modest, vivid narrative of his experiences and adventures. It seemed in the highest degree desirable that the American public should have an opportunity of reading this narrative from the pen of one in whose art so many of us take a profound interest. It also was apparent that since so little of an authentic nature had been heard from the Russo-Austrian field of warfare, this story would prove an important contribution to the contemporary history of the war.

After much persuasion, Mr. Kreisler reluctantly acceded to the suggestion that he write out his personal memories of the war for publication. He has completed his narrative in the midst of grave difficulties, writing it piecemeal in hotels and railway trains in the course of a concert tour through the country. It is offered by the publishers to the public with confidence that it will be found one of the most absorbing and informing narratives of the war that has yet appeared.

F. G.

CHAPTER I

IN trying to recall my impressions during my short war duty as an officer in the Austrian Army, I find that my recollections of this period are very uneven and confused. Some of the experiences stand out with absolute clearness; others, however, are blurred. Two or three events which took place in different localities seem merged into one, while in other instances recollection of the chronological order of things is missing. This curious indifference of the memory to values of time and space may be due to the extraordinary physical and mental stress under which the impressions I am trying to chronicle were received. The same state of mind I find is rather characteristic of most people I have met who were in the war. It should not be forgotten, too, that the gigantic upheaval which changed the fundamental condition of life overnight and threatened the very existence of nations naturally dwarfed the individual into nothingness, and the existing interest in the common welfare left practically no room for personal considerations. Then again, at the front, the extreme uncertainty of the morrow tended to lessen the interest in the details of to-day; consequently I may have missed a great many interesting happenings alongside of me which I would have wanted to note under other circumstances. One gets into a strange psychological, almost hypnotic, state of mind while on the firing line which probably prevents the mind's eye from observing and noticing things in a normal way. This accounts, perhaps, for some blank spaces in my memory. Besides, I went out completely resigned to my fate, without much thought for the future. It never occurred to me that I might ever want to write my experiences, and consequently I failed to take notes or to establish certain mnemo-technical landmarks by the aid of which I might now be able to reconstruct all details. I am, therefore, reduced to present an incoherent and rather piecemeal narrative of such episodes as forcibly impressed themselves upon my mind and left an ineradicable mark upon my memory.

The outbreak of the war found my wife and me in Switzerland, where we were taking a cure. On the 31st of July, on opening the paper, I read that the Third Army Corps, to which my regiment (which is stationed in Graz) belonged, had received an order for mobilization.

Although I had resigned my commission as an officer two years before, I immediately left Switzerland, accompanied by my wife, in order to report for duty. As it happened, a wire reached me a day later calling me to the colors.

We went by way of Munich. It was the first day of the declaration of the state of war in Germany. Intense excitement prevailed. In Munich all traffic was stopped; no trains were running except for military purposes. It was only due to the fact that I revealed my intention of rejoining my regiment in Austria that I was able to pass through at all, but by both the civil and military authorities in Bavaria I was shown the greatest possible consideration and passed through as soon as possible.

We reached Vienna on August first. A startling change had come over the city since I had left it only a few weeks before. Feverish activity everywhere prevailed. Reservists streamed in by thousands from all parts of the country to report at headquarters. Autos filled with officers whizzed past. Dense crowds surged up and down the streets. Bulletins and extra editions of newspapers passed from hand to hand. Immediately it was evident what a great leveler war is. Differences in rank and social distinctions had practically ceased. All barriers seemed to have fallen; everybody addressed everybody else.

I saw the crowds stop officers of high rank and well-known members of the aristocracy and clergy, also state officials and court functionaries of high rank, in quest of information, which was imparted cheerfully and patiently. The imperial princes could frequently be seen on the Ring Strasse surrounded by cheering crowds or mingling with the public unceremoniously at the cafes, talking to everybody. Of course, the army was idolized. Wherever the troops marched the public broke into cheers and every uniform was the center of an ovation.

While coming from the station I saw two young reservists, to all appearances brothers, as they hurried to the barracks, carrying their small belongings in a valise. Along with them walked a little old lady crying, presumably their mother. They passed a general in full uniform. Up went their hands to their caps in military salute, whereupon the old general threw his arms wide open and embraced them both, saying: "Go on, my boys, do your duty bravely and stand firm for your emperor and your country. God willing, you will come back to your old mother." The old lady smiled through her tears. A shout went up, and the crowds surrounding the general cheered him. Long after I had left I could hear them shouting.

A few streets farther on I saw in an open cafe a young couple, a reservist in field uniform and a young girl, his bride or sweetheart. They sat there, hands linked, utterly oblivious of their surroundings and of the world at large. When somebody in the crowd espied them, a great shout went up, the public rushing to the table and surrounding them, then breaking into applause and waving hats and handkerchiefs. At first the young couple seemed to be utterly taken aback and only slowly did they realize that the ovation was meant for them. They seemed confused, the young girl blushing and hiding her face in her hands, the young man rising to his feet, saluting and bowing. More cheers and applause. He opened his mouth as if wanting to speak. There was a sudden silence. He was vainly struggling for expression, but then his face lit up as if by inspiration. Standing erect, hand at his cap, in a pose of military salute, he intoned the Austrian national hymn. In a second every head in that throng was bared. All traffic suddenly stopped, everybody, passengers as well as conductors of the cars, joining in the anthem. The neighboring windows soon filled with people, and soon it was a chorus of thousands of voices. The volume of tone and the intensity of feeling seemed to raise the inspiring anthem to the uttermost heights of sublime majesty. We were then on our way to the station, and long afterwards we could hear the singing, swelling like a human organ.

What impressed me particularly in Vienna was the strict order everywhere. No mob disturbances of any kind, in spite of the greatly increased liberty and relaxation of police regulations. Nor was there any runaway chauvinism noticeable, aside from the occasional singing of patriotic songs and demonstrations like the one I just described. The keynote of popular feeling was quiet dignity, joined to determination, with an undercurrent of solemn gravity and responsibility.

I had stopped in Vienna only long enough to bid good-bye to my father, and left for the headquarters of my regiment in Graz. I reported there for duty and then went to join the Fourth Battalion, which was stationed at Leoben, one hour away from Graz, my orders being to take command of the first platoon in the sixteenth company. My platoon consisted of fifty-five men, two buglers, and an ambulance patrol of four.

In Leoben my wife and I remained a week, which was spent in organizing, equipping, requisitioning, recruiting, and preliminary drilling. These were happy days, as we officers met for the first time, friendships and bonds being sealed which subsequently were tested in common danger and amidst privation and stress. Many of the officers had brought their wives and soon delightful intercourse, utterly free from formality, developed, without any regard or reference to rank, wealth, or station in private life. Among the reserve officers of my battalion were a famous sculptor, a well-known philologist, two university professors (one of mathematics, the other of natural science), a prince, and a civil engineer at the head of one of the largest Austrian steel corporations. The surgeon of our battalion was the head of a great medical institution and a man of international fame. Among my men in the platoon were a painter, two college professors, a singer of repute, a banker, and a post official of high rank. But nobody cared and in fact I myself did not know until much later what distinguished men were in my platoon. A great cloak of brotherhood seemed to have enveloped everybody and everything, even differences in military rank not being so obvious at this time, for the officers made friends of their men, and in turn were worshipped by them.

My wife volunteered her services as Red Cross nurse, insisting upon being sent to the front, in order to be as near me as could be, but it developed later that no nurse was allowed to go farther than the large troop hospitals far in the rear of the actual operations. Upon my urgent appeal she desisted and remained in Vienna after I had left, nursing in the barracks, which are now used for hospital work. In fact, almost every third or fourth house, both private and public, as well as schools, were given to the use of the government and converted into Red Cross

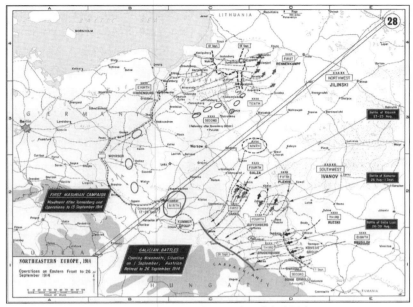

Eastern Front to September 26, 1914

stations.

The happy days in Leoben came to an abrupt end, my regiment receiving orders to start immediately for the front.

We proceeded to Graz, where we joined the other three battalions and were entrained for an unknown destination. We traveled via Budapest to Galicia, and left the train at Strij, a very important railroad center south of Lemberg. It must be understood that the only reports reaching us from the fighting line at that time were to the effect that the Russians had been driven back from our border, and that the Austrian armies actually stood on the enemy's soil. Strij being hundreds of miles away from the Russian frontier, we could not but surmise that we were going to be stationed there some time for the purpose of training and maneuvering. This belief was strengthened by the fact that our regiment belonged to the Landsturm, or second line of reserves, originally intended for home service. We were, however, alarmed that very same night and marched out of Strij for a distance of about twenty miles, in conjunction with the entire Third Army Corps. After a short pause for the purpose of eating and feeding the horses, we marched another twenty-two miles. This first day's march constituted a very strong test of endurance in consequence of our comparative softness and lack of training, especially as, in addition to his heavy rifle, bayonet, ammunition, and spade, each soldier was burdened with a knapsack containing emergency provisions in the form of tinned meats, coffee extract, sugar, salt, rice, and biscuits, together with various tin cooking and eating utensils; furthermore a second pair of shoes, extra blouse, changes of underwear, etc. On top of this heavy pack a winter overcoat and part of a tent were strapped, the entire weight of the equipment being in the neighborhood of fifty pounds. The day wore on. Signs of fatigue soon manifested themselves more and more strongly, and slowly the men dropped out one by one, from sheer exhaustion. No murmur of complaint, however, would be heard. Most of those who fell out of line, after taking a breathing space for a few minutes, staggered on again. The few that remained behind joined the regiment later on when camp was established. We wondered then at the necessity of such a forced march, being unable to see a reason for it, unless it was to put us in training.

Night had fallen when we reached a small monastery in the midst of a forest, where the peaceful surroundings and the monastic life, entirely untouched by the war fever, seemed strange indeed. Camp was established, tents erected, fires were lighted, and coffee made. Soon a life of bustling activity sprang up in the wilderness, in the midst of the forest which only a few hours before had been deserted.

It made a weird and impressive picture in the wonderful starlight night, these soldiers sitting around the camp fires softly singing in chorus; the fantastic outlines of the monastery half hidden in the woods; the dark figures of the monks moving silently back and forth amongst the shadows of the trees as they brought refreshments to the troops; the red glow of the camp fires illuminating the eager and enthusiastic faces of the young officers grouped around the colonel; the snorting and stamping of the horses nearby; an occasional melodic outcry of a sentinel out in the night; all these things merging into an unforgettable scene of great romanticism and beauty. That night I lay for a long while stretched near the smoldering ashes of the camp fire, with my cape as a blanket, in a state of lassitude and somnolence, my soul filled with exaltation and happiness over the beauty around me.

The rest, however, was of very short duration, for at six o'clock in the morning we were aroused, camp was broken up and soon afterwards we started on a forced march of twenty-two miles without a halt, during which we twice had to wade knee-deep through rivers. By midday most of the men were so exhausted that they could hardly crawl along. It was remarkable that the comparatively weaker and more refined city-bred people who had done little physical work in their lives, most of them being professional men, withstood hardships better than the sturdy and, to all appearances, stronger peasants; the only explanation for it being perhaps that the. city-bred people, in consequence of their better surroundings and by reason of their education, had more will power and nervous strength than the peasants.

At half-past two we reached a clearing in the midst of a wood through which a river flowed. Here camp was again established and a half hour later all the hardships of the march were once more forgotten in the bustle of camp life. This time we had a full rest until the next morning at four o'clock, when suddenly orders for marching were given. After we had been under way for about three hours we heard far-away, repeated rumbling which sounded like distant thunder. Not for a moment did we associate it with cannonading, being, as we supposed, hundreds of miles away from the nearest place where Russians could possibly be. Suddenly a mounted ordnance officer came rushing with a message to our colonel. We came to a halt and all officers were summoned to the colonel who, addressing us in his usual quiet, almost businesslike way, said: "Gentlemen, accept my congratulations, I have good news for you, we may meet the enemy to-day and I sincerely hope to lead you to the fight before evening." We were thunderstruck at the sudden realization that the Russians had penetrated so deeply into Galicia. The despondency which followed this startling revelation, however, was quickly replaced by the intense excitement of meeting the enemy so soon. We hurried back to our companies, imparting the news to the men, who broke forth into shouts of enthusiasm. All the fatigue so plainly noticeable only a few minutes before, suddenly vanished as if by magic, and every one seemed alert, springy, and full of spirit. We energetically resumed the march in the direction of the distant rumbling, which indicated that the artillery of our advance guard had engaged the enemy. My regiment then was part of the main body of a division. A second division advanced on the road parallel to ours, about a mile and a quarter to our left. Both columns belonged to the Third Army Corps and kept up constant communication with each other through mounted dispatch bearers and motor cycles.

The cannonading had meanwhile come perceptibly nearer, and in the midst of the dense forest we again came to a short halt. Orders were given to load rifles, and upon emerging from the woods we fell into open formation, the men marching abreast, the companies at a distance of three hundred yards, with the battalions at a distance of about a thousand yards. We were slowly entering the range of the Russian artillery. About a mile ahead we could see numbers of harmless looking round clouds, looking like ringlets of smoke from a huge cigar, indicating the places where shrapnel had exploded in mid-air. Our men, not being familiar with the spectacle, took no notice of it, but we officers knew its significance, and I daresay many a heart beat as wildly as mine did.

We marched on until the command was given for us to deploy, and soon afterwards the first shrapnel whizzed over our heads. It did no harm, nor did the second and third, but the fourth hit three men in the battalion in the rear of us. Our forward movement, however, was not interrupted, and we did not see or hear anything beyond two or three startled cries. The next shell burst right ahead of us, sending a shower of bullets and steel fragments around. A man about twenty yards to the right of my company, but not of my platoon, leaped into the air with an agonizing cry and fell in a heap, mortally wounded. As we were advancing very swiftly, I only saw it as in a dream, while running by. Then came in rapid succession four or five terrific explosions right over our heads, and I felt a sudden gust of cold wind strike my cheek as a big shell fragment came howling through the air, ploughing the ground viciously as it struck and sending a spray of sand around.

We ran on perhaps a quarter of a mile, when from the rear came the sharp command, "Down," and the next second we lay on the ground, panting and exhausted, my heart almost bursting with the exertion. Simultaneously the whizzing of a motor above our heads could be heard and we knew why the enemy's shrapnel had so suddenly found us. It was a Russian aeroplane which presumably had signaled our approach, together with the range, to the Russian gunners, and now was probably directing their fire and closely watching its effect, for a chain of hills was hiding us from the view of the enemy, who consequently had to fire indirectly. The air craft hovered above our heads, but we were forbidden to fire at it, the extremely difficult, almost vertical aim promising little success, aside from the danger of our bullets falling back among us. Our reserves in the rear had apparently sighted the air craft too, for soon we heard a volley of rifle fire from that direction and simultaneously the aeroplane arose and disappeared in the clouds.

Just then our own artillery came thundering up, occupied a little hill in the rear and opened fire on the enemy. The moral effect of the thundering of one's own artillery is most extraordinary, and many of us thought that we had never heard any more welcome sound than the deep roaring and crashing that started in at our rear. It quickly helped to disperse the nervousness caused by the first entering into battle and to restore self control and confidence. Besides, by getting into action, our artillery was now focusing the attention and drawing the fire of the Russian guns, for most of the latter's shells whined harmlessly above us, being aimed at the batteries in our rear. Considerably relieved by this diversion, we resumed our forward movement after about fifteen minutes of further rest, our goal being the little chain of hills which our advance guard had previously occupied pending our arrival. Here we were ordered to take up positions and dig trenches, any further advance being out of the question, as the Russian artillery overlooked and commanded the entire plain stretching in front of us.

We started at once to dig our trenches, half of my platoon stepping forward abreast, the men being placed an arm's length apart. After laying their rifles down, barrels pointing to the enemy, a line was drawn behind the row of rifles and parallel to it. Then each man would dig up the ground, starting from his part of the line backwards, throwing forward the earth removed, until it formed a sort of breastwork. The second half of the platoon was meanwhile resting in

Austro-Hungarian Field Artillery

the rear, rifle in hand and ready for action. After a half hour they took the place of the first division at work, and vice versa. Within an hour work on the trenches was so far advanced that they could be deepened while standing in them. Such an open trench affords sufficient shelter against rifle bullets striking from the front and can be made in a measure shell proof by being covered with boards, if at hand, and with sod.

In the western area of the theater of war, in France and Flanders, where whole armies were deadlocked, facing each other for weeks without shifting their position an inch, such trenches become an elaborate affair, with extensive underground working and wing connections of lines which almost constitute little fortresses and afford a certain measure of comfort. But where we were in Galicia at the beginning of the war, with conditions utterly unsteady and positions shifting daily and hourly, only the most superficial trenches were used. In fact, we thought ourselves fortunate if we could requisition enough straw to cover the bottom. That afternoon we had about half finished our work when our friend the aeroplane appeared on the horizon again. This time we immediately opened fire. It disappeared, but apparently had seen enough, for very soon our position was shelled. By this time, however, shrapnel had almost ceased to be a source of concern to us and we scarcely paid any attention to it. Human nerves quickly get accustomed to the most unusual conditions and circumstances and I noticed that quite a number of men actually fell asleep from sheer exhaustion in the trenches, in spite of the roaring of the cannon about us and the whizzing of shrapnel over our heads.

I, too, soon got accustomed to the deadly missiles,—in fact, I had already started to make observations of their peculiarities. My ear, accustomed to differentiate sounds of all kinds, had some time ago, while we still advanced, noted a remarkable discrepancy in the peculiar whine produced by the different shells in their rapid flight through the air as they passed over our heads, some sounding shrill, with a rising tendency, and the others rather dull, with a falling cadence. A short observation revealed the fact that the passing of a dull-sounding shell was invariably preceded by a flash from one of our own cannon in the rear on the hill, which conclusively proved it to be an Austrian shell. It must be understood that as we were advancing between the positions of the Austrian and Russian artillery, both kinds of shells were passing over our heads. As we advanced the difference between shrill and dull shell grew less and less perceptible, until I could hardly tell them apart. Upon nearing the hill the difference increased again more and more until on the hill itself it was very marked. After our trench was finished I crawled to the top of the hill until I could make out the flash of the Russian guns on the opposite heights and by timing flash and actual passing of the shell, found to my astonishment that now the Russian missiles had become dull, while on the other hand, the shrill shell was invariably heralded by a flash from one of our guns, now far in the rear. What had happened was this: Every shell describes in its course a parabolic line, with the first half of the curve ascending and the second one descending. Apparently in the first half of its curve, that is, its course while ascending, the shell produced a dull whine accompanied by a falling cadence, which changes to a rising shrill as soon as the acme has been reached and the curve points downward again. The acme for both kinds of shells naturally was exactly the half distance between the Russian and Austrian artillery and this was the point where I had noticed that the difference was the least marked. A few days later, in talking over my observation with an artillery officer, I was told the fact was known that the shells sounded different going up than when coming down, but this knowledge was not used for practical purposes. When I told him that I could actually determine by the sound the exact place where a shell coming from the opposing batteries was reaching its acme, he thought that this would be of great value in a case where the position of the opposing battery was hidden and thus could be located. He apparently spoke to his commander about me, for a few days later I was sent on a reconnoitering tour, with the object of marking on the map the exact spot where I thought the hostile shells were reaching their acme, and it was later on reported to me that I had succeeded in giving to our batteries the almost exact range of the Russian guns. I have gone into this matter at some length, because it is the only instance where my musical ear was of value during my service.

To return to my narrative, the losses which my battalion suffered that day seemed extraordinarily small when compared with the accuracy of the Russian artillery's aim and the number of missiles they fired. I counted seventy-four shrapnel that burst in a circle of half a mile around us in about two hours, and yet we had no more than about eighteen casualties. The most difficult part was to lie still and motionless while death was being dealt all about us and it was then and there that I had my first experience of seeing death next to me. A soldier of my platoon, while digging in the trench, suddenly leaned back, began to cough like an old man, a little blood broke from his lips, and he crumpled together in a heap and lay quite still. I could not realize that this was the end, for his eyes were wide open and his face wore the stamp of complete serenity. Apparently he had not suffered at all. The man had been a favorite with all his fellows by reason of his good humor, and that he was now stretched out dead seemed unbelievable. I saw a great many men die afterwards, some suffering horribly, but I do not recall any death that affected me quite so much as that of this first victim in my platoon.

CHAPTER II

THE artillery duel died out with the coming of darkness and we settled down to rest, half of the men taking watch while the others slept. At five o'clock in the morning our regiment suddenly received the order to fall in, and, together with two other regiments, was drawn out of the fighting line. Our commanding general had received news that an isolated detachment on the extreme right wing of our army, about fifteen miles east of us, had been entirely surrounded by a strong Russian body, and we were ordered to relieve them. It must not be forgotten that our men had been under a most incredible strain for the last three days with barely any rest during the nights and not more than one meal a day. They had actually welcomed entering the firing line, as a relief from the fatigues of marching with their heavy burdens. It is curious how indifferent one becomes to danger if one's organism is worn down and brain and faculty of perception numbed by physical exertion. It was, therefore, with badly broken-down strength that we started on this relief expedition, and it was good to see how unflinchingly the soldiers undertook their unexpected new task. All we had to say to our men was: "Boys, your brothers are needing you. They are cut off from all possible relief unless you bring it. Their lives are at stake, and as they are defending one of the most strategically important points—the right wing of our army—you can turn the tide of the whole battle in our favor; so go on." And on they went, staggering and stumbling, and at the end of a few hours almost crawling, but ever forward.

Suddenly we came up with another regiment which had been called to the same task, and the colonel of the new regiment, being older in rank than our colonel, took command of the newly formed brigade of two regiments. My company happened to march at the head of the regiment and the new brigadier rode for some time alongside of me. I was deeply impressed by his firm military and yet unassuming bearing and his deep glowing enthusiasm for his army and his men. He told me with pride that two of his sons were serving in the army, too, one as an artillery officer and the other one as an officer with the sappers. We were then approaching the point where we could hear distinctly the fire of our own batteries and the answer from the Russians, and here and there a volley of rifle fire. Our colonel urged us on to renewed energy, and knowledge that we were nearing our goal, seemed to give new strength to our men. Already we were witnessing evidences of the first fight that had passed here, for wounded men constantly passed us on stretchers. Suddenly I saw the face of the colonel riding next to me, light up with excitement as a wounded man was borne past. He addressed a few words to the stretcher-bearers and then turned to me, saying: "The regiment of my son is fighting on the hill. It is one of their men they have brought by." He urged us on again, and it seemed to me as if I noticed—or was it my imagination—a new note of appeal in his face. Suddenly another stretcher was brought past. The colonel at my side jumped from his horse, crying out, "My boy," and a feeble voice answered, "Father." We all stopped as if a command had been given, to look at the young officer who lay on the stretcher, his eyes all aglow with enthusiasm and joy, unmindful of his own wound as he cried out, "Father, how splendid that the relief should just come from you! Good. We held out splendidly. All we need is ammunition and a little moral support. Go on, don't stop for me, I am all right." The old colonel stood like a statue of bronze. His face had become suddenly ashen gray. He looked at the doctor and tried to catch his expression. The doctor seemed grave. But the young man urged us on, saying, "Go on, go on, I'll be all right to-morrow." The whole incident had not lasted more than five minutes, barely longer than it takes to write it. The colonel mounted his horse, sternly commanding us to march forward, but the light had died out of his eyes.

Within the next ten minutes a hail of shrapnel was greeting us, but hardly any one of us was conscious of it, so terribly and deeply were we affected by the scene of tragedy that had just been enacted before us. I remember foolishly mumbling something to the silent man riding next to me, something about the power of recuperation of youth, about the comparative harmlessness of the pointed, steelmantled rifle bullets which on account of their terrific percussion make small clean wounds and rarely cause splintering of the bone or blood poisoning. I remember saying that I had quite a medical knowledge and that it seemed to me that his son was not mortally wounded. But he knew better. He never said a word, only, a few minutes later, "He was my only hope"; and I can't express how ominous that word "was" sounded to me. But just then the command to deploy was given and the excitement that followed drowned for the time being all melancholy thoughts. We quickly ascended the hill where the isolated detachment of Austrians had kept the Russians at bay for fully twenty-four hours and opened fire on the enemy, while the second regiment tried to turn his left flank. The Russians slowly fell back but we followed them, and a sort of running fight ensued, during which my regiment lost about fifty— dead and wounded. The Russians temporarily resisted again, but soon the pressure from our other regiment on their flank began to be felt and they fled rather disorderly, leaving two machine guns, some ammunition, and four carriages full of provisions in our hands, while the regiment which had executed the flanking movement took two hundred and forty prisoners.

Around eight o'clock at night the fight was stopped for want of light, and we took up our newly acquired positions, entrenched them well, and began to make ready for the night. Orders for outpost duty were given and the officers were again called to the brigadier-colonel, who in a few words outlined the situation to us, thanking us for the pertinacity and bravery shown by the troops, and adding that the success of the expedition lay in the fact that we had arrived in time to save the situation.

Then the question of transporting prisoners to the rear came up, and while the brigadier's eyes were searching us I felt that he was going to entrust me with that mission. He looked at me, gave me the order in a short, measured way, but his eyes gazed searchingly and deeply into mine, and I thought I understood the unspoken message. So, tired as I was, I immediately set out with a guard of twenty men to transport the two hundred and forty Russian prisoners, among whom were two officers, back behind the fighting line. They seemed not unhappy over their lot—in fact, were smoking and chatting freely while we marched back. One of the Russian officers had a wound in his leg and was carried on a stretcher, but he, too, seemed quite at ease, conversing with me in French and congratulating me upon the bravery our isolated detachment had shown against the terrific onslaught. As soon as I had delivered them safely into the hands of the commander of our reserves, I inquired the way to the nearest field hospital in search of the young officer, the son of our brigadier-colonel. It was then about nine o'clock at night, and on entering the peasant's hut where the field hospital was established, I saw at a glance that I had come too late. He lay there still, hands folded over his breast with as serene and happy an expression as if asleep. His faithful orderly sat weeping next to him, and some kind hand had laid a small bunch of field flowers on his breast.

From the doctor I got the full information. He had received a shot in the abdomen and a rifle bullet had grazed his cheek. His last words had been a fervent expression of joy over the relief brought by his father and the knowledge that the position would not be taken by the Russians. He had died as simply as a child, without regret, and utterly happy. I took the orderly with me, asking him to carry all the belongings of the young officer with him in order to transmit them to his father.

When I returned with the orderly, the brigadier was issuing orders to his officers and conferring with them about the military situation. He saw me come, yet not a muscle moved in his face, nor did he interrupt his conversation. I was overwhelmed by the power this man showed at that minute, and admit I had not the courage to break the news to him, but it was unnecessary, for he understood. The faithful orderly stepped forward, as I had bidden him, presenting to the old man the pocketbook and small articles that belonged to his son. While he did so he broke forth into sobs, lamenting aloud the loss of his beloved lieutenant, yet not a muscle moved in the face of the father. He took my report, nodded curtly, dismissed me without a word, and turned back to his ordnance officers, resuming the conversation.

I assumed the command of my platoon which in the mean time had been assigned to do some outpost duty under the command of the sergeant. I inquired about their position and went out to join them. About midnight we were relieved, and when marching back, passed the place where the tent of the brigadier had been erected. I saw a dark figure lying on the floor, seemingly in deep sleep, and ordering my men to march on I crept silently forward. Then I saw that his shoulders were convulsively shaking and I knew that the mask of iron had fallen at last. The night was chilly so I entered his tent in search of his overcoat and laid it around his shoulders. He never noticed it. The next morning when I saw him his face was as immovable as it had been the night before, but he seemed to have aged by many years.

The next day was a comparatively restful one. We fortified the entrenchments which we had taken, and as our battle lines were extended to the right, from being the extreme right we became almost the center of the new position which extended for perhaps ten miles from northwest to southeast about eighteen miles south of Lemberg.

The next few days were given to repairs, provisioning, and resting, with occasional small skirmishes and shifting of positions. Then one night a scouting aeroplane brought news of a forward movement of about five Russian army corps, which seemed to push in the direction of our center. Against this force we could muster only about two army corps, but our strategical position seemed a very good one, both the extreme flanks of our army being protected by large and impassable swamps. Evidently the Russians had realized the impossibility of turning our flanks and were endeavoring to pierce our center by means of a vigorous frontal attack, relying upon their great superiority in numbers. Every preparation had been made to meet the onslaught during the night. Our trenches had been strengthened, the artillery had been brought into position, cleverly masked by means of transplanted bushes, the field in front of us had been cleared of objects obstructing the view, and the sappers had been feverishly busy constructing formidable barbed-wire entanglements and carefully measuring the shooting distances, marking the different ranges by bundles of hay or other innocent-looking objects, which were placed here and there in the field.

At nine o'clock in the morning everything was ready to receive the enemy, the men taking a short and well-deserved rest in their trenches, while we officers were called to the colonel, who acquainted us with the general situation, and, giving his orders, addressed us in a short, business-like way, appealing to our sense of duty and expressing his firm belief in our victory. We all knew that his martial attitude and abrupt manner were a mask to hide his inner self, full of throbbing emotion and tender solicitude for his subordinates, and we returned to our trenches deeply moved.

The camp was absolutely quiet, the only movements noticeable being around the field kitchens in the rear, which were being removed from the battle line. A half hour later any casual observer, glancing over the deserted fields might have laughed at the intimation that the earth around him was harboring thousands of men armed to their teeth, and that pandemonium of hell would break loose within an hour. Barely a sound was audible, and a hush of expectancy descended upon us. I looked around at my men in the trench; some were quietly asleep, some writing letters, others conversed in subdued and hushed tones. Every face I saw bore the unmistakable stamp of the feeling so characteristic of the last hour before a battle,—that curious mixture of solemn dignity, grave responsibility, and suppressed emotion, with an undercurrent of sad resignation. They were pondering over their possible fate, or perhaps dreaming of their dear ones at home.

By and by even the little conversation ceased, and they sat quite silent, waiting and waiting, perhaps awed by their own silence. Sometimes one would bravely try to crack a joke, and they laughed, but it sounded strained. They were plainly nervous, these brave men that fought like lions in the open when led to an attack, heedless of danger and destruction. They felt under a cloud in the security of the trenches, and they were conscious of it and ashamed. Sometimes my faithful orderly would turn his eye on me, mute, as if in quest of an explanation of his own feeling. Poor dear unsophisticated boy! I was as nervous as they all were, although trying my best to look unconcerned; but I knew that the hush that hovered around us like a dark cloud would give way like magic to wild enthusiasm as soon as the first shot broke the spell and the exultation of the battle took hold of us all.

Suddenly, at about ten o'clock, a dull thud sounded somewhere far away from us, and simultaneously we saw a small white round cloud about half a mile ahead of us where the shrapnel had exploded. The battle had begun. Other shots followed shortly, exploding here and there, but doing no harm. The Russian gunners evidently were trying to locate and draw an answer from our batteries. These, however, remained mute, not caring to reveal their position. For a long time the Russians fired at random, mostly at too short a range to do any harm, but slowly the harmless-looking white clouds came nearer, until a shell, whining as it whizzed past us, burst about a hundred yards behind our trench. A second shell followed, exploding almost at the same place. At the same time, we noticed a faint spinning noise above us. Soaring high above our position, looking like a speck in the firmament, flew a Russian aeroplane, watching the effect of the shells and presumably directing the fire of the Russian artillery. This explained its sudden accuracy. One of our aeroplanes rose, giving chase to the enemy, and simultaneously our batteries got into action. The Russians kept up a sharply concentrated, well-directed fire against our center, our gunners responding gallantly, and the spirited artillery duel which ensued grew in intensity until the entrails of the earth seemed fairly to shake with the thunder.

By one o'clock the incessant roaring, crashing, and splintering of bursting shells had become almost unendurable to our nerves, which were already strained to the snapping-point by the lack of action and the expectancy. Suddenly there appeared a thin dark line on the horizon which moved rapidly towards us, looking not unlike a huge running bird with immense outstretched wings. We looked through our field glasses; there could be no doubt,—it was Russian cavalry, swooping down upon us with incredible impetus and swiftness. I quickly glanced at our colonel. He stared open-mouthed. This was, indeed, good fortune for us,—too good to believe. No cavalry attack could stand before well-disciplined infantry, providing the latter keep cool and well composed, calmly waiting until the riders come sufficiently close to take sure aim.

There was action for us at last. At a sharp word of command, our men scrambled out of the trenches for better view and aim, shouting with joy as they did so. What a change had come over us all! My heart beat with wild exultation. I glanced at my men. They were all eagerness and determination, hand at the trigger, eyes on the approaching enemy, every muscle strained, yet calm, their bronzed faces hardened into immobility, waiting for the command to fire. Every subaltern officer's eye hung on our colonel, who stood about thirty yards ahead of us on a little hill, his figure well defined in the sunlight, motionless, the very picture of calm assurance and proud bearing. He scanned the horizon with his glasses. Shrapnel was hailing around him, but he seemed utterly unaware of it; for that matter we had all forgotten it, though it kept up its terrible uproar, spitting here and there destruction into our midst.

By this time the avalanche of tramping horses had come perceptibly nearer. Soon they would sweep by the bundle of hay which marked the carefully measured range within which our fire was terribly effective. Suddenly the mad stampede came to an abrupt standstill, and then the Cossacks scattered precipitately to the right and left, only to disclose in their rear the advancing Russian infantry, the movements of which it had been their endeavor to veil.

The infantry moved forward in loose lines, endlessly rolling on like shallow waves overtaking each other, one line running forward, then suddenly disappearing by throwing itself down and opening fire on us to cover the advance of the other line, and so on, while their artillery kept up a hellish uproar spreading destruction through our lines. Simultaneously a Russian aeroplane swept down upon us with a noise like an angered bird of prey and pelted us with bombs, the effects of which, however, were more moral than actual, for we had regained the security of the trenches and opened fire on the approaching enemy, who in spite of heavy losses advanced steadily until he reached our wire entanglements. There he was greeted by a deadly fire from our machine guns. The first Russian lines were mowed down as if by a gigantic scythe, and so were the reserves as they tried to advance. The first attack had collapsed. After a short time, however, they came on again, this time more cautiously, armed with nippers to cut the barbed wire and using the bodies of their own fallen comrades as a rampart. Again they were repulsed. Once more their cavalry executed a feigned attack under cover of which the Russian infantry rallied, strongly reinforced by reserves, and more determined than ever.

Supported by heavy artillery fire their lines rolled endlessly on and hurled themselves against the barbed-wire fences. For a short time it almost seemed, as if they would break through by sheer weight of numbers. At that critical moment, however, our reserves succeeded in executing a flanking movement. Surprised and caught in a deadly cross-fire, the Russian line wavered and finally they fled in disorder.

All these combined artillery, infantry, cavalry, and aeroplane attacks had utterly failed in their object of dislodging our center or shaking its position, each one being frustrated by the resourceful, cool alertness of our commanding general and the splendid heroism and stoicism of our troops. But the strain of the continuous fighting for nearly the whole day without respite of any kind, or chance for food or rest, in the end told on the power of endurance of our men, and when the last attack had been successfully repulsed they lay mostly prostrated on the ground, panting and exhausted. Our losses had been very considerable too, stretcher-bearers being busy administering first aid and carrying the wounded back to the nearest field hospital, while many a brave man lay stark and still.

By eight o'clock it had grown perceptibly cooler. We now had time to collect our impressions and look about us. The Russians had left many dead on the field, and at the barbed-wire entanglements which our sappers had constructed as an obstacle to their advance, their bodies lay heaped upon each other, looking not unlike the more innocent bundles of hay lying in the field. We could see the small Red Cross parties in the field climbing over the horribly grotesque tumuli of bodies, trying to disentangle the wounded from the dead and administer first aid to them.

Enthusiasm seemed suddenly to disappear before this terrible spectacle. Life that only a few hours before had glowed with enthusiasm and exultation, suddenly paled and sickened. The silence of the night was interrupted only by the low moaning of the wounded that came regularly to us. It was hideous in its terrible monotony. The moon had risen, throwing fantastic lights and shadows over the desolate landscape and the heaped-up dead. These grotesque piles of human bodies seemed like a monstrous sacrificial offering immolated on the altar of some fiendishly cruel, antique deity. I felt faint and sick at heart and near swooning away. I lay on the floor for some time unconscious of what was going on around me, in a sort of stupor, utterly crushed over the horrors about me. I do not know how long I had lain there, perhaps ten minutes, perhaps half an hour, when suddenly I heard a gruff, deep voice behind me—the brigadier, who had come around to inspect and to give orders about the outposts. His calm, quiet voice brought me to my senses and I reported to him. His self-assurance, kindness, and determination dominated the situation. Within five minutes he had restored confidence, giving definite orders for the welfare of every one, man and beast alike, showing his solicitude for the wounded, for the sick and weak ones, and mingling praise and admonition in just measure. As by magic I felt fortified. Here was a real man undaunted by nervous qualms or by over-sensitiveness. The horrors of the war were distasteful to him, but he bore them with equanimity. It was, perhaps, the first time in my life that I regretted that my artistic education had over-sharpened and overstrung my nervous system, when I saw how manfully and bravely that man bore what seemed to me almost unbearable. His whole machinery of thinking was not complicated and not for a moment did qualms of "Weltschmerz" or exaggerated altruism burden his conscience and interfere with his straight line of conduct which was wholly determined by duty and code of honor. In his private life he was an unusually kind man. His solicitude for his subordinates, for prisoners, and for the wounded was touching, yet he saw the horrors of the war unflinchingly and without weakening, for were they not the consequences of the devotion of men to their cause? The whole thing seemed quite natural to him. The man was clearly in his element and dominated it.

After having inspected the outposts, I went back, bedded myself in a soft sand-heap, covered myself up, and was soon fast and peacefully asleep. During the night the dew moistened the sand, and when I awoke in the morning I found myself encased in a plastering which could not be removed for days.

CHAPTER III

OUR hopes of getting a little rest and respite from the fighting were soon shattered, for a scouting aeroplane brought news that the Russians were again advancing in overwhelming strength. Our commanding general, coming to the conclusion that with the reduced and weakened forces at his command he could not possibly offer any effective resistance to a renewed onslaught, had determined to fall back slowly before their pressure. The consequence was a series of retreating battles for us, which lasted about ten days and which constituted what is now called the battle of Lemberg.

We were then terribly outnumbered by the Russians, and in order to extricate our army and prevent it from being surrounded and cut off, we constantly had to retreat, one detachment taking up positions to resist the advancing Russians, trying to hold them at all costs in order to give the rest of the army sufficient time to retire to safety. This maneuvering could not, of course, be carried out without the forces guarding the rear and covering the retreat suffering sometimes terrible losses.

These were depressing days, with rain and storm adding to the gloom. The men tramped wearily, hanging their heads, ashamed and humiliated by the retreat, the necessity of which they could not grasp, having, as they thought, successfully repulsed the enemy. It was difficult to make them understand that our regiment was only a cog in the huge wheel of the Austrian fighting machine and that, with a battle line extending over many miles, it was quite natural that partial successes could take place and yet the consideration of general strategy necessitate a retreat. Our arguing made little impression on the men; for they only shook their heads and said, "We were victorious, we should have gone on."

The spirit of retreating troops is vastly different from that shown by an advancing army, and it was probably in recognition of this well-known psychological state that our general staff had in the beginning attacked the Russians wherever they could, in spite of the overwhelming superiority of the foe, but the reinforcements the Russians were able to draw upon had swelled their ranks so enormously that any attack would have been little short of madness.

The real hardships and privations for us began only now. The few roads of Galicia, which at best are in bad condition, through the constant passing of heavy artillery and wagons of all kinds following each other in endless procession through constant rains, had become well-nigh impassable, the heavy mud constituting an additional impediment to the marching of troops. In order to get all of the train carrying provisions out of the possible reach of a sudden raid by the Russian cavalry, it had to be sent miles back of us, so as not to interfere with the movement of the troops. This caused somewhat of an interruption in the organization of the commissary department and very little food reached the troops, and that only at very long intervals.

The distribution of food to an army, even in peace and under the best conditions, is a very complicated and difficult undertaking. Provisions are shipped from the interior to the important railway centers, which serve as huge army depots and form the basis from which the different army corps draw their provisions and from which they are constantly replenished. They in turn supply the divisions and brigades wherefrom the regiments and battalions draw their provisions. So it is seen that the great aorta which leads from the interior to the big depots slowly subdivides itself into smaller arteries and feeders until they reach the ultimate destination, the extreme front.

This distribution of food had now become a formidable task, in consequence of the unforeseen movements and diversions which were forced upon us by the unexpected developments of the battle; and it often happened that food supplies intended for a certain detachment would reach their destination only after the departure of that detachment.

My platoon had by this time shrunk from fifty-five men to about thirty-four, but those remaining had become very hardened, efficient, and fit. It is astonishing how quickly the human organism adjusts itself, if need be, to the most difficult circumstances. So far as I was concerned, for instance, I adapted myself to the new life without any trouble at all, responding to the unusual demands upon me automatically, as it were. My rather impaired eyesight improved in the open, with only wide distances to look at. I found that my muscles served me better than ever before. I leaped and ran and supported fatigue that would have appalled me under other circumstances. In the field all neurotic symptoms seem to disappear as by magic, and one's whole system is charged with energy and vitality. Perhaps this is due to the open-air life with its simplified standards, freed from all the complex exigencies of society's laws, and unhampered by conventionalities, as well as to the constant throb of excitement, caused by the activity, the adventure, and the uncertainty of fate.

The very massing together of so many individuals, with every will merged into one that strives with gigantic effort toward a common end, and the consequent simplicity and directness of all purpose, seem to release and unhinge all the primitive, aboriginal forces stored in the human soul, and tend to create the indescribable atmosphere of exultation which envelopes everything and everybody as with a magic cloak.

It is extraordinary how quickly suggestions of luxury, culture, refinement, in fact all the gentler aspects of life, which one had considered to be an integral part of one's life are quickly forgotten, and, more than that, not even missed. Centuries drop from one, and one becomes a primeval man, nearing the cave-dweller in an incredibly short time. For twenty-one days I went without taking off my clothes, sleeping on wet grass or in mud, or in the swamps, wherever need be, and with nothing but my cape to cover me. Nothing disturbs one. One night, while sleeping, we were drenched to the skin by torrential rains. We never stirred, but waited for the sun to dry us out again. Many things considered necessities of civilization simply drop out of existence. A toothbrush was not imaginable. We ate instinctively, when we had food, with our hands. If we had stopped to think of it at all, we should have thought it ludicrous to use knife and fork.

We were all looking like shaggy, lean wolves, from the necessity of subsisting on next to nothing. I remember having gone for more than three days at a time without any food whatsoever, and many a time we had to lick the dew from the grass for want of water. A certain fierceness arises in you, an absolute indifference to anything the world holds except your duty of fighting. You are eating a crust of bread, and a man is shot dead in the trench next to you. You look calmly at him for a moment, and then go on eating your bread. Why not? There is nothing to be done. In the end you talk of your own death with as little excitement as you would of a luncheon engagement. There is nothing left in your mind but the fact that hordes of men to whom you belong are fighting against other hordes, and your side must win.

My memory of these days is very much blurred, every day being pretty nearly the same as the preceding one,—fatiguing marches, little rest and comparatively little fighting.

It is quite possible that our commander tried to divide the work of the troops in a just manner, and that in consequence of my regiment having borne the brunt of two terrible attacks, and having suffered considerable loss, we were now temporarily withdrawn from the fighting line, and not once during these days were assigned to the duty of a rear guard. Consequently we had only few and unimportant skirmishes in these days, twice while guarding the flank through having to repulse attacks of Cossacks, and once being harassed by an armored automobile. But the movements of an automobile being confined to the road, we had no difficulty in avoiding its fire, and as for the Cossacks with their eternal feigned attacks, we had reached the point where we almost ignored them.

We were in the first days of September, and upon reaching the swamps near Grodeck, south of Lemberg, a determined stand was decided upon by our commanding general. It seemed the most propitious place for a formidable defense, there being only few roads through otherwise impassable swamps. On September sixth my battalion was ordered to take up a position commanding a defile which formed one of the possible approaches for the enemy. Here we awaited the Russians, and they were not long in coming. First they violently shelled our position and silenced one of our batteries. Finding their artillery fire did not draw any answer from our side, they attempted to storm our position by means of frontal infantry attacks, combined with occasional raids of Cossacks, which were always repulsed. Finally the Russian infantry succeeded in establishing a number of trenches, the one opposite us not more than five hundred yards away. It was the first time we had come in close touch with the Russians, almost within hailing distance, and with the aid of our field glasses we could occasionally even get a glimpse of their faces and recognize their features. We stayed four days opposite each other, neither side gaining a foot of ground.

It was there and then that I made a curious observation. After the second day we had almost grown to know each other. The Russians would laughingly call over to us, and the Austrians would answer. The salient feature of these three days' fighting was the extraordinary lack of hatred. In fact, it is astonishing how little actual hatred exists between fighting men. One fights fiercely and passionately, mass against mass, but as soon as the mass crystallizes itself into human individuals whose features one actually can recognize, hatred almost ceases. Of course, fighting continues, but somehow it loses its fierceness and takes more the form of a sport, each side being eager to get the best of the other. One still shoots at his opponent, but almost regrets when he sees him drop.

By the morning of the third day we knew nearly every member of the opposing trench, the favorite of my men being a giant red-bearded Russian whose constant pastime consisted in jumping like a Jack-in-the-box from the trench, crying over to us as he did so. He was frequently shot at, but never hit. Then he grew bolder, showing himself longer and longer, until finally he jumped out of the trench altogether, shouting to us wildly and waving his cap. His good-humored jollity and bravado appealed to our boys and none of them attempted to shoot at him while he presented such a splendid target. Finally one of our men, who did not want to be second in bravery, jumped out of the trench and presented himself in the full sunlight. Not one attempt was made to shoot at him either, and these two men began to gesticulate at each other, inviting each other to come nearer. All fighting had suddenly ceased, and both opposing parties were looking on, laughing like boys at play. Finally the Russian would draw a step nearer, and our man boldly advanced too. Then the Russians urged on their man with shouts and laughter, and he made a big leap forward, standing still, whereupon the Austrian also jumped forward, and so, step by step, they approached until they nearly touched each other. They had left their rifles behind, and we thought that they were going to indulge in a fist fight, all of us being sorry for our champion, for he was a small and insignificant-looking man who looked as if he could be crushed with one blow by his gigantic opponent. But lo, and behold! The big Russian held out his hand which held a package of tobacco and our Austrian, seizing the tobacco, grasped the hand of the Russian, and then reaching in his pocket produced a long Austrian cigar, which he ceremoniously presented to the Russian. It was indeed a funny sight to see the small, wiry, lean Austrian talking in exaggerated terms of politeness to the blond Russian giant, who listened gravely and attentively, as if he understood every word.

By this time all precautions and even ideas of fighting had been forgotten, and we were surprised to find ourselves out of the shelter of our trenches and fully exposed to the Russians, who, in turn, leaned out of their own trenches and showed their heads in full. This unofficial truce had lasted about twenty minutes, and succeeded more in restoring good humor and joy of life among our soldiers than a trainload of provisions would have done. It was one of the incidents that helped to relieve the monotony of trench life and was heartily welcomed by all of us. The fighting, however, soon was resumed with all its earnestness and fierceness, but from this moment on a certain camaraderie was established between the two opposing trenches. Between skirmishes an unofficial truce would frequently be called for the purpose of removing the wounded. During these times when the stretcher-bearers were busy, no shot would be fired on either side.

Nor was this an isolated case, for similar intermittent truces, sometimes accompanied by actual intercourse between the opposing forces, were quite common all along the battle line. That very night I was hurriedly summoned to the trenches of the 13th Company, about half a mile east of us, in order to act as an interpreter between the major commanding that battalion and two singular guests he had just received, a Russian officer and his orderly. The pair, carrying a white flag, had hailed one of the numerous Austrian outposts placed during the night, in front of the trenches, and had been sent blindfolded back to the major. The Russian officer spoke only broken French. He commanded one of the opposing trenches, and from his narrative it appeared that his men had not received any food supplies for some days and were actually on the point of starvation. Not being able to stand their misery any longer, he had taken the bull by the horns and, with the utter confidence and straightforwardness of a fearless nature, had simply come over to us, the enemy, for help, offering a little barrel of water which his companion carried on his head and a little tobacco, in exchange for some provisions. The major seemed at first, perhaps, a little perplexed and undecided about this singular request, but his generous nature and chivalry soon asserted itself. One single look at the emaciated and worn faces of our guests sufficiently substantiated the truth of their story, for both men were utterly exhausted and on the verge of collapse. The next minute messengers were flying to the different trenches of the battalion to solicit and collect contributions, and the officers scrambled over each other in their noble contest to deplete their own last and cherished reserves for the supper of the guests. Soon the latter were seated as comfortably as circumstances permitted before a feast of canned beef, cheese, biscuits, and a slice of salami, my own proud contribution consisting of two tablets of chocolate, part of a precious reserve for extreme cases. It was a strange sight to see these two Russians in an Austrian trench, surrounded by cordiality and tender solicitude. The big brotherhood of humanity had for the time enveloped friend and foe, stamping out all hatred and racial differences. It is wonderful how the most tender flowers of civilization can go hand in hand with the most brutal atrocities of grim modern warfare.

In the mean while the messengers had returned almost staggering under the weight of a sack filled with the gifts of our soldiers to the enemy,—pieces of bread and biscuits with here and there a slice of bacon or a lump of cheese, all thrown pele-mele together. Many a man must have parted with his last piece of bread in order not to be outdone by the others in generosity, for our own provisions were running very low. It is true that the bread and biscuits were mildewed, the cheese stale, and the bacon as hard as stone, but the boys gave the best they could, the very poverty and humbleness of the gifts attesting their own desperate plight, and bearing proud witness to the extent of their sacrifice. With tears in their eyes and reiterated protestations of thanks, our guests staggered back through the night to their lines, undoubtedly carrying with them tender memories of Austrian generosity and hospitality.

On the morning of the next day a Russian detachment succeeded in storming a hill on our flank, commanding the strip of space between ourselves and our reserves in the rear, thus cutting us off from our main body. They established there a machine-gun battery, and, although we were under cover in our trench, we were now in a very precarious position, for no more provisions or ammunition could reach us, all attempts to do so breaking down under a terrific machine-gun fire, but we had orders to hold our position at all cost and to the last man. Unfortunately our ammunition was giving out, in spite of our husbanding it as much as possible and shooting only when we had a sure target. The Russians soon found that each shot meant a victim and took no chances on showing even the tips of their caps. Neither could we move the least bit without being the target for a volley from their side. Up to this day I cannot understand why they did not try to rush us, but apparently they were unaware of our comparative weakness.

Also for another reason our position had become more and more untenable. We were on swampy ground and the water was constantly oozing in from the bottom of the trench, so that we sometimes had to stand nearly knee-deep and were forced to bail the water out with our caps. It is difficult to imagine a more deplorable situation than to have to stay for four days in a foul trench, half filled with swamp water, constantly exposed to the destructive fire of the enemy, utterly isolated and hopeless.

Soon we were completely without any food or water and our ammunition was almost exhausted. During the night, here and there daring men would rush through the space swept by the Russian gun fire, which was kept up constantly, trying to bring us what scanty supplies they could procure from neighboring trenches better provided than we were, but the little they brought was nothing compared to our needs.

On the evening of that third day, knowing that our ammunition was

Russian infantry.

giving out, we felt that the next day would bring the end, and all our thoughts turned homewards and to the dear ones. We all wrote what we considered our parting and last farewell, each one pledging himself to deliver and take care of the letters of the others if he survived. It was a grave, sad, deeply touching moment, when we resigned ourselves to the inevitable, and yet somehow we all felt relieved and satisfied that the end might come and grimly resolved to sell our lives dearly.

Never before had I as much reason to admire the wonderful power of endurance and stoicism of our soldiers as on that night. Once resigned to the worst, all the old-time spirit returned, as if by magic. They sat together playing cards in as much moonlight as would fall into the deep trench, relating jokes and bolstering up one another's courage.

The fourth day broke gloomy, with a drizzling rain. At ten o'clock one of our men became suddenly insane, jumped out of the trench, danced wildly and divested himself of every stitch of clothing while doing so. Strange to say, the Russians must have realized that the man was insane, for they never fired at him, neither did they at the two men who jumped out to draw him back. We succeeded in comforting and

Cossacks of the Russian army during World War I

subduing him, and he soon fell into a stupor and remained motionless for some time. As soon as darkness fell we succeeded in conveying him back to the reserves and I understand that he got quite well again in a few days.

At five o'clock that afternoon we suddenly received orders through a running messenger, who was braving the incessant machine-gun fire, that our positions were about to be abandoned and that we were to evacuate our trench under the cover of darkness, at eleven o'clock. I cannot but confess that we all breathed more freely on the receipt of that information, but unfortunately the purpose could not be carried out. The Russians by this time evidently had realized our comparatively defenseless condition and utter lack of ammunition, for that same night we heard two shots ring out, being a signal from our sentinels that they were surprised and that danger was near. I hardly had time to draw my sword, to grasp my revolver with my left hand and issue a command to my men to hold their bayonets in readiness, when we heard a tramping of horses and saw dark figures swooping down upon us. For once the Cossacks actually carried out their attack, undoubtedly owing to their intimate knowledge of our lack of ammunition. My next sensation was a crushing pain in my shoulder, struck by the hoof of a horse, and a sharp knife pain in my right thigh. I fired with my revolver at the hazy figure above me, saw it topple over and then lost consciousness.

This happened, to the best of my recollection, at about half past ten at night. Upon coming to my senses I found my faithful orderly, kneeling in the trench by my side. He fairly shouted with delight as I opened my eyes. According to his story the Austrians, falling back under the cavalry charge, had evacuated the trench without noticing, in the darkness, that I was missing. But soon discovering my absence he started back to the trench in search of me. It was a perilous undertaking for him, for the Cossacks were still riding about, and he showed me with pride the place where a stray bullet had perforated his knapsack during the search. He revived me, gave me first aid, and succeeded with great difficulty in helping me out of the trench. For more than three hours we stumbled on in the night, trying to find our lines again. Twice we encountered a small troop of Cossacks, but upon hearing the tramping we quietly lay down on the wayside without a motion until they had passed. Happily we were not noticed by them, and from then we stumbled on without any further incident until we were hailed by an Austrian outpost and in safety.

By this time I was utterly exhausted and again lost consciousness. When I opened my eyes, I was in a little hut where our ambulance gave first aid. Therefrom I was transported to the nearest field hospital. This, however, had to be broken up and the wounded removed because of the Russian advance. We were hastily put on big ambulance wagons without springs, the jolting of which over the bad road caused us such suffering that we should have almost preferred to walk or crawl. We tried to reach the railway station at Komarno but found a Russian detachment had intercepted us. In the streets of the village a shell burst almost in front of our wagons, making the horses shy and causing a great deal of confusion. We had to turn back and after a long and wearisome detour reached our destination, the troop hospital in Sambor, in a state of great exhaustion. There I remained but a day. The less seriously wounded had to make place for the graver cases, and being among the former, I was transferred by hospital train to Miscolcy in Hungary. The same crowded conditions prevailed here as in

Sambor, and after a night's rest I again was put on board a Red Cross train en route to Vienna. We were met at the station by a number of Red Cross nurses and assistant doctors.

To my great joy my wife was among the former, having been assigned to that particular duty. A short official telegram to the effect that I was being sent home wounded on hospital train Number 16 was the first news she had received about me for fully four weeks. None of my field postcards had arrived and she was suffering extreme nervous strain from the long anxiety and suspense, which she had tried in vain to numb by feverish work in her hospital. I remained two weeks in Vienna and then was transferred to the sulphur bath of Baden nearby, where large hospitals had been established to relieve the overcrowding of Vienna. There I remained until the first of November when I was ordered to appear before a mixed commission of army surgeons and senior officers, for a medical examination. Two weeks later I received formal intimation that I had been pronounced invalid and physically unfit for army duty at the front or at home, and consequently was exempted from further service. My military experience ended there, and with deep regret I bade good-bye to my loyal brother officers, comrades, and faithful orderly, and discarded my well-beloved uniform for the nondescript garb of the civilian, grateful that I had been permitted to be of any, if ever so little, service to my Fatherland.

THEY SHALL NOT PASS

BY FRANK H. SIMONDS

CHAPTER I

MY TRIP TO VERDUN — GENERAL PÉTAIN FACE TO FACE — THE MEN WHO HOLD THE LINE — WHAT THEIR FACES TOLD OF THE PAST AND THE FUTURE OF FRANCE

MY road to Verdun ran through the Elysée Palace, and it was to the courtesy and interest of the President of the French Republic that I owed my opportunity to see the battle for the Meuse city at close range. Already through the kindness of the French General Staff I had seen the Lorraine and Marne battlegrounds and had been guided over these fields by officers who had shared in the opening battles that saved France. But Verdun was more difficult; there is little time for caring for the wandering correspondent when a decisive contest is going forward, and quite naturally the General Staff turned a deaf ear to my request.

Through the kindness of one of the many Frenchmen who gave time and effort to make my pilgrimage a success I was at last able to see M. Poincaré. Like our own American President, the French Chief Magistrate is never interviewed, and I mention this audience simply because it was one more and in a sense the final proof for me of the friendliness, the courtesy, the interest that the American will find to-day in France. I had gone to Paris, my ears filled with the warnings of those who told me that it was hard to be an American in Europe, in France, in the present hour. I had gone expecting, or at least fearing, that I should find it so.

Instead, from peasant to President I found only kindness, only gratitude, only a profound appreciation for all that Americans had individually done for France in the hour of her great trial. These things and one thing more I found: a very intense desire that Americans should be able to see for themselves; the Frenchman will not talk to you of what France has done, is doing; he shrinks from anything that might suggest the imitation of the German method of propaganda. In so far as it is humanly possible he would have you see the thing for yourself and testify out of your own mouth.

Thus it came about that all my difficulties vanished when I had been permitted to express to the President my desire to see Verdun and to go back to America—I was sailing within the week—able to report what I had seen with my own eyes of the decisive battle still going forward around the Lorraine city. Without further delay, discussion, it was promised that I should go to Verdun by motor, that I should go cared for by the French military authorities and that I should be permitted to see all that one could see at the moment of the contest.

We left Paris in the early afternoon; my companions were M. Henri Ponsot, chief of the Press Service of the Ministry of Foreign Affairs, and M. Hugues le Roux, a distinguished Frenchman of letters well known to many Americans. To start for the battlefield from a busy, peaceful city, to run for miles through suburbs as quiet and lacking in martial aspect as the regions beyond the Harlem, at home, was a thing that seemed almost unreal; but only for a brief moment, for war has come very near to Paris, and one may not travel far in Eastern France without seeing its signs.

In less than an hour we were passing the rear of the line held by the British at the Battle of the Marne, and barely sixty minutes after we had passed out through the Vincennes gate we met at Courtacon the first of the ruined villages that for two hundred miles line the roadways that lead from the capital to Lorraine and Champagne. Suddenly in the midst of a peaceful countryside, after passing a score of undisturbed villages, villages so like one to another, you come to one upon which the storm has burst, and instead of snug houses, smiling faces, the air of contentment and happiness that was France,

Western Battle Front, August 1916

there is only a heap of ruins, houses with their roofs gone, their walls torn by shell fire, villages abandoned partially or wholly, contemporary Pompeiis, overtaken by the Vesuvius of Krupp.

Coincidentally there appear along the roadside, in the fields, among the plough furrows, on every side, the crosses that mark the graves of those who died for France — or for Germany. Along the slope you may mark the passage of a charge by these crosses; those who fell were buried as they lay, French and Germans with equal care. Indeed, there is a certain pride visible in all that the French do for their dead foes. Alongside a hamlet wantonly burned, burned by careful labor and with German thoroughness; in villages where you will be told of nameless atrocities and shameful killings, you will see the German graves, marked by neat crosses, surrounded by sod embankments, marked with plaques of black and white; the French are marked by plaques of red, white and blue, and the latter invariably decorated with a flag and flowers.

Once you have seen these graves by the roadside going east you will hardly go a mile in two hundred which has not its graves. From the environs of Meaux, a scant twenty miles from Paris, to the frontier at the Seille, beyond Nancy, there are graves and more graves, now scattered, now crowded together where men fought hand to hand. Passing them in a swift-moving auto, they seem to march by you; there is the illusion of an army advancing on the hillside, until at last, beyond Nancy, where the fighting was so terrible, about little villages such as Corbessaux, you come to the great common graves, where a hundred or two hundred men have been gathered, where the trenches now levelled are but long graves, and you read, "Here rest 179 French soldiers," or across the road, "Here 196 Germans."

Take a map of France and from a point just south of Paris draw a straight line to the Vosges; twenty or thirty miles to the north draw another. Between the two is the black district of the Marne and Nancy battles. It is the district of ruined villages, destroyed farms; it is the region where every hillside—so it will seem to the traveller—is marked by these pathetic crosses. It is a region in which the sense of death and destruction is abroad. Go forty miles north again and draw two more lines, and this is the region not of the death and destruction of yesterday, but of to-day; this is the front, where the graves are still in the making, the region of the Oise to the Meuse, from Noyon to Verdun.

On this day our route led eastward through the villages which in September, 1914, woke from at least a century of oblivion, from the forgetting that followed Napoleon's last campaign in France to a splendid but terrible ten days: Courtacon, Sézanne, La-Fère

Champenoise, Vitry-le-François, the region where Franchet d'Esperey and Foch fought, where the "Miracle of the Marne" was performed. Mile after mile the countryside files by, the never-changing impression of a huge cemetery, the hugest in the world, the stricken villages, now and then striving to begin again, a red roof here and there telling of the first counter offensive of peace, of construction made against the whirlwind that had come and gone.

Always, too, nothing but old men and women, these and children, working in the broad fields, still partially cultivated, but no longer the fields of that perfectly cared for France of the other peace days. Women and children at the plough, old men bent double by age still spending such strength as is left in the tasks that war has set for them. This is the France behind the front, and, aside from the ruined villages and graves, the France that stretches from the Pyrenees to the Marne, a France from which youth and manhood are gone, in which age and childhood remain with the women. Yet in this land we were passing how much of the youth and manhood of France and Germany was buried in the graves the crosses demonstrated at every kilometre.

But a hundred miles east of Paris there begins a new world. The graves, the shell-cursed villages, remain, but this is no longer the France of the Marne fighting and of the war of two years ago. At Vitry-le-François you pass almost without warning into the region which is the back of the front to-day, the base of all the line of fire from Rheims to the Meuse, and suddenly along the road appear the canvas guideposts which bear the terse warning, "Verdun." You pass suddenly from ancient to contemporary history, from the killing of other years to the killing that is of to-day—the killing and the wounding—and along the hills where there are still graves there begin to appear Red Cross tents and signs, and ambulances pass you bearing the latest harvest.

And now every village is a garrison town. For a hundred miles there have been only women and old men, but now there are only soldiers; they fill the streets; they crowd the doorways of the houses. The fields are filled with tents, with horses, with all the impedimenta of an army. The whole countryside is a place of arms. Every branch of French service is about you—Tunisians, Turcos, cavalry, the black,

*With the Americans northwest of Verdun. The skipper and gunner of a
"whippet" tank, with the hatches open.*

the brown, and the white—the men who yesterday or last week were
in the first line, who rest and will return to-morrow or next day to fight
again.

Unmistakably, too, you feel that this is the business of war; you are
in a factory, a machine shop; if the product is death and destruction, it
is no less a matter of machinery, not of romance, of glamour. The back
of the front is a place of work and of rest for more work, but of parade,
of the brilliant, of the fascinating there is just nothing. Men with bright
but plainly weary faces, not young men, but men of thirty and above,
hard bitten by their experience, patently fit, fed, but somehow related
to the ruins and the destruction around them, they are all about you,
and wherever now you see a grave you will discover a knot of men
standing before it talking soberly. Wherever you see the vestiges of
an old trench, a hill that was fought for at this time twenty months ago,
you will see new practice trenches and probably the recruits, the "Class
of 1917," the boys that are waiting for the call, listening to an officer
explaining to them what has been done here, the mistake or the good
judgment revealed by the event. For France is training the youth that

remains to her on the still recent battlefields and in the presence of those who died to keep the ground.

Just as the darkness came we passed St. Dizier and entered at last upon the road to Verdun, the one road that is the life line of the city. For to understand the real problem of the defence of Verdun you must realize that there is lacking to the city any railroad. In September, 1914, the Germans took St. Mihiel and cut the railway coming north along the Meuse. On their retreat from the Marne the soldiers of the Crown Prince halted at Montfaucon and Varennes, and their cannon have commanded the Paris-Verdun-Metz Railroad ever since. Save for a crazy narrow-gauge line wandering along the hill slopes, climbing by impossible grades, Verdun is without rail communication.

It was this that made the defence of the town next to impossible. Partially to remedy the defect the French had reconstructed a local highway running from St. Dizier by Bar-le-Duc to Verdun beyond the reach of German artillery. To-day an army of a quarter of a million of men, the enormous parks of heavy artillery and field guns—everything is supplied by this one road and by motor transport.

Coming north from St. Dizier we entered this vast procession. Mile after mile the caravan stretched on, fifty miles with hardly a break of a hundred feet between trucks. Paris 'buses, turned into vehicles to bear fresh meat; new motor trucks built to carry thirty-five men and travelling in companies, regiments, brigades; wagons from the hood of which soldiers, bound to replace the killed and wounded of yesterday, looked down upon you, calmly but unsmilingly. From St. Dizier to Verdun the impression was of that of the machinery by which logs are carried to the saw in a mill. You felt unconsciously, yet unmistakably, that you were looking, not upon automobiles, not upon separate trucks, but upon some vast and intricate system of belts and benches that were steadily, swiftly, surely carrying all this vast material, carrying men and munitions and supplies, everything human and inanimate, to that vast grinding mill which was beyond the hills, the crushing machine which worked with equal remorselessness upon men and upon things.

Now and again, too, over the hills came the Red Cross ambulances; they passed you returning from the front and bringing within their carefully closed walls the finished product, the fruits of the day's grinding, or a fraction thereof. And about the whole thing there was a sense of the mechanical rather than the human, something that suggested an automatic, a machine-driven, movement; it was as if an unseen system of belts and engines and levers guided, moved, propelled this long procession upward and ever toward the mysterious front where the knives or the axes or the grinding stones did their work.

Night came down upon us along the road and brought a new impression. Mile on mile over the hills and round the curves, disappearing in the woods, reappearing on the distant summits of the hills, each showing a rear light that wagged crazily on the horizon, this huge caravan flowed onward, while in the villages and on the hillsides campfires flashed up and the faces or the figures of the soldiers could be seen now clearly and now dimly. But all else was subordinated to the line of moving transports. Somewhere far off at one end of the procession there was battle; somewhere down below at the other end there was peace. There all the resources, the life blood, the treasure in men and in riches of France were concentrating and collecting, were being fed into this motor fleet, which like baskets on ropes was carrying it forward to the end of the line and then bringing back what remained, or for the most part coming back empty, for more—for more lives and more treasure.

It was full night when our car came down the curved grades into Bar-le-Duc, halted at the corner, where soldiers performed the work of traffic policemen and steadily guided the caravan toward the road marked by a canvas sign lighted within by a single candle and bearing the one word, "Verdun." All night, too, the rumble of the passing transport filled the air and the little hotel shook with the jar of the heavy trucks, for neither by day nor by night is there a halt in the motor transport, and the sound of this grinding is never low.

It was little more than daylight when we took the road again, with a thirty-mile drive to Verdun before us. Almost immediately we turned into the Verdun route we met again the caravan of automobiles, of camions, as the French say. It still flowed on without break. Now, too, we entered the main road, the one road to Verdun, the road that had been built by the French army against just such an attack as was now in progress. The road was as wide as Fifth Avenue, as smooth as asphalt—a road that, when peace comes, if it ever does, will delight the motorist. Despite the traffic it had to bear, it was in perfect repair, and soldiers in uniform sat by the side breaking stone and preparing metal to keep it so.

The character of the country had now changed. We were entering the region of the hills, between the Aisne and the Meuse, a country reminiscent of New England. Those hills are the barrier which beyond the Meuse, under the names of the Côte de Meuse, have been the scene of so much desperate fighting. The roads that sidled off to the east bore battle names, St. Mihiel, Troyon, and the road that we followed was still marked at every turn with the magic word "Verdun." Our immediate objective was Souilly, the obscure hill town twenty miles, perhaps, south of the front, from which Sarrail had defended Verdun in the Marne days and from which Pétain was now defending Verdun against a still more terrible attack.

And in France to-day one speaks only of Verdun and Pétain. Soldiers have their day; Joffre, Castelnau, Foch, all retain much of the affection and admiration they have deserved, but at the moment it is the man who has held Verdun that France thinks of, and there was the promise for us that at Souilly we should see the man whose fame had filled the world in the recent great and terrible weeks. Upward and downward over the hills, through more ruined villages, more hospitals, more camps, our march took us until after a short hour we came to Souilly, general headquarters of the Army of Verdun, of Pétain, the centre of the world for the moment.

Few towns have done less to prepare for greatness than Souilly. It boasts a single street three inches deep in the clay mud of the spring—a single street through which the Verdun route marches almost contemptuously, the same nest of stone and plaster houses, one story high, houses from which the owners had departed to make room for generals and staff officers. This and one thing more, the Mairie, the town hall, as usual the one pretentious edifice of the French hamlet, and before the stairway of this we stopped and got out.

We were at headquarters. From this little building, devoted for perhaps a century to the business of governing the commune of Souilly, with its scant thousand of people, Pétain was defending Verdun and the fate of an army of 250,000 men at the least. In the upstairs room, where the town councillors had once debated parochial questions, Joffre and Castelnau and Pétain in the terrible days of the opening conflict had consulted, argued, decided—decided the fate of France, so the Germans had said, for they had made the fall of Verdun the assurance of French collapse.

Unconsciously, too, you felt the change in the character of the population of this village. There were still the soldiers, the eternal gray-blue uniforms, but there were also men of a different type, men of authority. In the street your guides pointed out to you General Herr, the man who had designed and planned and accomplished the miracle of the motor transport that had saved Verdun—with the aid of the brave men fighting somewhere not far beyond the nearest hills. He had commanded at Verdun when the attack came, and without hesitation he had turned over his command to Pétain, his junior in service and rank before the war, given up the glory and become the superintendent of transport. Men spoke to you of the fine loyalty of that action with unconcealed admiration.

And then out of the remoteness of Souilly there came a voice familiar to an American. Bunau-Varilla, the man of Panama, wearing the uniform of a commandant and the Croix de Guerre newly bestowed for some wonderful engineering achievement, stepped forward to ask for his friends and yours of the old "Sun paper." I had seen him last in the Sun office in the days when the war had just broken out and he was about to sail for home; in the days when the Marne was still unfought and he had breathed hope then as he spoke with confidence now.

Presently there arrived the two officers whose duty it was to take me to Verdun, Captain Henri Bourdeaux, a man of letters known to all Frenchmen; Captain Madelin, an historian, already documented in the history of the war making under his own eyes. To these gentlemen and their colleagues who perform this task that can hardly be agreeable, who risk their lives and give over their time with unfailing courtesy and consideration that the American newspaper correspondent may see, may report, it is impossible to return sufficient thanks, and every American newspaper reader who finds on his breakfast table the journal that tells him of the progress of the war owes something to some officer.

"Were we to see Verdun?" This was the first problem. I had been warned two days before that the bombardment was raging and that it was quite possible that it would be unsafe to go farther. But the news was reassuring; Verdun was tranquil. "And Pétain?" One could not yet say.

Even as we spoke there was a stirring in the crowd, general saluting, and I caught a glimpse of the commander-in-chief as he went quickly up the staircase. For the rest we must wait. But not for very long; in a few minutes there came the welcome word that General Pétain would see us, would see the stray American correspondent.

Since I saw Pétain in the little Mairie at Souilly I have seen many photographs of him, but none in any real measure give the true picture of the defender of Verdun. He saw us in his office, the bare upstairs room, two years ago the office of the Mayor of Souilly. Think of the Selectmen's office in any New England village and the picture will be accurate: a bare room, a desk, one chair, a telephone, nothing on the walls but two maps, one of the military zone, one of the actual front and positions of the Verdun fighting. A bleak room, barely heated by the most primitive of stoves. From the single window one looked down on the cheerless street along which lumbered the caravan of autos. On the pegs against the wall hung the General's hat and coat, weather-stained, faded, the clothes of a man who worked in all weathers. Of staff officers, of uniforms, of color there was just nothing; of war there was hardly a hint.

At the door the commander-in-chief met us, shook hands, and murmured clearly and slowly, with incisive distinctness, the formal words of French greeting; he spoke no English. Instantly there was the suggestion of Kitchener, not of Kitchener as you see him in flesh, but in photographs, the same coldness, decision. The smile that accompanied the words of welcome vanished and the face was utterly motionless, expressionless. You saw a tall, broad-shouldered man, with every appearance of physical strength, a clear blue eye, looking straight forward and beyond.

My French companion, M. Le Roux, spoke with Pétain. He had just come from Joffre and he told an interesting circumstance. Pétain listened. He said now and then "yes" or "no." Nothing more. Watching him narrowly you saw that occasionally his eyes twitched a little, the single sign of fatigue that the long strain of weeks of responsibility had brought.

It was hard to believe, looking at this quiet, calm, silent man, that you were in the presence of the soldier who had won the Battle of Champagne, the man whom the war had surprised in the last of his fifties, a Colonel, a teacher of war rather than a soldier, a professor like Foch.

No one of Napoleon's marshals had commanded as many men as obeyed this Frenchman, who was as lacking in the distinction of military circumstance as our own Grant. Napoleon had won all his famous victories with far fewer troops than were directed from the telephone on the table yonder.

Every impression of modern war that comes to one actually in touch with it is a destruction of illusion: this thing is a thing of mechanism rather than of brilliance; perhaps Pétain has led a regiment, a brigade, or a division to the charge. You knew instinctively in seeing the man that you would go or come, as he said, but there was neither dash nor fire, nothing of the suggestion of élan; rather there was the suggestion of the commander of a great ocean liner, the man responsible for the lives, this time of hundreds of thousands, not scores, for the safety of France, not of a ship, but the man of machinery and the master of the wisdom of the tides and the weather, not the Ney, or the Murat, not the Napoleon of Arcola. The impression was of a strong man whose life was a life beaten upon by storms; the man on the bridge, to keep to the rather ridiculously inadequate figure, but not by any chance the man on horseback.

My talk, our talk with Pétain was the matter of perhaps five minutes. The time was consumed by the words of M. Le Roux, who spoke very earnestly urging that more American correspondents be permitted to visit Verdun, and Pétain heard him patiently, but said just nothing. Once he had greeted us his face settled into that grim expression that never changed until he smiled his word of good wishes as we left. Yet I have since found that apart from one circumstance which I shall mention in a moment I have remembered those minutes most clearly of all of my Verdun experience. Just as the photograph does not reveal the face of the man, the word does not describe the sense of strength, of responsibility, that he gives.

In a childish sort of way, exactly as one thinks of war as a matter of dash and color and motion, one thinks of the French general as the leader of a cavalry charge or of a forlorn hope of infantry. And the French soldier of this war has not been the man of charge or of dash — not that he has not charged as well as ever in his history, a little more bravely, perhaps, for machine guns are new and something worse than other wars have had. What the French soldier has done has been to stand, to hold, to die not in the onrush but on the spot.

And Pétain in some curious way has fixed in my mind the impression of the new Frenchman, if there be a new one, or perhaps better of the French soldier of to-day, whether he wear the stars of the general or undecorated "horizon" blue of the Poilu. The look that I saw in his eyes, the calm, steady, utterly emotionless looking straight forward, I saw everywhere at the front and at the back of the front. It embodied for me an enduring impression of the spirit and the poise of the French soldier of the latest and most terrible of French struggles. And I confess that, more than all I saw and heard at the front and in Paris, the look of this man convinced me that Verdun would not fall, that France herself would not either weary or weaken.

In Paris, where one may hear anything, there are those that will tell you that Joffre's work is done and that France waits for the man who will complete the task; that the strain of the terrible months has wearied the general who won the Battle of the Marne and saved France. They will tell you, perhaps, that Pétain is the man; they will certainly tell you that they hope that the man has been found in Pétain. As to the truth of all this I do not pretend to know. I did not see Joffre, but all that I have read of Joffre suggests that Pétain is of his sort, the same quiet, silent man, with a certain coldness of the North, a grimness of manner that is lacking in his chief.

There was a Kitchener legend in Europe, and I do not think it survives save a little perhaps in corners of England. There was a legend of a man of ice and of iron, a man who made victory out of human material as a man makes a wall of mortar and stone, a man to whom his material was only mortar and stone, even though it were human. This legend has perished so far as Kitchener is concerned, gone with so much that England trusted and believed two years ago, but I find myself thinking now of Pétain as we all thought of Kitchener in his great day.

If I were an officer I should not like to come to the defender of Verdun with the confession of failure. I think I should rather meet the Bavarians in the first line trenches, but I should like to know that when I was obeying orders I was carrying out a minor detail of something Pétain had planned; I should expect it to happen, the thing that he had arranged, and I should feel that those clear, steel-blue eyes had foreseen all that could occur, foreseen calmly and utterly, whether it entailed the death of one or a thousand men, of ten thousand men if necessary, and had willed that it should happen.

I do not believe Napoleon's Old Guard would have followed Pétain as they followed Ney. I cannot fancy him in the Imperial uniform, and yet, now that war is a thing of machines, of telephones, of indirect fire and destruction from unseen weapons at remote ranges, now that the whole manner and circumstance of conflict have changed, it is but natural that the General should change, too. Patently Pétain is of the new, not the old, but no less patently he was the master of it.

We left the little Mairie, entered our machines and slid out swiftly for the last miles, climbed and curved over the final hill and suddenly looked down on a deep, trenchlike valley marching from east to west and carrying the Paris-Verdun-Metz Railroad, no longer available for traffic. And as we coasted down the hill we heard the guns at last, not steadily, but only from time to time, a distant boom, a faint billowing up of musketry fire. Some three or four miles straight ahead there were the lines of fire beyond the brown hills that flanked the valley.

At the bottom of the valley we turned east, moved on for a mile, and stopped abruptly. The guns were sounding more clearly, and suddenly there was a sense not of soldiers, but of an army. On one side of the road a column was coming toward us, a column of men who

German infantry at the top of le mort homme, Verdun

were leaving the trenches for a rest, the men who for the recent days had held the first line. Wearily but steadily they streamed by; the mud of the trenches covered their tunics; here and there a man had lost his steel helmet and wore a handkerchief about his head, probably to conceal a slight wound that but for the helmet had killed him.

These men were smiling as they marched; they carried their full equipment and it rattled and tinkled; they carried their guns at all angles, they wore their uniforms in the strangest of disorders; they seemed almost like miners coming from the depths of the earth rather than soldiers returning from a decisive battle, from the hell of modern shell fire.

But it was the line on the other side of the road that held the eye. Here were the troops that were going toward the fire, toward the trenches, that were marching to the sound of the guns, and as one saw them the artillery rumble took on a new distinctness.

Involuntarily I searched the faces of these men as they passed. They were hardly ten feet from me. Platoon after platoon, company after company, whole regiments in columns of fours. And seeing the faces brought an instant shock; they all wore the same calm, steady, slightly weary expression, but there was in the whole line scarcely a young man. Here were men of the thirties, not the twenties; men still in the prime of strength, of health, but the fathers of families, the men of full manhood.

Almost in a flash the fact came home. This was what all the graves along the road had meant. This was what the battlefields and the glories of the twenty months had spelled—France had sent her youth and it was spent; she was sending her manhood now.

In the line no man smiled and no man straggled; the ranks were closed up and there were neither commands nor any visible sign of authority. These men who were marching to the sound of the guns had been there before. They knew precisely what it meant. Yet you could not but feel that as they went a little wearily, sadly, they marched willingly. They would not have it otherwise. Their faces were the faces of men who had taken the full measure of their own fate.

You had a sense of the loathing, the horror, above all the sadness that was in their hearts that this thing, this war, this destruction had to be. They had come back here through all the waste of ruined villages and shell-torn hillsides; all the men that you saw would not measure the cost of a single hour of trench fighting if the real attack began. This these men knew, and the message of the artillery fire, which was only one of unknown terrors for you, was intelligible to the utmost to each of them.

And yet with the weariness there was a certain resignation, a certain patience, a certain sense of comprehending sacrifice that more than all else is France to-day, the true France. This, and not the empty forts, not even the busy guns, was the wall that defended France, this line of men. If it broke there would come thundering down again out of the north all the tornado of destruction that had turned Northeastern France into a waste place and wrecked so much of the world's store of the beautiful and the inspiring.

Somehow you felt that this was in the minds of all these men. They had willed to die that France might live. They were going to a death that sounded ever more clearly as they marched. This death had eaten up all that was young, most of what was young at the least, of France; it might yet consume France, and so these men marched to the sound of the guns, not to martial music, not with any suggestion of dash, of enthusiasm, but quietly, steadily, all with the same look upon their faces—the look of men who have seen death and are to see it again.

Instinctively I thought of what Kipling had said to me in London:

"Somewhere over there," he had said, "the thing will suddenly grip your throat and your heart; it will take hold of you as nothing in your life has ever done or ever will." And I know that I never shall forget those lines of quiet, patient, middle-aged men marching to the sound of the guns, leaving at their backs the countless graves that hold the youth of France, the men who had known the Marne, the Yser, Champagne, who had known death for nearly two years, night and day, almost constantly. Yet during the fifteen minutes I watched there was not one order, not one straggler; there was a sense of the regularity with which the blood flows through the human arteries in this tide, and it was the blood of France.

So many people have asked me, I had asked myself, the question before I went to France: "Are they not weary of it? Will the French not give up from sheer exhaustion of strength?" I do not think so, now that I have seen the faces of these hundreds of men as they marched to the trenches beyond Verdun. France may bleed to death, but I do not think that while there are men there will be an end of the sacrifice. No pen or voice can express the horror that these men, that all Frenchmen, have of this war, of all war, the weariness. They hate it; you cannot mistake this; but France marches to the frontier in the spirit that men manned the walls against the barbarians in the other days; there is no other way; it must be.

Over and over again there has come the invariable answer; it would have come from scores and hundreds of these men who passed so near me I could have touched their faded uniforms if I had asked—"It is for France, for civilization; it must be, for there is no other way; we shall die, but with us, with our sacrifice, perhaps this thing will end." You cannot put it in words quite, I do not think even any Frenchman has quite said it, but you can see it, you can feel it, you can understand it, when you see a regiment, a brigade, a division of these men of thirty, some perhaps of forty, going forward to the war they hate and will never quiet until that which they love is safe or they and all of their race are swallowed up in the storm that now was audibly beating beyond the human walls on the nearby hillsides.

Presently we moved again, we slipped through the column, topped the last incline, shot under the crumbling gate of the Verdun fortress, and as we entered a shell burst just behind us and the roar drowned out all else in its sudden and paralyzing crash. It had fallen, so we learned a little later, just where we had been watching the passing troops; it had fallen among them and killed. But an hour or two later, when we repassed the point where it fell, men were still marching by. Other regiments of men were still marching to the sound of the guns, and those who had passed were already over the hills and beyond the river, filing into the trenches in time, so it turned out, to meet the new attack that came with the later afternoon.

I went to Verdun to see the forts, the city, the hills, and the topography of a great battle; I went in the hope of describing with a little of clarity what the operation meant as a military affair. I say, and I shall hereafter try to describe this. But I shall never be able to describe this thing which was the true Verdun for me—these men, their faces, seen as one heard the shell fire and the musketry rolling, not steadily but intermittently, the men who had marched over the roads that are lined with graves, through villages that are destroyed, who had come of their own will and in calm determination and marched unhurryingly and yet unshrinkingly, the men who were no longer young, who had left behind them all that men hold dear in life, home, wives, children, because they knew that there was no other way.

I can only say to all those who have asked me, "What of France?" this simple thing, that I do not believe the French will ever stop. I do not believe, as the Germans have said, that French courage is weakening, that French determination is abating. I do not believe the Kaiser himself would think this if he had seen these men's faces as they marched toward his guns. I think he would feel as I felt, as one must feel, that these men went willingly, hating war with their whole soul, destitute of passion or anger. I never heard a passionate word in France, because there had entered into their minds, into the mind and heart of a whole race, the belief that what was at stake was the thing that for two thousand years of history had been France.

CHAPTER II

MY TRIP TO VERDUN — A DYING, SHELL-
RIDDEN CITY — THE VAUBAN CITADEL, IN
THE SHELTER OF WHICH FALLING SHELLS
CANNOT FIND YOU — HOUSES AND BLOCKS
THAT ARE VANISHING HOURLY — "BUT
WILLIAM WILL NOT COME" — WAR THAT IS
INVISIBLE — A LUNCHEON UNDERGROUND
WITH A TOAST TO AMERICA — THE LAST
COURTESY FROM A GENERAL AND A
HOST — NOTHING THAT WAS NOT
BEAUTIFUL

THE citadel of Verdun, the bulwark of the eastern frontier in ancient days, rises out of the meadows of the Meuse with something of the abruptness of the sky-scraper, and still preserves that aspect which led the writers of other wars to describe all forts as "frowning." It was built for Louis XIV by Vauban. He took a solid rock and blasted out redoubts and battlements. The generations that followed him dug into the living rock and created within it a whole city of catacombs, a vast labyrinth of passages and chambers and halls; even an elevator was added by the latest engineers, so that one can go from floor to floor, from the level of the meadow to the level of the summit of the rock, possibly a hundred feet above.

By reason of the fact that many correspondents have visited this fortress since the war began the world has come to know of the underground life in Verdun, to think of the city as defended by some wonderful system of subterranean works; to think of Verdun, in fact, as a city or citadel that is defensible either by walls or by forts. But the truth is far different: even the old citadel is but a deserted cave; its massive walls of natural rock resist the shells as they would repulse an avalanche; but the guns that were once on its parapets are gone, the garrison is gone, gone far out on the trench lines beyond the hills. The Vauban citadel is now a place where bread is baked, where wounded men are occasionally brought, where live the soldiers and officers whose important but unromantic mission it is to keep the roads through the town open, to police the ashes of the city, to do what remains of the work that once fell to the lot of the civil authorities.

To glide swiftly to the shelter of this rock from a region in which a falling shell has served to remind you of the real meaning of Verdun of the moment, to leave the automobile and plunge into the welcome obscurity of this cavern—this was perhaps the most comfortable personal incident of the day. The mere shadow of the rock gave a sense of security; to penetrate it was to pass to safety.

Some moments of wandering by corridors and stairways into the very heart of the rock brought us to the quarters of our host, General Dubois; to his kind attention I was to owe all my good fortune in seeing his dying city; to him, at the end, I was to owe the ultimate evidence of courtesy, which I shall never forget.

Unlike Pétain or Joffre, General Dubois is a little man, possibly a trifle older than either. A white-haired, bright-eyed, vigorous soldier, who made his real fame in Madagascar with Joffre and with Gallieni, and when the storm broke was sent to Verdun by these men, who knew him, to do the difficult work that there was to be performed behind the battle line. There is about General Dubois a suggestion of the old, as well as the new, of the French general. The private soldiers to whom he spoke as he went his rounds responded with a "Oui, mon Général" that had a note of affection as well as of discipline; he was rather as one fancied were the soldiers of the Revolution, of the Empire, of the Algerian days of Père Bugeaud whose memory is still green.

Our salutations made, we returned through the winding corridors to inspect the bakeries, the water and light plant, the unsuspected resources of this rock. In one huge cavern we saw the men who provided 30,000 men with bread each day, men working as the stokers in an ocean steamer labor amidst the glare of fires; we tasted the bread and found it good, as good as all French bread is, and that means a little better than all other bread.

Then we slipped back into daylight and wandered along the face of the fortress. We inspected shell holes of yesterday and of last month; we inspected them as one inspects the best blossoms in a garden; we studied the angle at which they dropped; we measured the miniature avalanche that they brought with them. But always, so far, there was the subconscious sense of the rock between us and the enemy. I never before understood the full meaning of that phrase "a rock in a weary land."

All this was but preliminary, however. Other automobiles arrived; the General entered one. I followed in the next and we set out to visit Verdun, to visit the ruins, or, rather, to see not a city that was dead, but a city that was visibly, hourly dying—a city that was vanishing by blocks and by squares—but was not yet fallen to the estate of Ypres or Arras; a city that in corners, where there were gardens behind the walls, still smiled; a city where some few brave old buildings still stood four square and solid, but only waiting what was to come.

Before I visited Verdun I had seen many cities and towns which had been wholly or partially destroyed, either by shell fire or by the German soldiers in their great invasion before the Marne. One shelled town is much like another, and there is no thrill quite like that you experience when you see the first. But these towns had died nearly two years ago; indeed, in most the resurrection had begun: little red roofs were beginning to shine through the brown trees and stark ruins. Children played again in the squares. It was like the sense you have when you see an old peasant ploughing among the cross-marked graves of a hard-fought battle corner—the sense of a beginning as well as of death and destruction.

But at Verdun it was utterly different. Of life, or people, of activity beginning again or surviving there was nothing. Some time in the recent past all the little people who lived in these houses had put upon wagons what could be quickly moved and had slipped out of their home, that was already under sentence of death. They were gone into the distance, and they had left behind them no stragglers. The city was empty save for a few soldiers who passed rapidly along the streets, as one marches in a heavy snowstorm.

Yet Verdun was not wholly dead. Shell fire is the most inexplicable of all things that carry destruction. As you passed down one street the mark of destruction varied with each house. Here the blast had come and cut the building squarely; it had carried with it into ruin behind in the courtyard all that the house contained, but against the wall the telephone rested undisturbed; pictures—possibly even a looking glass—hung as the inhabitants had left it, hung as perhaps it had hung when the last woman had taken her ultimate hurried glance at her hat before she departed into the outer darkness.

But the next house had lost only the front walls; it stood before you as if it had been opened for your inspection by the removal of the façade. Chairs, beds—all the domestic economy of the house—sagged visibly outward toward the street, or stood still firm, but open to the four winds. It was as if the scene were prepared for a stage and you sat before the footlights looking into the interior. Again, the next house and that beyond were utterly gone—side walls, front walls, everything swallowed up and vanished—the iron work twisted into heaps, the stone work crumbled to dust; the whole mass of ruin still smoked, for it was a shell of yesterday that had done this work.

Down on the Riviera, where the mistral blows—all the pine trees lean away from the invariable track of this storm wind—you have the sense, even in the summer months, of a whole countryside bent by the gales. In the same fashion you felt in Verdun, felt rather than saw, a whole town not bent, but crumbled, crushed—and the line of fall was always apparent; you could tell the direction from which each storm of shells had come, you could almost feel that the storm was but suspended, not over, that at any moment it might begin again.

Yet even in the midst of destruction there were enclaves of unshaken structures. On the Rue Mazel, "Main Street," the chief clothing store rose immune amid ashes on all sides. Its huge plate-glass window was not even cracked. And behind the window a little mannikin, one of the familiar images that wear clothes to tempt the purchaser, stood erect. A French soldier had crept in and raised the stiff arm of the mannikin to the salute, pushed back the hat to a rakish angle. The mannikin seemed alive and more than alive, the embodiment of the spirit of the place. Facing northward toward the German guns it seemed to respond to them with a "morituri

Reserves crossing a river on the way to Verdun. "They shall not pass" is a phrase which for all time will be associated with the heroic defense of Verdun. To future generations of French people it will bring a thrill of pride even surpassing that enkindled by the glorious "The Old Guard dies, it never surrenders." The guardians of the great fortress on the Meuse have proved themselves invincible in attack, invulnerable in defense.

salutamus." "The last civilian in Verdun," the soldiers called him, but his manner was rather that of the Poilu.

We crossed the river and the canal and stopped by the ruin of what had once been a big factory or warehouse. We crawled through an open shell-made breach in the brick wall and stood in the interior. The ashes were still hot, and in corners there were smoking fires. Two days ago, at just this time, your guides told you, men had been working here; making bread, I think. At the same time we had come to the ruins — the same time of day, that is — the Germans had dropped a half-dozen incendiary shells into the building and it had burned in ten minutes. Most of the men who had been there then were still there, under the smoking mass of wreckage; the smell of burned human flesh was in the air.

A few steps away there was a little house standing intact. On the floor there were stretched four rolls of white cloth. The General and those with him took off their hats as they entered. He opened one of the packages and you saw only a charred black mass, something that looked like a half-burned log taken from the fireplace. But two days ago it had been a man, and the metal disk of identification had already been found and had served to disclose the victim's name. These were the first bodies that had been removed from the ruins.

Taking our cars again we drove back and stopped before the Mairie, and passing under the arch entered the courtyard. The building had fared better than most, but there were many shell marks. In the courtyard were four guns. Forty-six years before another German army had come down from the North, another whirlwind of artillery had struck the town and laid it in ashes, but even under the ashes the town had held out for three weeks. Afterward the Republic of France had given these guns to the people of Verdun in recognition of their heroism.

In the courtyard I was presented to a man wearing the uniform and helmet of a fireman. He was the chief of the Verdun fire department. His mission, his perilous duty, it was to help extinguish the fires that flamed up after every shell. In all my life I have never seen a man at once so crushed and so patently courageous. He was not young, but his blue Lorraine eyes were still clear. Yet he looked at you, he looked out upon the world with undisguised amazement. For a generation his business had been to fight fires. He had protected his little town from conflagrations that might sometimes, perhaps once, possibly twice, have risen to the dignity of a "three alarm." For the rest he had dealt with blazes.

Now out of the skies and the darkness and out of the daylight, too, fire had descended upon his town. Under an avalanche of incendiary shells, under a landslide of fire, his city was melting visibly into ashes. He had lived fire and dreamed fire for half a century, but now the world had turned to fire—his world—and he looked out upon it in dazed wonder. He could no longer fight this fire, restrain it, conquer it; he could only go out under the bursting shells and strive to minimize by some fraction the destruction; but it was only child's play, this work of his which had been a man's business. And there was no mistaking the fact that this world was now too much for him. He was a brave man; they told me of things he had done; but his little cosmos had gone to chaos utterly.

We entered our cars again and went to another quarter of the city. Everywhere were ashes and ruin, but everywhere the sense of a destruction that was progressive, not complete: it still marched. It was as Arras had been, they told me, before the last wall had tumbled and the Artois capital had become nothing but a memory. We climbed the slope toward the cathedral and stopped in a little square still unscathed, the Place d'Armes, the most historic acre of the town. After a moment I realized what my friends were telling me. It was in this square that the Crown Prince was to receive the surrender of the town. Along the road we had climbed he was to lead his victorious army through the town and out the Porte de France beyond. In this square the Kaiser was to stand and review the army, to greet his victorious son. The scene as it had been arranged was almost rehearsed for you in the gestures of the French officers.

"But William has not come," they said, "and he will not come now." This last was not spoken as a boast, but as a faith, a conviction.

Still climbing we came to the cathedral. It is seated on the very top pinnacle of the rock of Verdun, suggesting the French cities of Provence. Its two towers, severe and lacking ornamentation, are the landmarks of the countryside for miles around. When I came back to America I read the story of an American correspondent whom the Germans had brought down from Berlin to see the destruction of Verdun. They had brought him to the edge of the hills and then thrown some incendiary shells into the town, the very shells that killed the men whose bodies I had seen. The black smoke and flames rushed up around these towers and then the Germans brought the correspondent over the hills and showed him the destruction of Verdun. He described it vividly and concluded that the condition of the town must be desperate.

They are a wonderful people, these Germans, in their stage management. Of course this was precisely the thing that they desired that he should feel. They had sent their shells at the right moment, the whole performance had gone off like clockwork. Those poor blackened masses of humanity in the house below were the cost that was represented in the performance. And since there is much still left to burn in Verdun, the Germans may repeat this thing whenever they desire.

But somewhere three or four miles from here, and between Verdun and the Germans, are many thousands of Frenchmen, with guns and cannon, and hearts of even finer metal. They cannot even know that Verdun is being shelled or is burning, and if it burns to ultimate ashes it will not affect them or their lines. This is the fallacy of all the talk of the destruction of Verdun city and the desperate condition of its defenders. The army left Verdun for the hills when the war began; the people left when the present drive began in February. Even the dogs and cats, which were seen by correspondents in earlier visits, have been rescued and sent away. Verdun is dead, it is almost as dead as are Arras and Ypres; but neither of these towns after a year and a half bombardment has fallen.

The correspondent who was taken up on a hill by the Germans to see Verdun burn, after it had been carefully set on fire by shell fire, was discovered by French gunners and shelled. He went away taking with him an impression of a doomed city. This picture was duly transmitted to America. But two days later, when I visited the city, there was no evidence of desperation, because there was no one left to be desperate. Doubtless on occasion we shall have many more descriptions of the destruction of this town, descriptions meant to impress Americans or encourage Germans. The material for such fires is not exhausted. The cathedral on the top of the hill is hardly shell-marked at all, and it will make a famous display when it is fired as was Rheims, as were the churches of Champagne and Artois. But there is something novel in the thought of a city burned, not to make a Roman or even German holiday, but burned to make the world believe that the Battle of Verdun had been a German victory.

For two hours we wandered about the town exploring and estimating the effect of heavy gunfire, for the Germans are too far from the city to use anything but heavy guns effectively. The impressions of such a visit are too numerous to recall. I shall mention but one more. Behind the cathedral are cloisters that the guide books mention; they inclose a courtyard that was once decorated with statues of saints. By some accident or miracle—there are always miracles in shelled towns—one of these images, perhaps that of the Madonna, has been lifted from its pedestal and thrown into the branches of a tree, which seems almost to hold it with outstretched arms.

At length we left the town, going out by the Porte de France, which cuts the old Vauban ramparts, now as deserted as those of Paris, ramparts that had been covered with trees and were now strewn with the débris of the trees that had fallen under the shell fire. In all this time not a shell had fallen in Verdun; it was the first completely tranquil morning in weeks; but there was always the sense of impending destruction, there was always the sense of the approaching shell. There was an odd subconscious curiosity, and something more than curiosity, about the mental processes of some men, not far away, who were beside guns pointed toward you, guns which yesterday or the day before had sent their destruction to the very spot where you stood.

Yet, oddly enough, in the town there was a wholly absurd sense of security, derived from the fact that there were still buildings between you and those guns. You saw that the buildings went to dust and ashes whenever the guns were fired; you saw that each explosion might turn a city block into ashes, and yet you were glad of the buildings and there was reassurance in their shadows. Now we travelled in the open country; we began to climb across the face of a bare hill, and it was the face that fronted the Germans.

Presently the General's car stuck in the mud and we halted, for a minute perhaps; then we went on; we passed a dead horse lying in the road, then of a sudden came that same terrible grinding, metallic crash. I have never seen any description of a heavy shell explosion that fitted it. Behind us we could see the black smoke rising from the ground in a suburb through which we had just come. I saw three explosions. A moment later we were at the gate of Fort de la Chaume, and we were warned not to stop, but to hasten in, for the Germans, whenever they see cars at this point, suspect that Joffre has arrived, or President Poincaré, and act accordingly. We did not delay.

Fort de la Chaume is one of the many fortifications built since the Franco-Prussian War and intended to defend the city. Like all the rest, it ceased to have value when the German artillery had shown at Liège

Fort Doaumont 1916

and at Namur that it was the master of the fort. Then the French left their forts and went out to trenches beyond and took with them the heavy guns that the fort once boasted. To-day Fort de la Chaume is just an empty shell, as empty as the old Vauban citadel in the valley below. And what is true of this fort is true of all the other forts of that famous fortress of Verdun, which is no longer a fortress, but a sector in the trench line that runs from the North Sea to Switzerland.

From the walls of the fort staff officers showed me the surrounding country. I looked down on the city of Verdun, hiding under the shadow of its cathedral. I looked across the level Meuse Valley, with its little river; I studied the wall of hills beyond. Somewhere in the tangle on the horizon was Douaumont, which the Germans held. Down the valley of the river in the haze was the town of Bras, which was French; beyond it the village of Vachereauville, which was German. Beyond the hills in the centre of the picture, but hidden by them, were Le Mort

Homme and Hill 304.

Verdun is like a lump of sugar in a finger bowl, and I was standing on the rim. It seemed utterly impossible that any one should even think of this town as a fortress or count its ashes as of meaning in the conflict.

Somewhere in the background a French battery of heavy guns was firing, and the sound was clear; but it did not suggest war, rather a blasting operation. The German guns were still again. There was a faint billowing roll of gunfire across the river toward Douaumont, but very faint. As for trenches, soldiers, evidences of battle, they did not exist. I thought of Ralph Pulitzer's vivid story of riding to the Rheims front in a military aeroplane and seeing, of war, just nothing.

The geography of the Verdun country unrolled before us with absolute clarity; the whole relation of hills and river and railroads was unmistakable. But despite the faint sound of musketry, the occasional roar of a French gun, I might have been in the Berkshires looking down on the Housatonic. Six miles to the north around Le Mort Homme that battle which has not stopped for two months was still going on. Around Douaumont the overture was just starting, the overture to a stiff fight in the afternoon, but of all the circumstances of battle that one has read of, that one still vaguely expects to see, there was not a sign. If it suited their fancy the Germans could turn the hill on which I stood into a crater of ruin, as they did with Fort Loncin at Liège. We were well within range, easy range; we lived because they had no object to serve by such shooting, but we were without even a hint of their whereabouts.

I have already described the military geography of Verdun. I shall not attempt to repeat it here, but it is the invisibility of warfare, whether examined from the earth or the air, which impresses the civilian. If you go to the trenches you creep through tunnels and cavities until you are permitted to peer through a peephole, and you see yellow dirt some yards away. You may hear bullets over your head, you may hear shells passing, but what you see is a hillside with some slashings. That is the enemy. If you go to an observation post back of the trenches, then you will see a whole range of country, but not even the trenches of your own side.

From the Grand Mont east of Nancy I watched some French batteries shell the German line. I didn't see the French guns, I didn't see the German trenches, I didn't see the French line. I did see some black smoke rising a little above the underbrush, and I was told that the shells were striking behind the German lines and that the gunners were searching for a German battery. But I might as well have been observing a gang of Italians at blasting operations in the Montclair Mountains. And the officer with me said: "Our children are just amusing themselves."

From Fort de la Chaume we rode back to the citadel; and there I was the guest of the General and the officers of the town garrison; their guest because I was an American who came to see their town. I shall always remember that luncheon down in the very depths of this rock in a dimly lighted room. I sat at the General's right, and all around me were the men whose day's work it was to keep the roads open, the machinery running in the shell-cursed city. Every time they went out into daylight they knew that they might not return. For two months the storm had beaten about this rock, it had written its mark upon all these faces, and yet it had neither extinguished the light nor the laughter; the sense of strength and of calmness was inescapable, and never have I known such charming, such thoughtful hosts.

When the champagne came the old General rose and made me a little speech. He spoke in English, with absolute correctness, but as one who spoke it with difficulty. He welcomed me as an American to Verdun, he thanked me for coming, he raised his glass to drink to my country and the hope that in the right time she would be standing with France—in the cause of civilization. Always in his heart, in his thought, in his speech, the Frenchman is thinking of that cause of civilization; always this is what the terrible conflict that is eating up all France means to him.

Afterward we went out of this cavern into daylight, and the officers came and shook hands with me and said good-bye. One does not say au revoir at the front; one says bonne chance—"good luck; it may and it may not—we hope not." We entered our cars and were about to start, when suddenly, with a blinding, stunning crash, a whole salvo landed in the meadow just beyond the road, we could not see where, because some houses hid the field. It was the most suddenly appalling crash I have ever heard.

Instantly the General ordered our drivers to halt. He explained that it might be the beginning of a bombardment or only a single trial, a detail in the intermittent firing to cut the road that we were to take. We sat waiting for several moments and no more shots came. Then the General turned and gave an order to his car to follow, bade our drivers go fast, and climbed into my car and sat down. The wandering American correspondent was his guest. He could not protect him from the shell fire. He could not prevent it. But he could share the danger. He could share the risk, and so he rode with me the mile until we passed beyond the danger zone. There he gave me another bonne chance and left me, went back to his shell-cursed town with its ruins and its agonies.

I hope I shall see General Dubois again. I hope it will be on the day when he is made Governor of Strassburg.

As we left Verdun the firing was increasing; it was rolling up like a rising gale; the infantry fire was becoming pronounced; the Germans were beginning an attack upon Le Mort Homme. Just before sunset we passed through the Argonne Forest and came out beyond. On a hill to the north against the sky the monument of Valmy stood out in clear relief, marking the hill where Kellerman had turned back another Prussian army. Then we slipped down into the Plain of Châlons, where other Frenchmen had met and conquered Attila. At dark we halted in Montmirail, where Napoleon won his last victory before his empire fell. The sound of the guns we had left behind was still in our ears and the meaning of these names in our minds. Presently my French companion said to me: "It is a long time, isn't it?" He meant all the years since the first storm came out of the north, and I think the same thought is in every Frenchman's mind. Then he told me his story.

"I had two boys," he said; "one was taken from me years ago in an accident; he was killed and it was terrible. But the other I gave.

"He was shot, my last boy, up near Verdun, in the beginning of the war. He did not die at once and I went to him. For twenty days I sat beside him in a cellar waiting for him to die. I bought the last coffin in the village, that he might be buried in it, and kept it under my bed.

We talked many times before he died, and he told me all he knew of the fight, of the men about him and how they fell.

"My name is finished, but I say to you now that in all that experience there was nothing that was not beautiful." And as far as I can analyze or put in words the impression that I have brought away from France, from the ruin and the suffering and the destruction, I think it is expressed in those words. I have seen nothing that was not beautiful, too, because through all the spirit of France shone clear and bright.

CHAPTER III

BATTLE OF VERDUN ANOTHER GETTYSBURG — FAILURE OF CROWN PRINCE LIKENED BY FRENCH TO "HIGH TIDE" OF CONFEDERACY

"THE parallel between Gettysburg in your Civil War and Verdun in the present contest is unmistakable and striking." This was said to me by General Delacroix, one of Joffre's predecessors as chief of the French General Staff and the distinguished military critic of the Paris Temps now that because of age he has passed to the retired list.

What General Delacroix meant was patent and must have already impressed many Americans. Our own Gettysburg was the final bid for decision of a South which had long been victorious on the battlefield, which still possessed the armies that seemed the better organized and the generals whose campaigns had been wonderfully successful. But it was the bid for decision of a Confederacy which was outnumbered in men, in resources, in the ultimate powers of endurance, and was already beginning to feel the growing pinch both in numbers and credit.

At Gettysburg Lee made his final effort to destroy the army which he had frequently defeated but never eliminated. Victory meant the fall of Washington, the coming of despair to the North, an end of the Civil War, which would bring independence and the prize for which they had contended to the Confederates. And Lee failed at Gettysburg, not as Napoleon failed at Waterloo or as MacMahon failed at Sedan, but he failed, and his failure was the beginning of the end. The victory of Gettysburg put new heart, new assurance into the North; it broke the long illusion of an invincible Confederacy; it gave to Europe, to London, and to Paris, even more promptly than to Washington, the unmistakable message that the North was bound to win the Civil War.

I mean in a moment to discuss the military aspects of this conflict about the Lorraine fortress, but before the military it is essential to grasp the moral consequences of Verdun to France, to the Allies, to Germany. Not since the Marne, not even then—because it was only after a long delay that France really knew what had happened in this struggle—has anything occurred that has so profoundly, so indescribably, heartened the French people as has the victory at Verdun. It is not too much to say that the victory has been the most immediately inspiring thing in French national life since the disaster at Sedan and that it has roused national confidence, hope, faith, as nothing else has since the present conflict began.

In this sense rather than in the military sense Verdun was a decisive battle and its consequences of far-reaching character. France as a whole, from the moment when the attack began, understood the issue; the battle was fought in the open and the whole nation watched the communiqués day by day. It was accepted as a terrible if not a final test, and no Frenchman fails to recognize in all that he says the strength, the power, the military skill of Germany.

And when the advance was checked, when after the first two weeks the battle flickered out as did the French offensive in Champagne and the former German drive about Ypres a year ago, France, which had held her breath and waited, hoped, read in the results at Verdun the promise of ultimate victory, felt that all that Germany had, all that she could produce, had been put to the test and had failed to accomplish the result for which Germany had striven—or any portion thereof.

War is something beyond armies and tactics, beyond strategy and even military genius, and the real meaning of Verdun is not to be found in lines held or lost, not to be found even in the ashes of the old town that France and not Germany holds. It is to be found in the spirit of France, now that the great trial is over and the lines have held.

It was Germany and not France that raised the issue of Verdun. The Germans believed, and all their published statements show this, that France was weary, disheartened, ready to quit, on fair terms. They believed that there was needed only a shining victory, a great moral demonstration of German strength to accomplish the end—to bring victorious peace. In this I think, and all with whom I talked in France felt, that the Germans were wrong, that France would have endured defeat and gone on. But conversely, the Germans knew, must have known, that to try and to fail was to rouse the whole heart of France, to destroy any pessimism, and this is precisely what the failure has done.

The battle for Verdun was a battle for moral rather than military values, and the moral victory remains with the French. It was a deliberate and calculated effort to break the spirit of France, and it roused the spirit of France as perhaps nothing has raised the spirit of this people since Valmy, where other Frenchmen met and checked another German invasion, brought to a halt the army of Frederick the Great, which still preserved the prestige of its great captain who was dead, turned it back along the road that was presently to end at Jena.

Beside the moral value of Verdun the military is just nothing. To appreciate its meaning you must understand what it has meant to the French, and you must understand it by recalling what Gettysburg meant to the North, invaded as is France, defeated at half a dozen struggles in Virginia as France has been defeated in the past months of this war. Gettysburg was and remains the decisive battle of our Civil War, although the conflict lasted for nearly two years more. For France Verdun is exactly the same thing. Having accepted the moral likeness, you may find much that is instructive and suggestive in the military, but this is of relatively minor importance.

Now, on the military side it is necessary to know first of all that when the Germans began their gigantic attack upon Verdun the French high command decided not to defend the city. Joffre and those who with him direct the French armies were agreed that the city of Verdun was without military value comparable with the cost of defending it, and that the wisest and best thing to do was to draw back the lines to the hills above the city and west of the Meuse. Had their will prevailed there would have been no real battle at Verdun and the Germans would long ago have occupied the ashes of the town.

Joffre's view was easily explicable, and it was hardly possible to quarrel with the military judgment it discloses. To the world Verdun is a great fortress, a second Gibraltar, encircled by great forts, furnished with huge guns, the gateway to Paris and the key to the French eastern frontier. And this is just what Verdun was until the coming of the present war, when the German and Austrian siege guns levelled the forts of Antwerp, of Maubeuge, of Liège. But after that Verdun ceased to be anything, because all fortresses lost their value with the revelation that they had failed to keep pace with the gun.

After the Battle of the Marne, when the trench war began, the French took all their guns out of the forts of Verdun, pushed out before the forts, and Verdun became just a sector in the long trench line from the sea to Switzerland. It was defended by trenches, not forts. It was neither of more importance nor less than any other point in the line and it was a place of trenches, not of forts. The forts were empty and remain empty, monuments to the past of war, quite as useless as the walls of Rome would be against modern artillery.

The decline of Verdun was even more complete. From the strongest point in French defence it became the weakest. When the Germans took St. Mihiel in September, 1914, they cut the north and south railroad that binds Verdun to the Paris-Nancy Railroad. When they retreated from the Marne they halted at Varennes and Montfaucon, and from these points they command the Paris-Verdun-Metz Railroad. Apart from a single narrow-gauge railroad of minor value, which wanders among the hills, climbing at prohibitive grades, Verdun is isolated from the rest of France. Consider what this means in modern war when the amount of ammunition consumed in a day almost staggers belief. Consider what it means when there are a quarter of a million men to be fed and munitioned in this sector.

More than all this, when the lines came down to the trench condition Verdun was a salient, it was a narrow curve bulging out into the German front. It was precisely the same sort of military position as Ypres, which the Germans have twice before selected as the point for a great attack. In the Verdun sector the French are exposed to a converging fire; they are inside the German semicircle. Moreover, the salient is so narrow that the effect of converging fire is not to be exaggerated.

When the French attacked the Germans in Champagne last fall they advanced on a wide front from a line parallel to the German line. As

American advance northwest of Verdun. The ruined church on the crest of the captured height of Montfaucon. This was the condition of the site after the Americans finally drove the Germans out from it.

they pierced the first German lines they were exposed to the converging fire of the Germans, because they were pushing a wedge in. Ultimately they got one brigade through all the German lines, but it was destroyed beyond by this converging fire. But as the Germans advanced upon Verdun they were breaking down a salient and possessed the advantage they had had on the defensive in Champagne.

Finally, one-half the French army of Verdun fought with its back to a deep river, connected with the other half only by bridges, some of which presently came under German fire, and there was every possibility that these troops might be cut off and captured if the German advance were pushed home far enough on the west bank of the Meuse and the German artillery was successful in interrupting the passage of the river. It was a perilous position and there were some days when the situation seemed critical.

Accordingly, when the German drive at Verdun was at last disclosed in its real magnitude Joffre prepared to evacuate the town and the east bank of the river, to straighten his line and abolish the salient and give over to the Germans the wreck of Verdun. The position behind the river was next to impregnable; the lines would then be parallel; there would be no salient, and in the new position the French could concentrate their heavy artillery while the Germans were moving up the guns that they had fixed to the north of the old front.

But at this point the French politician interfered. He recognized the wisdom of the merely military view of Joffre, but he saw also the moral value. He recognized that the French and the German public alike would not see Verdun as a mere point in a trench line and a point almost impossible to defend and destitute of military value. He saw that the French and German publics would think of Verdun as it had been thought of before the present war changed all the conditions of conflict. He recognized that the German people would be roused to new hope and confidence by the capture of a great fortress, and that the French would be equally depressed by losing what they believed was a great fortress.

You had therefore in France for some hours, perhaps for several days, something that approximated a crisis growing out of the division of opinion between the civil and the military authorities, a division of opinion based upon two wholly different but not impossible equally correct appraisals. Joffre did not believe it was worth the men or the risk to hold a few square miles of French territory, since to evacuate would strengthen, not weaken, the line. The French politicians recognized that to lose Verdun was to suffer a moral defeat which would almost infallibly bring down the Ministry, might call into existence a new Committee of Public Safety, and would fire the German heart and depress the French.

In the end the politicians had their way and Castelnau, Joffre's second in command, came over to their view and set out for Verdun to organize the defence for the position at the eleventh hour. He had with him Pétain, the man who had commanded the French army in the Battle of Champagne and henceforth commanded the army that was hurried to the Verdun sector. France now took up definitely the gage of battle as Germany had laid it down. Verdun now became a battle in the decisive sense of the word, although still on the moral side. Nothing is more preposterous than to believe that there ever was any chance of a German advance through Verdun to Paris. One has only to go to Verdun and see the country and the lines behind the city and miles back of the present front to realize how foolish such talk is.

Meantime the German advance had been steady and considerable. All these attacks follow the same course—Ypres, Artois, Champagne, Dunajec. There is first the tremendous artillery concentration of the assailant; then the bombardment which abolishes the first and second line trenches of the defenders; then the infantry attack which takes these ruined trenches and almost invariably many thousands of prisoners and scores of guns. But now the situation changes. The assailant has passed beyond the effective range of his own heavy artillery, which cannot be immediately advanced because of its weight; he encounters a line of trenches that has not been levelled, he has come under the concentrated fire of his foe's heavy and light artillery without the support of his own heavy artillery, and all the advantage of surprise has gone.

What happened at Verdun is what happened in the Champagne. The German advance was quite as successful—rather more successful than the French last September; it covered three or four miles on a considerable front, and it even reached Douaumont, one of the old forts and the fort which was placed on the highest hill in the environs of Verdun. Thousands of prisoners had been captured and many guns taken. But at this point the French resistance stiffened, as had the German last year. French reserves and artillery arrived. Pétain and Castelnau arrived. There was an end of the rapid advance and there began the pounding, grinding attack in which the advantage passed to the defender. It was just what happened at Neuve Chapelle so long ago when we first saw this kind of fighting exemplified completely.

In the new attacks the Germans still gained ground, but they gained ground because the French withdrew from positions made untenable through the original German advance at other points. They consolidated their line, organized their new front. Ten days after the attack had begun it had ceased to be a question of Verdun, just as in a shorter time the French had realized last September that they could not break the German line in Champagne. But like the French in Champagne, like the British at Neuve Chapelle, the Germans persevered, and in consequence suffered colossal losses, exactly as the

French and British had.

To understand the German tactics you must recognize two things. The Germans had expected to take Verdun, and they had unquestionably known that the French military command did not intend at the outset to hold the town. They had advertised the coming victory far and wide over the world; they had staked much upon it. Moreover, in the first days, when they had taken much ground, when they had got Douaumont and could look down into Verdun, they had every reason to believe that they possessed the key to the city and that the French high command was slowly but steadily drawing back its lines and would presently evacuate the city.

Knowing these things you can understand why the Germans were so confident. They did not invent stories of coming victory which they did not believe. They believed that Verdun was to fall because they knew, and the same thing was known and mentioned in London. I heard it there when the battle was in its earlier stages — that the French high command intended to evacuate Verdun. What they did not know and could not know was that the French politicians, perhaps one should say statesmen this time, had interfered, that the French high command had yielded and that Verdun was to be defended to the last ditch.

When this decision was made the end of the real German advance was almost instantaneous. All that has happened since has been nothing but active trench war, violent fighting, desperate charge and counter charge, a material shortening of the French line at certain points, the abolition of minor salients, but of actual progress not the smallest. The advance stopped before lines on which Pétain elected to make his stand when he came with his army to defend Verdun. The Germans are still several miles outside of Verdun itself, and only at Douaumont have they touched the line of the exterior forts, which before the war were expected to defend the city.

In Paris and elsewhere you will be told that Douaumont was occupied without resistance and that it was abandoned under orders before there had been a decision to hold Verdun. I do not pretend to know whether this is true or not, although I heard it on authority that was wholly credible, but the fact that the map discloses, that I saw for myself at Verdun, is that, save for Douaumont, none of the old forts have been taken and that the Germans have never been able to advance a foot from Douaumont or reach the other forts at any other point. And this is nothing more or less than the French experience at Champagne, the German experience about Ypres in 1915.

In a later chapter I hope to discuss the situation at Verdun as I saw it on April 6th, and also the miracle of motor transport which played so great a part in the successful defence of the position. But the military details are wholly subordinate to the moral. All France was roused by a successful defence of a position attacked by Germany with the advertised purpose of breaking the spirit of the French people. The battle was fought in the plain daylight without the smallest concealment, and the least-informed reader of the official reports could grasp the issue which was the fate of the city of Verdun.

The fact, known to a certain number of Frenchmen only, that the defence was improvised after the decision had been made to evacuate the whole salient, serves for them to increase the meaning of the victory as it increases the real extent of the French exploit. But this is a detail. The Germans openly, deliberately, after long preparation, announced their purpose, used every conceivable bit of strength they could bring to bear to take Verdun, and told their own people not merely that Verdun would fall, but at one moment that it had fallen. They did this with the firm conviction that it would fall—was falling.

The French were steadily aware that Verdun might be lost. They knew from letters coming daily from the front how terrible the struggle was, and it is impossible to exaggerate the tension of the early days, although it was not a tension of panic or fear. Paris did not expect to see the invader, and there was nothing of this sort of moonshine abroad. But it was plain that the fall of the town would bring a tremendous wave of depression and if not despair yet a real reduction of hope. Instead, Verdun defended itself, the lines were maintained several miles on the other side of the town and all substantial advance came to an end in the first two weeks. The army itself, the military observers, were convinced that all danger was over as early as the second week in March, when correspondents of French newspapers were being taken to Verdun to see the situation and tell the people the facts.

All over Northern France, and I was in many towns and cities, the "lift" that Verdun had brought was unmistakable and French confidence was everywhere evident. It showed itself in a spontaneous welcome to Alexander of Serbia in Paris, which, I am told, was the first thing of the sort in the war period. Frenchmen did not say that Verdun was the beginning of the end, and they did not forecast the prompt collapse of Germany. They did not even forecast the immediate end of the fighting about Verdun. They did not regard the victory as a Waterloo or a Sedan or any other foolish thing. But they did rather coolly and quite calmly appraise the thing and see in it the biggest German failure since the Marne, and a failure in a fight which the Germans had laid down all the conditions in advance and advertised the victory that they did not achieve as promising the collapse of French endurance and spirit.

The Battle of Verdun was a battle for moral values, and the possession of the town itself was never of any real military value. Verdun commands nothing, and behind it lie well-prepared fortifications on dominating heights, positions that are ten times as easy to defend as those which the French have defended. It was not a battle for Paris, and there was never a prospect of the piercing of the French line; Germany was never as near a great military success as she was at Ypres after the first gas attack a year ago. The French army leaders judged the Verdun position as not worth the cost of defending. They were overruled by the politicians and they defended it successfully. But their first decision is the best evidence of the wholly illusory value that has been attached to the possession of Verdun itself.

The politicians were unquestionably right as to the moral value, and it is possible if not probable that the relinquishment of the city voluntarily might have precipitated the fall of the Briand Ministry and the creation of a Committee of Public Safety—not to make peace, but to make war successfully. The will to defend Verdun came from the French people, it imposed itself upon the army and it resulted in a moral victory the consequences of which cannot be exaggerated and have given new heart and confidence to a people whose courage and determination must make an enduring impression on any one who sees France in the present terrible but glorious time.

CHAPTER IV

VERDUN, THE DOOR THAT LEADS NOWHERE — THE BATTLE AND THE TOPOGRAPHY OF THE BATTLEFIELD — AN ANALYSIS OF THE ATTACK AND DEFENCE

I N a preceding article I have endeavored to explain the tremendous moral "lift" that the successful defence of the city of Verdun has brought to France, a moral "lift" which has roused French confidence and expectation of ultimate victory to the highest point since the war began. I have also tried to demonstrate how utterly without value the fortress of Verdun was, because the forts were of no use in the present war, were as useless against German heavy artillery as those of Antwerp and Maubeuge, and had been evacuated by the French a full eighteen months before the present battle began. Finally I have indicated that so little military value was attached to Verdun by the French high command that it was prepared to evacuate the whole position, which is the most difficult to defend on the whole French front, and was only persuaded to give over his purpose by the arguments of the politicians, who believed that the moral effect of the evacuation would be disastrous to France and inspiriting to Germany.

I now desire to describe at some length the actual topographical circumstances of Verdun and later I shall discuss the fashion in which an automobile transport system was improvised to meet the situation created by the interruption of traffic by German artillery fire along the two considerable railroad lines. It was this system which actually saved the town and is the real "miracle of Verdun," if one is to have miracles to explain what brave and skilful men do.

I saw Verdun on April 6th. I went through the city, which was little more than a mass of ashes, with General Dubois, the military governor of the town itself, and with him I went to Fort de la Chaume, on one of the highest hills near Verdun, and from this vantage point had the whole countryside explained to me. The day on which I visited Verdun was the first completely quiet day in weeks, and I was thus fortunate in being able to see and to go about without the disturbing or hindering circumstances which are incident to a bombardment.

The city of Verdun is situated at the bottom of the Meuse Valley on both sides of the river. But the main portion of the town is on the west bank and surrounds a low hill, crowned by the cathedral and old Vauban citadel. The town is surrounded by old ramparts, long ago deprived of military value and belonging, like the citadel, to eighteenth century warfare. The Valley of the Meuse is here several miles wide, as flat as your hand, and the river, which is small but fairly deep, a real obstacle since it cannot be forded, wanders back and forth from one side of the valley to the other. Below Verdun it is doubled, as a military obstacle, by the Canal de l'Est.

If you put a lump of sugar in a finger bowl you will pretty fairly reproduce the Verdun topography. The lump of sugar will represent Verdun, the rim of the bowl the hills around the city, the interior of the bowl the little basin in which the city stands. This rim of hills, which rise some five or six hundred feet above the town itself, is broken on the west by a deep and fairly narrow trough which comes into the Meuse Valley and connects it some thirty miles to the west with the Plain of Châlons. If you should look down upon this region from an aeroplane this furrow would look like a very deep gutter cutting far into the tangle of hills.

Now in the warfare of other centuries the value of the Verdun fortress was just this: the furrow which I have described is the one avenue available for an invading army coming from the east out of Metz or south from Luxemburg and aiming to get into the Plain of Châlons to the west. It is the way the Prussians came in 1792 and were defeated at Valmy, at the western entrance of the trough about thirty miles away. They took Verdun on their way—so did the Germans in 1870.

Verdun in French hands closed this trough to the invaders.

It closed it because the low hill which bears the town was strongly fortified and was surrounded by lower ground. Such artillery as was in existence was not of a sufficiently long range to place upon the hills about Verdun which we have described as the rim of the bowl. The town of Verdun was situated on both sides of the river and commanded all the bridges. It was, in fact, the stopple in the mouth of the bottleneck passage leading into North Central France, the passage through which ran the main road and, later, the railway from the frontier nearest Paris to the capital.

But when the modern developments of artillery came, then Verdun, the old fortress that Vauban built for Louis XIV, lost its value. It was commanded by the surrounding hills and the French moved out of the town and the Vauban fortifications and built on the surrounding hills, on the rim, to go back to our figure, the forts which were the defence of the town when the present war began, forts arranged quite like those of Liège or Antwerp and some four or five miles away from the town. But bear in mind these forts were designed, like the old fortress and fortifications of the eighteenth century, to bar the road from the Meuse and from Germany to the Plain of Châlons and the level country west of the Argonne. When the Germans came south through Belgium and got into the Plain of Châlons from the north they had turned the whole Verdun position and had got into the region it barred by another route; they had come in by the back door; Verdun was the front. Not only that, but they are there now and have been there ever since the first days of September, 1914.

When one hears about Verdun as the gateway to Paris or anything else one hears about the Verdun of the past. It was not the door to Paris but the outer door to the region around Paris, to the Plains of Champagne and Châlons. But as the Germans are already in these plains the taking of Verdun now would not bring them nearer to Paris; they are only fifty miles away at Noyon, on the Oise, and they would be 160 at Verdun if they took the city. If they took Verdun they would get control of the Paris-Metz Railway, and if they then drove the French away from the trough we have been describing they would get a short line into France, and a line coming from German territory directly, not passing through Belgium. But they would not be nearer to Paris.

When the French saw, in the opening days of the war, that forts

French soldiers of the 87th Regiment, 6th Division, at Côte 304, (Hill 304), northwest of Verdun, 1916

were of no permanent value against the German guns they left the forts on the hills above Verdun as they had abandoned the Vauban works and moved north for a few miles. Here they dug trenches, mounted their guns in concealed positions, and stood on the defensive, as they were standing elsewhere from Belgium to Switzerland. There was now no fortress of Verdun, and Verdun city was nothing but a point behind the lines of trenches, a point like Rheims, or Arras. The forts of the rim were equally of no more importance and were now empty of guns or garrisons. If the Germans, by a sudden attack, broke all the way through the French trenches here it would be quite as serious as if they broke through at other points, but no more so. There was no fortress of Verdun and the Verdun position commanded nothing.

The Battle of Verdun, as it is disclosed to an observer who stands on Fort de la Chaume, a mile or two west and above Verdun and in the mouth of the trough we have described, was this: On the west bank of the Meuse, four or five miles northwest of the town, there is a steep ridge going east and west and perhaps 1,100 feet high. This is the crest of Charny, and it rises sharply from the flat valley and marches to the west without a break for some miles. On it are the old forts of the rim.

Three or four miles still to the north is a line of hills which are separated from each other by deep ravines leading north and south. Two of these hills, Le Mort Homme (Dead Man's Hill) and Hill 304, have been steadily in the reports for many weeks. They are the present front of the French. Between one and two miles still to the north are other confused and tangled hills facing north, and it was here that the French lines ran when the great attack began in the third week of February. On this side the Germans have advanced rather less than two miles; they have not reached the Charny Ridge, which is the true and last line of defence of the Verdun position, and they have not captured the two hills to the north, which are the advanced position, now the first line.

When I was in Paris before I went to Verdun there was a general belief that the French might ultimately abandon the two outer hills, Dead Man's and 304, and come back to the Charny Ridge, which is a wall running from the river west without a break for miles. Apparently this has not been found necessary, but what is worth noting is that if these hills were evacuated it would not mean the withdrawal from Verdun but only to the best line of defence (the last line, to be sure), which includes the town itself.

Now, east of the river the situation is materially different. Between the Meuse and the level plateau, which appears in the dispatches from the front as the Woevre, is a long, narrow ridge, running from north to south for perhaps thirty-five or forty miles. This is the Côte de Meuse, or, translated, the Hills of the Meuse. The range is never more than ten miles wide and at many points less than half as wide. On the west it rises very sharply from the Meuse and on the east it breaks down quite as abruptly into the Woevre Plain. It cannot be effectively approached from the Woevre, because the Woevre is an exceedingly marshy plain, with much sub-surface water and in spring a mass of liquid clay.

Now the French, when the German drive began, stood on this ridge some eight miles, rather less, perhaps, to the north of the town of Verdun; their line ran from the Meuse straight east along this ridge and then turned at right angles and came south along the eastern edge of the Meuse Hills and the shore of the Woevre Plain until it touched the river again at St. Mihiel, twenty miles to the south, where the Germans had broken through the Meuse Hills and reached the river. The German attack came south along the crest of this ridge because the German heavy artillery could not be brought over the Woevre.

About halfway between the French front and Verdun, on a little crest somewhat higher than the main ridge, the French had erected a line of forts, just as they had on the Charny Ridge, Forts Douaumont and Vaux, familiar names now, were the forts most distant from Verdun. But the French here, as on the other side of the river, had come out of these forts, abandoned and dismantled them, and taken to trenches much to the north. It was upon these trenches that the main German attack fell, and in the first days the French were pushed back until their trench line followed the crests that bear the old forts, and at one point, at Douaumont, the Germans had actually got possession of one of the old forts; but the French trenches pass in front of this fort at a distance of but a few hundred yards.

Now, in the first days of the battle the position of the French on the east bank of the Meuse was just this: the troops facing north were meeting and slowly yielding to a terrific drive coming south and southwest; the rest of the troops that faced east toward the Woevre were not attacked severely. But as the Germans came south, and when they took Douaumont, they were able to reach the bridges across the Meuse behind the French troops on the Meuse Hills and to destroy them by indirect fire, and these French troops, more than a hundred thousand probably, were fighting with their backs to a deep river and exposed to destruction in case their lines did not hold.

In this situation Joffre proposed to take his troops behind the Meuse and on the hills to the west and above the city, leaving the city to the Germans. The French line would thus come north behind the Meuse from St. Mihiel and then turn west above Verdun, following either the Charny Ridge or else the Hills of Regret and Chaume, on either side of the trough, described above, which the road to Paris follows.

If Verdun were a fortress actually; if either the old town or the circle of forts outside had been of value, Joffre would not have proposed this thing. But they were of no value. Verdun was once a fortress barring the way to the Plain of Châlons, but the Germans were in the plain, having come through Belgium by the back door, as it were. The forts outside the city on the rim of the basin had already been abandoned because they could have been destroyed by German heavy artillery, as were those of Liège and Antwerp. Verdun was just a position; but it was a difficult position to defend because of the river, which cut off one-half the army and could be crossed only by bridges, which were under indirect fire.

If the French had come back to the Charny Ridge, or even to the Regret Hills south of the trough followed by the Paris-Metz road, they would have stood on hills of patent military value; the trough is a natural ditch in front. These hills are all trenched and prepared for defence. The French would merely have shortened their lines and taken an easy position to defend, instead of holding a bad position. But ultimately this would have meant the relinquishing of Verdun, the little town down in the valley below, now become a heap of ruins and having lost its military value thirty years earlier, when heavy artillery began its decisive success over the old fortifications.

The French did not retire, because the civil government overruled the military; decided that the moral effect of the withdrawal from Verdun would be disastrous to the French and advantageous to the Germans. Instead of retiring, the French stood and held the hills beyond the Charny Ridge, Dead Man's and 304; they hold them still and seem determined to keep them. But remember that they can still retire to the Charny Ridge if they choose, and only then find their best line west of the Meuse, if they mean to hold on to the city of Verdun.

On the other hand, east of the River Meuse the French are approximately in their last line. The hills and crests they hold upon the Meuse Hills are some three or four miles from Verdun, but if the French retired far they would begin to come down hill, with a deep river at their backs. In consequence, whenever you hear that the Germans have made some slight gain, taken a trench about Douaumont or Vaux, you are certain to hear at once that the French have counter attacked and retaken the lost ground.

The essential thing to remember is that the defence of Verdun is not the defence of a position that has a great military value. The French would be better off, would lose fewer men and run smaller risk of considerable losses if they should quit the east bank of the Meuse and occupy the hills back of Verdun on the west bank. On the west bank the Germans have never made any material gain, and they have not come within reach of the hills that bear the old forts. But the French Government has decided that for political reason, for reasons that affect the moral, not the military, situation, Verdun must not be surrendered; hence the army is holding it at a cost of men less than the Germans are paying to take it, but at a far greater cost than would be necessary to hold the better positions west of the river.

The Germans have not made any gain of importance in nearly two months. The French are very sure they will not come farther south. They are as confident as men could be. But if the Germans should come farther south and at last force the French to come back behind the river and to the hills above the town, they would only win a moral victory. The military situation would not be changed, unless they should also pierce the French lines on the west of the river, and this is absolutely unthinkable now.

If you think of Verdun city as a fortress you will put yourself in the eighteenth century. It is just an abandoned town, mostly ashes and completely ruined by a useless bombardment after the main German advance had been checked. If you think of Verdun as a fortified position, like Liège, which, if it fell, would bring disaster, as did the fall of Liège, you are thinking in terms of the situation before the war. The forts of this position have all been abandoned and the French are fighting in trenches in all points save one outside this circle of forts.

If you think of Verdun as the gateway to anything, you are thinking of something that doesn't exist. It was a gateway to Central France, to the Plain of Châlons, from the German frontier before the Germans came down into the Plain of Châlons from the north through Belgium.

But if you think of Verdun as a place which has a great sentimental value for both the French and the Germans; if you think of it as a place which by reason of its importance in other days still preserves a value in the minds of the mass of the French and German publics, a town the taking of which would as a result of this wholly false appraisal be reckoned in Germany as a great victory, which would vastly encourage German masses and would be accepted in France as a great defeat which would equally depress the French public, you will think of the battle for Verdun as it is.

If you go to Verdun you will see that the estimate that the world has placed upon it is illusory. You will see it is an abandoned town. You will see, as I did, that great and famous forts are without guns, and you will see, as I did, that the positions which the French have prepared behind the Meuse and above the town are vastly stronger than those which they have held successfully, in Lorraine or any other place where the attacks have been bitter, for nearly two years.

There are no forts, fortifications, fortresses, in this war. There are just trenches, and the Verdun sector is no exception. Verdun is not surrounded; it is not invested. I went to the town from Bar-le-Duc in an automobile without difficulty, and I ran back to Paris by another road, through Châlons, with equal ease. The Germans have never got within three miles of the town on any side; to the west of the River Meuse they are not within six miles of it. They are not gaining, and have not been gaining for weeks; they are merely fighting a desperate trench campaign, and the French are fighting back, retaking trenches on the east of the river, because they are in their last line on this bank of the river, but paying less attention to German trench gains on the west because the Germans are still far from the Charny Ridge, their main position.

If Verdun falls, that is, if the French are compelled under pressure or as a result of the cost of holding their present awkward position to go back behind the river, they will lose fifty or a hundred square miles of French territory, they will lose all the tremendous value of the moral "lift" which the successful defence has brought, but they will lose nothing else; and when the Germans have taken Verdun, the ashes, the ruins, they will stop, because there is no object or value in further attack. They are fighting for moral values, and the French politician has overruled the French soldier and compelled him to accept battle on unfavorable ground for this same moral value, but against his military judgment. He has done it successfully. He expects and France expects that he will continue to do it successfully, but in the wholly remote contingency that he failed (I can only say that it is a contingency no longer considered in France), a loss in moral advantage would be the only consequence.

CHAPTER V

IN SIGHT OF THE PROMISED LAND—
ON THE LORRAINE BATTLEFIELD

IN the third week of August, 1914, a French army crossed the frontier of Alsace-Lorraine and entered the Promised Land, toward which all Frenchmen had looked in hope and sadness for forty-four years. The long-forgotten communiqués of that early period of the war reported success after success, until at last it was announced that the victorious French armies had reached Sarrebourg and Morhange, and were astride the Strassburg-Metz Railroad. And then Berlin took up the cry, and France and the world learned of a great German victory and of the defeat and rout of the invading army. Even Paris conceded that the retreat had begun and the "army of liberation" was crowding back beyond the frontier and far within French territory.

Then the curtain of the censorship fell and the world turned to the westward to watch the terrible battle for Paris. In the agony and glory of the Marne the struggle along the Moselle was forgotten; the Battle of Nancy, of Lorraine, was fought and won in the darkness, and when the safety of Paris was assured the world looked toward the Aisne, and then toward Flanders. So it came about that one of the greatest battles of the whole war, one of the most important of the French victories, the success that made the Marne possible, the rally and stand of the French armies about Nancy, escaped the fame it earned. Only in legend, in the romance of the Kaiser with his cavalry waiting on the hills to enter the Lorraine capital, did the battle live.

When I went to France one of the hopes I had cherished was that I might be permitted to visit this battlefield, to see the ground on which a great battle had been fought, that was still unknown country, in the main, for those who have written on the war. The Lorraine field was the field on which France and Germany had planned for a generation to fight. Had the Germans respected the neutrality of Belgium, it is by

Nancy, by the gap between the Vosges and the hills of the Meuse, that they must have broken into France. The Marne was a battlefield which was reached by chance and fought over by hazard, but every foot of the Lorraine country had been studied for the fight long years in advance. Here war followed the natural course, followed the plans of the general staff prepared years in advance. Indeed, I had treasured over years a plan of the Battle of Nancy, contained in a French book written years ago, which might serve as the basis for a history of what happened, as it was written as a prophecy of what was to come.

When the Great General Staff was pleased to grant my request to see the battlefield of Nancy I was advised to travel by train to that town accompanied by an officer from the General Staff, and informed that I should there meet an officer of the garrison, who would conduct me to all points of interest and explain in detail the various phases of the conflict. Thus it fell out, and I have to thank Commandant Leroux for the courtesy and consideration which made this excursion successful.

In peace time one goes from Paris to Nancy in five hours, and the distance is about that from New York to Boston, by Springfield. In war all is different, and the time almost doubled. Yet there are compensations. Think of the New York-Boston trip as bringing you beyond New Haven to the exact rear of battle, of battle but fifteen miles away, with the guns booming in the distance and the aeroplanes and balloons in full view. Think also of this same trip, which from Hartford to Worchester follows the line of a battle not yet two years old, a battle that has left its traces in ruined villages, in shattered houses. On either side of the railroad track the graves descend to meet the embankments; you can mark the advance and the retreat by the crosses which fill the fields. The gardens that touch the railroad and extend to the rear of houses in the little towns are filled with graves. Each enclosure has been fought for at the point of the bayonet, and every garden wall recalls the Château of Hougoumont, at Waterloo.

All this was two years ago, but there is to-day, also. East of Bar-le-Duc the main line is cut by German shell fire now. From Fort Camp des Romains above St. Mihiel German guns sweep the railroad near Commercy, and one has to turn south by a long detour, as if one went to Boston by Fitchburg, travel south through the country of Jeanne d'Arc and return by Toul, whose forts look out upon the invaded land. Thus one comes to Nancy by night, and only by night, for twenty miles beyond there are Germans and a German cannon, which not so long ago sent a shell into the town and removed a whole city block beside the railroad station. It is the sight of this ruin as you enter the town which reminds you that you are at the front, but there are other reminders.

As we ate our dinner in the café, facing the beautiful Place Stanislas, we were disturbed by a strange and curious drumming sound. Going out into the square, we saw an aeroplane, or rather its lights, red and green, like those of a ship. It was the first of several, the night patrol, rising slowly and steadily, and then sweeping off in a wide curve toward the enemy's line. They were the sentries of the air which were to guard us while we slept, for men do sentry-go in the air as well as on the earth about the capital of Lorraine. Then the searchlights on the hills began to play, sweeping the horizon toward that same mysterious region where beyond the darkness there is war.

The next morning I woke with the sense of Fourth of July. Bang! Bang! Bang! Such a barking of cannon crackers I had never heard. Still drowsy, I pushed open the French windows and looked down on the square. There I beheld a hundred or more men, women, and children, their eyes fixed on something in the air above and behind the hotel. Still the incessant barking of guns, with the occasional boom of something more impressive. With difficulty I grasped the fact. I was in the midst of a Taube raid. Somewhere over my head, invisible to me because of the wall of my hotel, a German aeroplane was flying, and all the anti-aircraft guns were shooting at it. Was it carrying bombs? Should I presently see or feel the destruction following the descent of these?

But the Taube turned away, the guns fired less and less frequently, the people in the streets drifted away, the children to school, the men to work, the women to wait. It was just a detail in their lives, as familiar as the incoming steamer to the commuters on the North River ferryboats. Some portion of war has been the day's history of Nancy for nearly two years now. The children do not carry gas masks to school with them as they do at Pont-à-Mousson, a dozen miles to the north, but women and children have been killed by German shells, by bombs, brought by Zeppelins and by aeroplanes. There is always excitement of sorts in the district of Nancy.

After a breakfast, broken by the return of the aeroplanes we had seen departing the night before for the patrol, we entered our cars and set out for the front, for the near-front, for the lines a few miles behind the present trenches, where Nancy was saved but two years ago. Our route lay north along the valley of the Meurthe, a smiling broad valley, marching north and south and meeting in a few miles that of the Moselle coming east. It was easy to believe that one was riding through the valley of the Susquehanna, with spring and peace in the air. Toward the east a wall of hills shut out the view. This was the shoulder of the Grand Couronné, the wall against which German violence burst and broke in September, 1914.

Presently we came to a long stretch of road walled in on the river side by brown canvas, exactly the sort of thing that is used at football games to shut out the non-paying public. But it had another purpose here. We were within the vision of the Germans, across the river, on the heights behind the forest, which outlined itself at the skyline; there were the Kaiser's troops and that forest was the Bois-le-Prêtre, the familiar incident in so many communiqués since the war began. Thanks to the canvas, it was possible for the French to move troops along this road without inviting German shells. Yet it was impossible to derive any large feeling of security from a canvas wall, which alone interposed between you and German heavy artillery.

We passed through several villages and each was crowded with troops; cavalry, infantry, all the branches represented; it was still early and the soldiers were just beginning their day's work; war is so completely a business here. Transport wagons marched along the roads, companies of soldiers filed by. Interspersed with the soldiers were civilians, the women and children, for none of the villages are evacuated. Not even the occasional boom of a gun far off could give to this thing the character of real war. It recalled the days of my soldiering in the militia camp at Framingham in Massachusetts. It was simply impossible to believe that it was real. Even the faces of the soldiers were smiling. There was no such sense of terribleness, of strain and weariness as I later found about Verdun. The Lorraine front is now inactive, tranquil; it has been quiet so long that men have forgotten all the carnage and horror of the earlier time.

We turned out of the valley and climbed abruptly up the hillside. In a moment we came into the centre of a tiny village and looked into a row of houses, whose roofs had been swept off by shell fire. Here and there a whole house was gone; next door the house was undisturbed and the women and children looked out of the doors. The village was St. Geneviève, and we were at the extreme front of the French in August, and against this hill burst the flood of German invasion. Leaving the car we walked out of the village, and at the end of the street a sign warned the wayfarer not to enter the fields, for which we were bound: "War—do not trespass." This was the burden of the warning.

Once beyond this sign we came out suddenly upon an open plateau, upon trenches. Northward the slope descended to a valley at our feet. It was cut and seamed by trenches, and beyond the trenches stood the posts that carried the barbed-wire entanglements. Here and there, amidst the trenches, there were graves. I went down to the barbed-wire entanglements and examined them curiously. They at least were real. Once thousands of men had come up out of the little woods a quarter of a mile below; they had come on in that famous massed attack, they had come on in the face of machine gun and "seventy-fives." They had just reached the wires, which marked high water. In the woods below, the Bois de Facq, in the fields by the river 4,000 Germans had been buried.

Looking out from the trenches the whole country unfolded. Northward the little village of Atton slept under the steep slope of Côte-de-Mousson, a round pinnacle crowned with an ancient château. From the hill the German artillery had swept the ground where I stood. Below the hill to the west was Pont-à-Mousson, the city of 150 bombardments, which the Germans took when they came south and lost later. Above it was the Bois-le-Prêtre, in which guns were now booming occasionally. Far to the north was another hill, just visible, and its slope toward us was cut and seamed with yellow slashes: Those were the French trenches, then of the second or third line; beyond there was still another hill, it was slightly blurred in the haze, but it was not over five miles away, and it was occupied by the Germans. From the slope above me on a clear day it is possible to see Metz, so near are French and German lines to the old frontier.

Straight across the river to the west of us was another wood, with a glorious name, the Forest of the Advance Guard. It swept to the south of us. In that wood the Germans had also planted their guns on the day of battle. They had swept the trenches where I stood from three sides. Plainly it had been a warm corner. But the French had held on. Their commander had received a verbal order to retreat. He insisted that it should be put in writing, and this took time. The order came. It had to be obeyed, but he obeyed slowly. Reluctantly the men left the trenches they had held so long. They slipped southward along the road by which we had come. But suddenly their rear guards discovered the Germans were also retreating. So the French came back and the line of St. Geneviève was held, the northern door to Nancy was not forced.

Looking down again it was not difficult to reconstitute that German assault, made at night. The thing was so simple the civilian could grasp it. A road ran through the valley and along it the Germans had formed; the slope they had to advance up was gentle, far more gradual than that of San Juan. They had been picked troops selected for a forlorn hope, and they had come back four times. The next morning the whole forest had been filled with dead and dying. Not less than a division— 20,000 men—had made the terrible venture. Now there was a strange sense of emptiness in the country; war had come and gone, left its graves, its trenches, its barbed-wire entanglements; but these were all disappearing already. On this beautiful spring morning it was impossible to feel the reality of what happened here, what was happening now, in some measure, five miles or more to the north. Nature is certainly the greatest of all pacifists; she will not permit the signs of war to endure nor the mind to believe that war itself has existed and exists.

From St. Geneviève we went to the Grand Mont d'Amance, the most famous point in all the Lorraine front, the southeast corner of the Grand Couronné, as St. Geneviève is the northern. Here, from a hill some 1,300 feet high, one looks eastward into the Promised Land of France—into German Lorraine. In the early days of August the great French invasion, resting one flank upon this hill, the other upon the distant Vosges, had stepped over the frontier. One could trace its route to the distant hills among which it had found disaster. In these hills the Germans had hidden their heavy guns, and the French, coming under their fire without warning, unsupported by heavy artillery, which was lacking to them, had broken. Then the German invasion had rolled back. You could follow the route. In the foreground the little Seille River could be discerned; it marked the old frontier. Across this had come the defeated troops. They had swarmed down the low, bare hills; they had crossed and vanished in the woods just at my feet; these woods were the Forest of Champenoux. Into this forest the Germans had followed by the thousand, they were astride the main road to Nancy, which rolled white and straight at my feet. But in the woods the French rallied. For days there was fought in this stretch of trees one of the most terrible of battles.

As I stood on the Grand Mont I faced almost due east. In front of me and to the south extended the forest. Exactly at my feet the forest reached up the hill and there was a little cluster of buildings about a fountain. All was in ruins, and here, exactly here, was the high water mark of the German advance. They had occupied the ruins for a few moments and then had been driven out. Elsewhere they had never emerged from the woods; they had approached the western shore, but the French had met them with machine guns and "seventy-fives." The brown woods at my feet were nothing but a vast cemetery; thousands of French and German soldiers slept there.

In their turn the Germans had gone back. Now, in the same woods, a French battery was shelling the Germans on the other side of the Seille. Under the glass I studied the little villages unfolding as on a map; they were all destroyed, but it was impossible to recognize this. Some were French, some German; you could follow the line, but there were no trenches; behind them French shells were bursting occasionally and black smoke rose just above the ground. Thousands of men faced each other less than four miles from where I stood, but all that there was to be detected were the shell bursts; otherwise one saw a pleasant country, rolling hills, mostly without woods, bare in the spring, which had not yet come to turn them green. In the foreground ran that arbitrary line Bismarck had drawn between Frenchmen forty-six years before—the frontier—but of natural separation there was none. He had cut off a part of France, that was all, and one looked upon what had been and was still a bleeding wound.

I asked the French commandant about the various descriptions made by those who have written about the war. They have described the German attack as mounting the slope of the Grand Mont, where we stood. He took me to the edge and pointed down. It was a cliff almost as steep as the Palisades. "C'est une blague," he smiled. "Just a story." The Germans had not charged here, but in the forest below, where the Nancy road passed through and enters the valley of the Amezeule. They had not tried to carry but to turn the Grand Mont. More than 200,000 men had fought for days in the valley below. I asked him about the legend of the Kaiser, sitting on a hill, waiting in white uniform with his famous escort, waiting until the road was clear for his triumphal entrance into the capital of Lorraine. He laughed. I might choose my hill; if the Emperor had done this thing the hill was "over there," but had he? They are hard on legends at the front, and the tales that delight Paris die easily on the frontiers of war.

But since I had asked so much about the fighting my commandant promised to take me in the afternoon to the point where the struggle had been fiercest, still farther to the south, where all the hills break down and there is a natural gateway from Germany into France, the beginning of the famous Charmes Gap, through which the German road to Paris from the east ran, and still runs. Leaving Nancy behind us, and ascending the Meurthe valley on the eastern bank, turning out of it before Saint Nicholas du Port, we came presently to the most completely war-swept fields that I have ever seen. On a perfectly level plain the little town of Haraucourt stands in sombre ruins. Its houses are nothing but ashes and rubble. Go out of the village toward the east and you enter fields pockmarked by shell fire. For several miles you can walk from shell hole to shell hole. The whole country is a patchwork of these shell holes. At every few rods a new line of old

Members of the 101st Field Signal Battalion (formerly 1st Massachusetts Field Signal Battalion) at outdoor church services in the ruins of a church destroyed by shell fire. Verdun, 18th October 1918

trenches approaches the road and wanders away again. Barbed-wire entanglements run up and down the gently sloping hillsides.

Presently we came out upon a perfectly level field. It was simply torn by shell fire. Old half-filled trenches wandered aimlessly about, and beyond, under a gentle slope, the little village of Courbessaux stood in ruins. The commandant called my attention to a bit of woods in front.

"The Germans had their machine guns there," said he. "We didn't know it, and a French brigade charged across this field. It started at 8:15, and at 8:30 it had lost more than 3,000 out of 6,000. Then the Germans came out of the woods in their turn, and our artillery, back at Haraucourt, caught them and they lost 3,500 men in a quarter of an hour." Along the roadside were innumerable graves. We looked at one. It was marked: "Here 196 French." Twenty feet distant was another; it was marked: "Here 196 Germans." In the field where we stood I was told some 10,000 men are buried. They were buried hurriedly, and even now when it rains arms and legs are exposed.

Two years had passed, almost two years, since this field had been fought for. The Germans had taken it. They had approached Haraucourt, but had not passed it. This was the centre and the most vital point in the Lorraine battle. What Foch's troops had done about La Fère Champenoise, those of Castelnau had done here. The German wave had been broken, but at what cost? And now, after so many months, the desolation of war remained. But yet it was not to endure. Beside the very graves an old peasant was ploughing, guiding his plough and his horses carefully among the tombs. Four miles away more trenches faced each other and the battle went on audibly, but behind this line, in this very field where so many had died, life was beginning.

Later we drove south, passing within the lines the Germans had held in their great advance, we travelled through Lunéville, which they had taken and left unharmed, save as shell fire had wrecked an eastern suburb. We visited Gerbéviller, where in an excess of rage the Germans had burned every structure in the town. I have never seen such a headquarters of desolation. Everything that had a shape, that had a semblance of beauty or of use, lies in complete ruin, detached houses, a château, the blocks in the village, all in ashes. Save for Sermaize, Gerbéviller is the most completely wrecked town in France.

You enter the village over a little bridge across the tiny Mortagne. Here some French soldiers made a stand and held off the German advance for some hours. There was no other battle at Gerbéviller, but for this defence the town died. Never was death so complete. Incendiary material was placed in every house, and all that thoroughness could do to make the destruction complete was done. Gerbéviller is dead, a few women and children live amidst its ashes, there is a wooden barrack by the bridge with a post-office and the inevitable postcards, but only on postcards, picture postcards, does the town live. It will be a place of pilgrimage when peace comes.

From Gerbéviller we went by Bayon to the Plateau of Saffais, the ridge between the Meurthe and the Moselle, where the defeated army of Castelnau made its last and successful stand. The French line came south from St. Geneviève, where we had been in the morning, through the Grand Mont, across the plain by Haraucourt and Corbessaux, then crossed the Meurthe by Dombasle and stood on the heights from

Rossières south. Having taken Lunéville, the Germans attempted to cross the Meurthe coming out of the Forest of Vitrimont.

Standing on the Plateau of Saffais and facing east, the whole country unfolded again, as it did at the Grand Mont. The face of the plateau is seamed with trenches. They follow the slopes, and the village of Saffais stands out like a promontory. On this ridge the French had massed three hundred cannon. Their army had come back in ruins, and to steady it they had been compelled to draw troops from Alsace. Mülhausen was sacrificed to save Nancy. Behind these crests on which we stood a beaten army, almost routed, had in three days found itself and returned to the charge.

In the shadow of the dusk I looked across the Meurthe into the brown mass of the Forest of Vitrimont. Through this had come the victorious Germans. They had debouched from the wood; they had approached the river, hidden under the slope, but, swept by the hell of this artillery storm, they had broken. But few had lived to pass the river, none had mounted the slopes. There were almost no graves along these trenches. Afterward the Germans had in turn yielded to pressure from the south and gone back. Before the Battle of the Marne began the German wave of invasion had been stopped here in the last days of August. A second terrific drive, coincident with the Marne, had likewise failed. Then the Germans had gone back to the frontier. The old boundary line of Bismarck is now in many instances an actual line of fire, and nowhere on this front are the Germans more than three or four miles within French territory.

If you should look at the map of the wholly imaginary Battle of Nancy, drawn by Colonel Boucher to illustrate his book, published before 1910, a book describing the problem of the defence of the eastern frontier, you will find the lines on which the French stood at Saffais indicated exactly. Colonel Boucher had not dreamed this battle, but for a generation the French General Staff had planned it. Here they had expected to meet the German thrust. When the Germans decided to go by Belgium they had in turn taken the offensive, but, having failed, they had fought their long-planned battle.

Out of all the region of war, of war to-day and war yesterday, one goes back to Nancy, to its busy streets, its crowds of people returning from their day's work. War is less than fifteen miles away, but Nancy is as calm as London is nervous. Its bakers still make macaroons; even Taube raids do not excuse the children from punctual attendance at school. Nancy is calm with the calmness of all France, but with just a touch of something more than calmness, which forty-six years of living by an open frontier brings. Twenty-one months ago it was the gauge of battle, and half a million men fought for it; a new German drive may approach it at any time. Out toward the old frontier there is still a German gun, hidden in the Forest of Bézange, which has turned one block to ashes and may fire again at any hour. Zeppelins have come and gone, leaving dead women and children behind them, but Nancy goes on with to-day.

And to-morrow? In the hearts of all the people of this beautiful city there is a single and a simple faith. Nancy turns her face toward the ancient frontier, she looks hopefully out upon the shell-swept Grand Couronné and beyond to the Promised Land. And the people say to you, if you ask them about war and about peace, as one of them said to me: "Peace will come, but not until we have our ancient frontier, not until we have Metz and Strassburg. We have waited a long time, is it not so?"

AN ONLOOKER IN FRANCE 1917-1919

BY WILLIAM ORPEN

PREFACE

THIS book must not be considered as a serious work on life in France behind the lines, it is merely an attempt to record some certain little incidents that occurred in my own life there.

The only thought I wish to convey is my sincere thanks for the wonderful opportunity that was given me to look on and see the fighting man, and to learn to revere and worship him—that is the only serious thing. I wish to express my worship and reverence to that gallant company, and to convey to those who are left my most sincere thanks for all their marvellous kindness to me, a mere looker on.

CHAPTER I

TO FRANCE (APRIL 1917)

THE boat was crowded. Khaki, everywhere khaki; lifebelts, rain and storm, everything soaked. Destroyers, churning through the waves, played strange games all round us. Some old-time Tommies, taking everything for granted, smoked and laughed and told funny stories. Others had the look of dumb animals in pain, going to what they knew only too well. The new hands for France asked many questions, pretended to laugh, pretended not to care, but for the most part were in terror of the unknown.

It was strange to watch this huddled heap of humanity, study their faces and realise that perhaps half of them would meet a bloody end before a new moon was over, and wonder how they could do it, why they did it—Patriotism? Yes, and perhaps it was the chance of getting home again when the war was over. Think of the life they would have! The old song:—

"We don't want to lose you,
But we think you ought to go,
For your King and your Country
Both need you so.
"We shall-want you and miss you,
But with all our might and main
We shall cheer you, thank you, kiss you,
When you come back again."

Did they think of that, and all the joys it seemed to promise them? I pray not.

What a change had come over the world for me since the day before! On that evening I had dined with friends who had laughed and talked small scandal about their friends. One, also, was rather upset because he had an appointment at 10.30 the next day—and there was I, a few hours later, being tossed about and soaked in company with men who knew they would run a big chance of never seeing England again, and were certainly going to suffer terrible hardships from cold,

Men resting. La Boisselle.

filth, discomfort and fatigue. There they stood, sat and lay—a mass of humanity which would be shortly bundled off the boat at Boulogne like so many animals, to wait in the rain, perhaps for hours, before being sent off again to whatever spot the unknown at G.H.Q. had allotted for them, to kill or to be killed; and there was I among them, going quietly to G.H.Q., everything arranged by the War Office, all in comfort. Yet my stomach was twitching about with nerves. What would I have been like had I been one of them?

At Boulogne we lunched at the "Mony" (my companion, Aikman, had been to France before during the war and knew a few things). It was an excellent lunch, and, as we were not to report at G.H.Q. till the next day, we walked about looking at lorries and trains, all going off to the unknown, filled with humanity in khaki weighed down with their packs.

The following morning at breakfast at the "Folkestone Hotel" we sat at the next table to a Major with red tabs. He did not speak to us, but after breakfast he said: "Is your name Orpen?" "Yes, sir," said I. "Have you got your car ready?" "Yes, sir," said I. "Well, you had better drive back with me. Pack all your things in your car." "Yes, sir," said I. He explained to me that he had come to Boulogne to fetch General Smuts' luggage, otherwise he gave us no idea of who or what he was, and off we drove to the C.-in-C.'s house, where he went in with the General's luggage and left us in the car for about an hour. Then we went on to Hesdin, where he reported us to the Town Major, who said he had found billets for us. The Red Tab Major departed, as he said he was only just in time for his lunch, and told us to come to Rollencourt soon and report to the Colonel. The Town Major brought us round to our billet—the most filthy, disgusting house in all Hesdin, and the owner, an old woman, cursed us soundly, hating the idea of people being billeted with her. Anyway, there he left us and went off to his "Mess."

This was all very depressing, so we talked together and went on a voyage of discovery and found an hotel; then we went back to the billet and said "good-bye" to Madame and moved our stuff there. But the hotel wasn't a dream—at least we had no chance of dreaming— bugs, lice and all sorts of little things were active all night. I had been told by the War Office to go slow and not try to hustle people, so we decided we would not go and report to the Colonel till the next day after lunch.

Looking into the yard from my window in the afternoon, I saw two men I knew, one an artist from Chelsea, the other a Dublin man, who used to play lawn tennis. They were "Graves." My Dublin friend was "Adjutant, Graves," in fact he proudly told me that "Adjutant, Graves, B.E.F., France," would always find him. We dined with them that night at H.Q. Graves. They were very friendly, and said we could travel all over the back of the line by going from one "Graves" to another "Graves." All good chaps, I'm sure, and cheerful, but we did not do it.

The next day after lunch we drove to Rollencourt, and found the Major in his office (a hut on the lawn in front of the château). He left, and returned to say the Colonel could not see us then. Would we come back at 5 p.m.? So off we went and sat by the side of the road for two hours. Then again to the Major's at 5 p.m., when he informed us the Colonel had gone out. Would we come back at 7 p.m.? (No tea offered.) This we did and waited until 7.50, when the Major informed us that the Colonel would not see us that evening, but we were to report the next morning at 9 a.m. (No dinner offered.) We left thinking very hard—things did not seem so simple after all. We reported at 9 a.m. and waited, and got a message at 11 a.m. that the Colonel would see us, and we were shown in to a wizened, sour-faced little man, his breast ablaze with strange colours. I explained to him that I did not like the billets at Hesdin, that Hesdin was too far away from anything near the front, and that I intended to go to Amiens at once. To my surprise he did not seem to object, and just as we were leaving, he said: "By the way, General Charteris wants you to go and see him this morning. You had better go at once." So that was it! If General Charteris had not sent that message I might not have been admitted to the presence of the Colonel for weeks. Off we went, full of hope, packed our bags and on to G.H.Q. proper, and got in to see the General at once—a bluff, jovial fellow who said: "You go anywhere you like, do anything you like, but don't ask me to get any Generals to sit to you; they're fed up with artists." I said: "That's the last thing I want." "Right," said he, "off you go." So we "offed" it to Amiens, arriving there about 7 p.m. on a cold, black, wet night. We went to see the Allied Press "Major," to find out some place to stop in, etc. Again we were rather depressed. The meeting was very chilly, the importance of the Major was great—the full weight and responsibility of the war seemed on him. "The Importance of being Ernest" wasn't in it with him. As I learnt afterwards, when he came in late for a meal all the other officers and Allied Press correspondents stood up. Many a time I got a black look for not doing so. However, he advised the worst and most expensive hotel in the town, and off we went (no dinner offered), rather depressed and sad.

CHAPTER II
THE SOMME (APRIL 1917)

AMIENS was the one big town that could be reached easily from the Somme front for dinner, so every night it was crowded with officers and men who had come back in cars, motor-bikes, lorries or any old thing in or on which they could get a lift. After dinner they would stand near the station and hail anything passing, till they found something that would drop them near their destination. As there was an endless stream of traffic going out over the Albert and Péronne Roads during that time (April 1917), it was easy.

Amiens is a dirty old town with its seven canals. The cathedral, belfry and the theatre are, of course, wonderful, but there is little else except the dirt.

I remember later lunching with John Sargent in Amiens, after which I asked him if he would like to see the front of the theatre. He said he would. When we were looking at it he said: "Yes, I suppose it

A Tank. Pozières.

is one of the most perfect things in Europe. I've had a photograph of it hanging over my bed for the last thirty years."

But Amiens was a danger trap for the young officer from the line, also for the men. "Charlie's Bar" was always full of officers; mirth ran high, also the bills for drinks—and the drink the Tommies got in the little cafés was terrible stuff, and often doped.

Then, when darkness came on, strange women—the riff-raff from Paris, the expelled from Rouen, in fact the badly diseased from all parts of France—hovered about in the blackness with their electric torches, and led the unknowing away to blackened side-streets and up dim stairways—to what? Anyway, for an hour or so they were out of the rain and mud, but afterwards? Often did I go with Freddie Fane, the A.P.M., to these dens of filth to drag fine men away from disease.

The wise ones dined well—if not too well—at the "Godbert," with its Madeleine, or the "Cathedral," with its Marguerite, who was the queen of the British Army in Picardy, or, not so expensively, at the "Hôtel de la Paix." Some months later the club started, a well-run place. I remember a Major who used to have his bath there once a week at 4 p.m. It was prepared for him, with a large whisky-and-soda by its side. What more comfort could one wish? Then there were dinners at the Allied Press, after which the Major would give a discourse amid heavy silence; then music. The favourite song at that time was:—

"Jackie Boy!
Master?
Singie well?
Very well.
Hey down,
Ho down,
Derry, Derry down,
All among the leaves so green, O.
"With my Hey down, down,
With my Ho down, down,
Hey down,
Ho down,
Derry, Derry down,

All among the leaves so green, O."

Later, perhaps, if the night was fine, the Major would retire to the garden and play the flute. This was a serious moment—a great hush was felt, nobody dared to move; but he really didn't play badly. And old Hale would tell stories which no one could understand, and de Maratray would play ping-pong with extraordinary agility. It would all have been great fun if people had not been killing each other so near. Why, during that time, the Boche did not bomb Amiens, I cannot understand, it was thick every week-end with the British Army. One could hardly jamb oneself through the crowd in the Place Gambetta or up the Rue des Trois Cailloux. It was a struggling mass of khaki, bumping over the uneven cobblestones. What streets they were! I remember walking back from dinner one night with a Major, the agricultural expert of the Somme, and he said, "Don't you think the pavement is very hostile to-night?"

I shall never forget my first sight of the Somme battlefields. It was snowing fast, but the ground was not covered, and there was this endless waste of mud, holes and water. Nothing but mud, water, crosses and broken Tanks; miles and miles of it, horrible and terrible, but with a noble dignity of its own, and, running through it, the great artery, the Albert-Bapaume Road, with its endless stream of men, guns, food lorries, mules and cars, all pressing along with apparently unceasing energy towards the front. Past all the little crosses where their comrades had fallen, nothing daunted, they pressed on towards the Hell that awaited them on the far side of Bapaume. The mud, the cold, the noise, the misery, and perhaps death;—on they went, plodding through the mud, those wonderful men, perhaps singing one of their cheer-making songs, such as:—

"I want to go home.

I want to go home.

I don't want to go to the trenches no more,

Where the Whizz-bangs and Johnsons do rattle and roar.

Take me right over the sea,

Where the Allemande can't bayonet me.

Oh, my!

I don't want to die,

Warwickshires entering Péronne.

I want to go home."

How did they do it? "I want to go home."—Does anyone realise what those words must have meant to them then? I believe I do now — a little bit. Even I, from my back, looking-on position, sometimes felt the terrible fear, the longing to get away. What must they have felt? "From battle, murder and sudden death, Good Lord, deliver us."

On up the hill past the mines to Pozières. An Army railway was then running through Pozières, and the station was marked by a big wooden sign painted black and white, like you see at any country station in England, with POZIÈRES in large Roman letters, but that's all there was of Pozières except a little red in the mud. I remember later, at the R.F.C. H.Q., Maurice Baring showed me a series of air-photographs of Pozières as it was in 1914, with its peaceful little streets and rows of trees. What a contrast to the Pozières as it was in 1917 — MUD. Further on, the Butte stood out on the right, a heap of chalky mud, not a blade of grass round it then — nothing but mud, with a white cross on the top. On the left, the Crown Prince's dug-out and Gibraltar — I suppose these have gone now — and Le Sars and

No Man's Land.

Grévillers, at that time General Birdwood's H.Q., where the church had been knocked into a fine shape. I tried to draw it, but was much put off by air fighting. It seemed a favourite spot for this.

Bapaume must always have been a dismal place, like Albert, but Péronne must have been lovely, looking up from the water; and the main Place must have been most imposing, but then it was very sad. The Boche had only left it about three weeks, and it had not been "cleaned up." But the real terribleness of the Somme was not in the towns or on the roads. One felt it as one wandered over the old battlefields of La Boisselle, Courcelette, Thiepval, Grandcourt, Miraumont, Beaumont-Hamel, Bazentin-le-Grand and Bazentin-le-Petit—the whole country practically untouched since the great day when the Boche was pushed back and it was left in peace once more.

A hand lying on the duckboards; a Boche and a Highlander locked in a deadly embrace at the edge of Highwood; the "Cough-drop" with the stench coming from its watery bottom; the shell-holes with the shapes of bodies faintly showing through the putrid water—all these things made one think terribly of what human beings had been through, and were going through a bit further on, and would be going through for perhaps years more—who knew how many?

I remember an officer saying to me, "Paint the Somme? I could do it from memory—just a flat horizon-line and mud-holes and water, with the stumps of a few battered trees," but one could not paint the smell.

Early one morning in Amiens I got a message from Colonel John Buchan asking me to breakfast at the "Hôtel du Rhin." While we were having breakfast, there was a great noise outside—an English voice was cursing someone else hard and telling him to get on and not make an ass of himself. Then a Flying Pilot was pushed in by an Observer. The Pilot's hand and arm were temporarily bound up, but blood was dropping through. The Observer had his face badly scratched and one of his legs was not quite right. They sat at a table, and the waiter brought them eggs and coffee, which they took with relish, but the Pilot was constantly drooping towards his left, and the drooping always continued, till he went crack on the floor. Then the Observer would curse him soundly and put him back in his chair, where he would eat again till the next fall. When they had finished, the waiter put a cigarette in each of their mouths and lit them. After a few minutes four men walked in with two stretchers, put the two breakfasters on the stretchers, and walked out with them—not a word was spoken.

I found out afterwards that the Pilot had been hit in the wrist over the lines early that morning and missed the direction back to his aerodrome. Getting very weak, he landed, not very well, outside Amiens. He got his wrist bound up and had asked someone to telephone to the aerodrome to tell them that they were going to the "Rhin" for breakfast, and would they send for them there?

After I had been in Amiens for about a fortnight, going out to the Somme battlefields early in the morning and coming back when it got dark, I received a message one evening from the Press "Major" to go to his château and ring up the "Colonel" at Rollencourt, which I did. The following was the conversation as far as I remember:—

"Is that Orpen?"

"Yes, sir."

"What do you mean by behaving this way?"

"What way, please, sir?"

"By not reporting to me."

"I'm sorry, sir, but I do not understand."

"Don't you know you must report to me, and show me what work you have been doing?"

"I've practically done nothing yet, sir."

"What have you been doing?"

"Looking round, sir."

"Are you aware you are being paid for your services?"

"Yes, sir."

"Well, report to me and show me your work regularly.—Tell the Major to speak to me."

The Major spoke, and I clearly heard him say my behaviour was damnable.

This wonderful Colonel expected me to work all day, and apparently, in the evening, to take what I had done and show it to him—the distance by motor to him and back was something like 110 miles!

I saw there was nothing for it, if I wanted to do my work, but to fight, so I decided to lay my views of people and things before those who were above the Colonel. This I did, and had comparative peace, but the seed of hostility was sown in the Colonel's Intelligence (F) Section, G.H.Q., as I think it was then called, and they made me suffer as much as was in their power.

"BEAUMONT-HAMEL"

A MEMORY OF THE SOMME (SPRING 1917)

A fair spring morning—not a living soul is near,
Far, far away there is the faint grumble of the guns;
The battle has passed long since—
All is Peace.
At times there is the faint drone of aeroplanes as
They pass overhead, amber specks, high up in the blue;
Occasionally there is the movement of a rat in the
Old battered trench on which I sit, still in the
Confusion in which it was hurriedly left.
The sun is baking hot.

Three Weeks in France. Shell shock.

Strange odours come from the door of a dug-out
With its endless steps running down into blackness.
The land is white—dazzling.
The distance is all shimmering in heat.
A few little spring flowers have forced their way
Through the chalk.
He lies a few yards in front of the trench.
We are quite alone.
He makes me feel very awed, very small, very ashamed.
He has been there a long, long time—
Hundreds of eyes have seen him,
Hundreds of bodies have felt faint and sick

Because of him.
Then this place was Hell,
But now all is Peace.
And the sun has made him Holy and Pure—
He and his garments are bleached white and clean.
A daffodil is by his head, and his curly, golden
Hair is moving in the slight breeze.
He, the man who died in "No Man's Land," doing
Some great act of bravery for his comrades and
Country—
Here he lies, Pure and Holy, his face upward turned;
No earth between him and his Maker.
I have no right to be so near.

CHAPTER III

AT BRIGADE HEADQUARTERS AND ST. POL (MAY-JUNE 1917)

ABOUT this time Freddie Fane (Major Fane, A.P.M.) sent me up to his old division, which was then fighting in front of Péronne. We arrived on a lovely afternoon at Divisional H.Q., which were in a pretty fir-wood, and consisted of beautifully camouflaged little huts. The guns were booming a few miles off, but everything was very peaceful there, and the dinner was excellent; but, just as we finished, the first shell shrieked overhead, and this I was told afterwards went on all night. Personally I had another large whisky-and-soda, and slept like a log.

The next morning the General's A.D.C. motored me to a village about four kilometres off and handed me over to a 2nd Lieutenant, who walked me off to Brigade H.Q. These were behind an old railway embankment. Everyone was most kind, but I saw no quiet place to work. Everyone was rushing about, and the noise of the guns was terrific. The young 2nd Lieutenant advised me to take the men I wanted to draw and to go to the other side of the embankment. He said that there was no one there and that I could work in peace, and he was right. The noise from our batteries immediately gave me a bad headache, but apparently the Boche did not respond at all till the afternoon. Then they started, and the noise was HELL. Whenever there was a big bang I couldn't help giving a jump. The old Tommy I was drawing said, "It's all right, Guv'ner, you'll get used to it very soon." I didn't think so, but to make conversation I said: "How long is it since you were home?"

"Twenty-two months," said he.

"Twenty-two months!" said I.

"Yes," said he, "but one can't complain. That bloke over there hasn't been home for twenty-eight."

What a life! Twenty-four hours of it was enough for me at a time. Before evening came my head felt as if it were filled with pebbles

Man in the Glare. Two miles from the Hindenburg Line.

which were rattling about inside it. After lunch I sat with the Brigadier for a time and watched the men coming out from the trenches. Some sick; some with trench feet; some on stretchers; some walking; worn, sad and dirty—all stumbling along in the glare. The General spoke to each as they passed. I noticed that their faces had no change of expression. Their eyes were wide open, the pupils very small, and their mouths always sagged a bit. They seemed like men in a dream, hardly realising where they were or what they were doing. They showed no sign of pleasure at the idea of leaving Hell for a bit. It was as if they had gone through so much that nothing mattered. I was glad when I was back at Divisional H.Q. that evening. We had difficulty on one part of the road, as a "Sausage" had been brought down across it.

Shortly afterwards I went to live at St. Pol, a dirty little town, but full of character. The hotel was filthy and the food impossible. We ate tinned tongue and bully-beef for the most part. Here I met Laboreur, a Frenchman, who was acting as interpreter—a very good artist. I think his etchings are as good as any line work the war has produced. A most amusing man. We had many happy dinners together at a little restaurant, where the old lady used to give us her bedroom as a private sitting-room dining-room. It was a bit stuffy, but the food was eatable.

One fine morning I got a message, "Would I ring up the P.S. of the C.-in-C. at once?" so I went to the Camp Commandant's office. No one was there except a corporal, so I asked him to get through to Sir Philip Sassoon, and said that I would wait outside till he did so. Presently he called me in, and Sassoon said I was to paint the Chief, and would I come to lunch the next day at Advanced H.Q., G.H.Q.? after which we talked and laughed a bit. When I hung up the receiver, I turned round, and there was a large A.S.C. Colonel glaring at me. I was so taken aback, as I had not heard him come in, that I didn't even salute him. He roared at me, "Are you an S.S.O.?" (Senior Supply Officer). "No," said I, "I'm a painter!" I never saw a man in such a fury in my life. I thought he was going to hit me. However, I made him understand in the end that I really was speaking the truth and in no way wanted to be cheeky.

I had lunch at Advanced G.H.Q. the next day. The C.-in-C. was very kind, and brought me into his room afterwards, and asked me if everything was going all right with me. I told him I had a few troubles and was not very popular with certain people. He said: "If you get any more letters that annoy you, send them to me and I'll answer them." I went back to St. Pol with my head in the air. A great weight seemed to have been lifted off me.

Sir Douglas was a strong man, a true Northerner, well inside himself—no pose. It seemed it would be impossible to upset him, impossible to make him show any strong feeling, and yet one felt he understood, knew all, and felt for all his men, and that he truly loved them; and I knew they loved him. Never once, all the time I was in

France, did I hear a "Tommy" say one word against "'Aig." Whenever it became my honour to be allowed to visit him, I always left feeling happier — feeling more sure that the fighting men being killed were not dying for nothing. One felt he knew, and would never allow them to suffer and die except for final victory.

When I started painting him he said, "Why waste your time painting me? Go and paint the men. They're the fellows who are saving the world, and they're getting killed every day."

The second time I was there, just after lunch, the Chief had gone to his room, and several Generals, Colonel Fletcher, Sassoon and myself were standing in the hall, when suddenly a most violent explosion went off, all the windows came tumbling in, and there was great excitement, as they thought the Boche had spotted the Chiefs whereabouts. The explosions went on, and out came the Chief. He walked straight up to me, laid his hand on my shoulder and said: "That's the worst of having a fellow like you here, Major. I thought the Huns would spot it," and, having had his joke, went back to his work. He was a great man. It turned out to be a munition dump which had exploded near by, and the noise was deafening for about eight hours.

This was the time of the great fight round the chemical works at Rœux, and I was drawing the men as they came out for rest. They were mostly in a bad state, but some were quite calm. One, I remember, was quite happy. He had ten days' leave and was going back to some village near Manchester to be married. He showed me her photograph, a pretty girl. Perhaps he was killed afterwards.

The view from Mont St. Eloy was fine, with the guns belching out flame on the plain in the midday sun.

One day I was painting the C.-in-C., and at lunch-time the news came in that General Trenchard was there. The C.-in-C. said: "Orpen must see 'Boom,' he's great," so I was taken off and we met him in the garden. A huge man with a little head and a great personality, proud of one thing only, that is, that he is a descendant of Jack Sheppard. With him, to my delight, was Maurice Baring (his A.D.C.). The General was told that I wanted to see the aerodromes, and Maurice shyly said: "May I take Orpen round, sir? I know him." Gee! How

Air-Marshal Sir H. M. Trenchard, Bart., K.C.B., etc.

happy I was when the General said: "All right, you see to it, Baring."

I painted "Boom" a few days later in a beautiful château with the most wonderful old stables. They have all been burnt down since. "Boom" worked hard all the time I painted. A few days later Baring told me that he had spoken to "Boom" and told him how much I admired his head. "Boom" replied: "Damned if he showed it in his painting." And yet he was worshipped by all the flying boys.

About this time I had sent from England Maurice Baring's "In Memoriam" to Lord Lucas. It made a tremendous impression on me then, and still does. I think it is one of the greatest poems ever written, and by far the greatest work of art the war has produced.

Baring took me out for a great day round the aerodromes. We visited several and lunched with a Wing-Commander, Colonel Freeman, who was most kind, a great lover of books, a lot of which Maurice used to supply him with. After this, we visited a squadron where there was to be a test fight between a German Albatross, which had been captured intact, and one of our machines. The fight was a failure, however, as just after they got up something went wrong with the radiator of the Albatross; but later Captain Little did some wonderful stunts on a triplane. I also saw Robert Gregory there, but had no chance to speak to him. But I learnt that he was doing very well and was most popular in the squadron, and that he had painted some fine scenery for their theatre.

St. Pol possessed an open-air swimming-bath, a strange thing for St. Pol, but there it was—a fine large swimming-bath, full of warm water which came from some chemical works. I used to swim there every evening when I got back from work. The one thing that struck me at that time was the difference between nudity and uniform—while bathing one could look at and study all these fine lads, and I would think of one, "Gee! there's an aristocrat. What a figure! What refinement!" and of another, "What a badly-bred, vulgar, common brute!" Later they would both come out of their bathing-boxes, and the "brute" would be a smartly dressed officer carrying himself with ease and distinction, and the "aristocrat" would be an untidy, uncouth "Tommy" shambling along. Truly on sight one should never judge a man with his clothes on.

CHAPTER IV

THE YPRES SALIENT
(JUNE-JULY 1917)

IT was about this time we moved to Cassel. Nothing very interesting in the journey till one comes to Arques and St. Omer (at one time Lord French's G.H.Q.). The road from Arques to the station at the foot of Cassel Hill was always lined on each side by lorries, guns, pontoons and all manner of war material. A gloomy road, thick with mud for the most part, if not dust. It was always a pleasure to start climbing Cassel Hill, past the seven windmills and up to the little town perched on the summit.

Cassel is a picturesque little spot, with its glazed tiles and sprinkling of Spanish buildings, and the view from it is marvellous. On a clear day one could see practically the whole line from Nieuport

Howitzer in Action.

German 'Planes visiting Cassel.

to Armentières and the coast from Nieuport to Boulogne. At that time, the 2nd Army H.Q. were in the one-time casino, which was the summit of the town, and from its roof one got a clear view all round. Cassel was to the Ypres Salient what Amiens was to the Somme, and the little "Hôtel Sauvage" stood for the "Godbert," the "Cathedral" and "Charlie's Bar" all in one. The dining-room, with its long row of windows showing the wonderful view, like the Rubens landscape in the National Gallery, was packed every night for the most part with fighting boys from the Salient, who had come in for a couple of hours to eat, drink, play the piano and sing, forgetting their misery and discomfort for the moment. It was enormously interesting to watch and study what happened in that room. One saw gaiety, misery, fear, thoughtfulness and unthoughtfulness all mixed up like a kaleidoscope. It was a well-run, romantic little hotel, built round a small courtyard, which was always noisy with the tramp of cavalry horses and the rattle of harness. The hotel was managed by Madame Loorius and her two daughters, Suzanne and Blanche, who were known as "The Peaches."

Suzanne was undoubtedly the Queen of the Ypres Salient, as sure as Marguerite was that of the Somme. One look from the eyes of Suzanne, one smile, and these wonderful lads would go back to their gun-pits—or who knows where?—proud.

Suzanne wore an R.F.C. badge on her breast. She was engaged to be married to an R.F.C. officer at that time. Whether the marriage ever came off I know not. Certainly not before the end of the war, and now Madame is dead, and they have given up the "Sauvage," and are, as far as I am concerned, lost.

Here the Press used to come when any particular operation was going on in the North. In my mind now I can look clearly from my room across the courtyard and can see Beach Thomas by his open window, in his shirt-sleeves, writing like fury at some terrific tale for the Daily Mail. It seemed strange his writing this stuff, this mild-eyed, country-loving dreamer; but he knew his job.

Philip Gibbs was also there—despondent, gloomy, nervy, realising to the full the horror of the whole business; his face drawn very fine, and intense sadness in his very kind eyes; also Percival Phillips—that deep thinker on war, who probably knew more about it than all the rest of the correspondents put together.

The people of Cassel loved the Tommy, so the latter had a good time there.

One day I drew German prisoners at Bailleul. They had just been captured, 3,500 in one cage, all covered with lice—3,500 men, some nude, some half-nude, trying to clean the lice off themselves. It was a strange business. The Boche at the time were sending over Jack Johnsons at the station, and these men used to cheer as each shell shrieked overhead.

It was at Cassel I first began to realise how wonderful the women of the working class in France were, how absolutely different and infinitely superior they were to the same class at home; in fact no class in England corresponded to them at all. Clean, neat, prim women, working from early dawn till late at night, apparently with unceasing energy, they never seemed to tire and usually wore a smile.

I remember one girl, a widow; her name was Madame Blanche, who worked at the "Hôtel Sauvage." She was about twenty-two years of age, and she owned a house in Cassel. A few months before I arrived there her husband had contracted some sort of poisoning in the trenches and had been brought back to Cassel, where he died. Madame Blanche interested me; she was very slim and prim and neat and tightly laced. Her fair hair was always very carefully crimped. She looked like a girl out of a painting by Metsu or Van Meer. I could see her posing at a piano for either, calm, gentle and silent; and could imagine her in the midst of all the refined surroundings in which these artists would have painted her. But now her surroundings were khaki, and her background was the wonderful Flemish view from the windows — miles and miles of country, with the old sausage balloons floating sleepily in the distance.

I must have looked at Madame Blanche a lot—perhaps too much. I remember she used to smile at me; but that was as far as our friendship could get—smiles, as I only knew about ten words of French, and she less of English.

But one day she surprised me, and left me thinking and wondering more of the strange, unbelievable things that happen to one in this world.

It was after lunch one Sunday: I had just got back to my room to work when there was a knock on the door, and in walked Madame Blanche, who, after much trouble to us both, I gathered wished me to go for a walk with her. Impossible! I, a major, a Field Officer, to walk at large through the streets of Cassel, 2nd Army H.Q., with a serving-girl from the "Hôtel Sauvage"! I succeeded in explaining this after some time; and then, to my amazement, she broke down and wept. The convulsive sobbing continued, and I thought and wondered, and in the end decided that I was crazy to make a woman weep because I would not go for a walk with her. So I told her I would do so; and she dried her eyes and asked me to meet her in the hotel yard in ten

Soldiers and Peasants, Cassel.

minutes.

When I got down to the yard the rain was coming down in torrents, and there she was, dressed in her widow's weeds and holding in her arms a mass of flowers. Solemnly we went out into the streets. Not a civilian, not a soldier, not even a military policeman was to be seen. All other human beings had taken refuge from the deluge: we were quite alone. Right through the town we went and out to the little cemetery, into which she brought me and led to her husband's grave, on which she placed the mass of flowers, and then knelt in the mud and prayed for about half an hour in the pouring rain; after which we walked solemnly and silently back to the hotel, soaked through and through. It was a strange affair. I may be stupid, but I cannot yet see her reason for wishing to take me out in the wet.

After working up there for about six weeks I began to feel very tired, and thought I would go for a change; so I decided to run away and go and see some "Bases"—Dieppe, Le Havre and Rouen. The day after I reached Dieppe I received a telegram from the "Colonel": "When do you return?" to which I replied: "Return where, please?" to which apparently no reply could be made. But two days later I received a letter from him saying he was moving to another job, but would always remember the honour of his having had me working under him. This was a nasty one for me, and I had no answer to give. About the same time I received a telegram from Sir Philip Sassoon: "Where the devil are you? aaa Philip." Months later he sent me a great parcel of correspondence as to whether this telegram, sent by the P.S. of the C.-in-C., could be regarded as an official telegram, its language, etc. The minutes were signed by Lieutenants, Captains, Majors, Colonels, all up to the last one, which was signed by a General, and ran thus: "What the — — hell were you using this disgusting language for, Philip?"

After a week I went back to Cassel, packed up and went south to Amiens.

CHAPTER V

THE SOMME IN SUMMER-TIME (AUGUST 1917)

NEVER shall I forget my first sight of the Somme in summer-time. I had left it mud, nothing but water, shell-holes and mud—the most gloomy, dreary abomination of desolation the mind could imagine; and now, in the summer of 1917, no words could express the beauty of it. The dreary, dismal mud was baked white and pure—dazzling white. White daisies, red poppies and a blue flower, great masses of them, stretched for miles and miles. The sky a pure dark blue, and the whole air, up to a height of about forty feet, thick with white butterflies: your clothes were covered with butterflies. It was like an enchanted land; but in the place of fairies there were thousands of little white crosses, marked "Unknown British Soldier," for the most part. (Later, all these bodies were taken up and nearly all were identified and re-buried in Army cemeteries.) Through the masses of white butterflies, blue dragon-flies darted about; high up the larks sang; higher still the aeroplanes droned. Everything shimmered in the heat. Clothes, guns, all that had been left in confusion when the war passed on, had now been baked by the sun into one wonderful combination of colour—white, pale grey and pale gold. The only dark colours were the deep red bronze of the "wire" and one black cat which lived in a shelter in what once was the main street of Thiepval. It was strange, this black cat living there all alone. No humans, or those of her own species, lived within miles of her. It took me days to make friends and get her to come to me; and when at last I succeeded, the friendship did not last long. No matter where I worked round that district, the black cat of Thiepval would find me, and would approach silently, and would suddenly jump on my knees and dig all her long nails deeply into my flesh, with affection. I stood it for a little time, and then gave her a good smack, after which I never saw my little black friend again.

Thiepval Château, one of the largest in the north of France, was

German Prisoners.

practically flattened. What little mound was left was covered with flowers. Some bricks had been collected from it and marked the grave of "An Unknown British Soldier." Even Albert, that deadly uninteresting little town, looked almost beautiful and cheerful. Flowers grew by the sides of the streets; roses were abundant in what were once back-gardens; a hut was up at the corner by the Cathedral and Daily Mails were sold there every evening at four o'clock, and the golden leaning Lady holding her Baby, looking down towards the street, gleamed in the sun on top of the Cathedral tower.

A family had come back from Corbie and re-started their restaurant—a father and three charming girls. They patched up the little house by the station and did a roaring trade, and some few other families came back. Once more a skirt could be seen, even a few silk stockings occasionally tripping about.

Péronne was now like a polished skeleton—very clean, but very brittle: a little breeze, and whole houses would tumble to bits. I started painting, one day, a little picture from the hall of the College for Young Ladies. When I went the next day I found my point of view had been raised several feet: the top walls had come down. But here again they had patched up a great big house as a club. It was airy, not intentionally so, but on a hot day it was ideal, with its view down over the Somme.

Bully-beef pie, cheese and beer—if one could only have had French coffee instead of that terrible black mixture imported from England, things would have been more perfectly complete.

About August, a burial party worked round Thiepval. Lieutenant Clark was in charge of it, a sturdy little Scot. During the month or so they worked there, they dug up, identified and re-buried thousands of bodies. Some could not be identified, and what was found on these in the way of money, knives, etc., was considered fair spoil for the burial party.

Often, coming down Thiepval Hill in the evening, everything golden in the sunlight, one would come across a little group of men, sitting by the side of the battered Hill Road, counting out and dividing the spoils of the day. It was a sordid sight, but for a non-combatant job, to be a member of a burial party was certainly not a pleasant one, and I do not think anyone could grudge them whatever pennies they made, and most of them would have to go back in the trenches when their burial party disbanded.

Down in the Valley of the Ancre, just beside the Thiepval Hill Road, there was a great colony of Indians. They were all Catholics, and were headed by an old padre who had worked in India for forty-five years—a fine old fellow. He held wonderful services each Sunday afternoon on the side of the Hill in the open air; he had an altar put up with wonderful coloured draperies behind it, which hung from a structure about thirty feet high. In the mornings, it was a very beautiful sight to see these nut-brown men washing themselves and their bronze vessels among the reeds in the Ancre; one could hardly believe one was in France. And where was one? Surely in a place and seeing a life that never existed before, and never will again. The rapidity with which these Indians (they were a cleaning-up party) changed the whole face of Thiepval and that part of the Ancre Valley was incredible.

When working in the Valley of the Ancre region, coming home in the evening, we would bring the car down to the water near Aveluy. It is a long stretch of water, and the Tommies had put up a springboard. It was a joy to take off one's clothes in the car and jump into the cool water and watch all these wonderful young men stripping, diving, swimming, drying and dressing in the evening sun, all full of life and health. At one period, Joffroy, a very good French artist, who had lost a leg, right up to his trunk, early in the War, used to swim there with me. He had been a great athlete, and had a very strong arm-stroke, and possessed one of the most beautifully-developed bodies I have ever seen. One evening, after bathing, as we were driving back to Amiens in the car, he stretched out his arms and said, "Orpen, I feel like a young Greek god!" And, after a pause, added: "But only a fragment, you know, only a fragment." He was a great man, and could clamber over trenches with his wooden stump in a marvellous way.

I remember that summer a strange thing happened. One day I found, and started painting, the remains of a Britisher and a Boche — just skulls, bones, garments — up by the trenches at Thiepval. I was all alone. My faithful Howlett was about half a mile away with the car. When I had been working about a couple of hours I felt strange. I cannot say even now what I felt. Afraid? Of what? The sun shone fiercely. There was not a breath of air. Perhaps it was that — a touch of the sun. So I stopped painting and went and sat on the trunk of a blown-up tree close by, when suddenly I was thrown on the back of my head on the ground. My heavy easel was upset, and one of the skulls went through the canvas. I got up and thought a lot, but came to the conclusion I had better just go on working, which I did, and nothing further strange happened. That night I happened to meet Joffroy, and told him about these skulls, and how peculiar one was, as it had a division in the frontal bone (the Britisher's). He said he would like to go and make a study of it; so I brought him out the next morning to the place, I myself working that day in Thiepval Wood, about half a mile further up the hill. I left him, saying I would come back and bring him lunch from the car, as it was difficult for him to get about. When I did get back I found him lying down, not very near the place, saying he felt very ill and he thought it was the smell "from those remains." He had done no work, and refused even to try to eat till we got a long way away from the skulls. I explained to him that there was no smell, and he said, "But didn't you see one has an eye still?" But I knew that all four eyes had withered away months before. There must have been something strange about the place.

Most of these summer months John Masefield was working on the

Adam and Eve at Péronne.

Somme battlefields. He preferred to work out there on the spot. He would get a lift out from Amiens in the morning on a motor or lorry, work all day by himself at some spot like La Boisselle, and walk back to the bridge at Albert and look out for a lift back to Amiens. If we worked out in this direction, on the way home our eye was always kept on the look-out for him; but really it never appeared to matter to him if he got back or not. I don't believe he minded where he was as long as he could ponder over things all alone.

The small towns and villages in this part of the country, behind the old fighting line of 1916, were, for the most part, dirty and usually uninteresting; but once clear of them the plains of Picardy had much charm and beauty, great, undulating, rolling plains, cut into large chequers made by the different crops. When a hill became too steep to work on, it was cut into terraces, like one sees in many of the vineyards in the South; these often have great decorative charm. A fair country—I remember Joffroy sometimes used the word "graceful" regarding different views in those parts, and the word gives the impression well.

There is a beautiful valley on the left, as one goes from Amiens to Albert: one looked down into it from the road, a patchwork of greens, browns, greys and yellows. I remember John Masefield said one day it looked to him like a post-impressionist table-cloth; later, white zigzagging lines were cut all through it—trenches.

In the spring of 1917 it was strange motoring out from Amiens to Albert. Just beyond this valley everything changed. Suddenly one felt oneself in another world. Before this point one drove through ordinary natural country, with women and children and men working in the fields; cows, pigs, hens and all the usual farm belongings. Then, before one could say "Jack Robinson!" not another civilian, not another crop, nothing but a vast waste of land; no life, except Army life; nothing but devastation, desolation and khaki.

CHAPTER VI
THE SOMME (SEPTEMBER 1917)

ABOUT this time I got a telegram from Lord Beaverbrook asking me to meet him the next morning at Hesdin (Canadian Representatives' H.Q.); so I left Amiens early, arriving at Hesdin about 11.45 a.m. There they handed me a letter from him explaining to me that something very important had happened, and that he had left for Cassel. Would I have some lunch and follow him there? I lunched alone at the H.Q. and started for Cassel, where I arrived about 2.30, and found a letter telling me that he found that the aerodrome from which he wanted to get the news he desired was not near Cassel, so he had left, but would I meet him at the "Hôtel du Louvre," Boulogne, at 4 p.m., as his boat left at 4.20? Away I went to Boulogne, and walked up and down outside the "Louvre." About ten minutes past four up breezed a car, and in it was a slim little man with an enormous head and two remarkable eyes. I saluted and tried to make military noises with my boots. Said he: "Are you Orpen?" "Yes, sir," said I. "Are you willing to work for the Canadians?" said he. "Certainly, sir," said I. "Well," said he, "that's all right. Jump in, and we'll go and have a drink." So down to the buffet we went, and we had a bottle of champagne in very quick time, and away he went on to the boat, without another word, smiling; and the smile continued till I lost sight of him round the corner of the jetty. A strange day: I wondered a lot on the way back to Amiens, where I arrived about 9.45. I never knew then what a good friend I had met.

As before, in Cassel, I first began to realise how wonderful the workwomen of France were, so in Amiens I began to realise how different the young men of France were to what one was brought up at home to imagine. I had always been led to believe that an Englishman was a far finer example of the human race than a Frenchman; but it certainly is not so now. The young Frenchman is a keen, strong, hardy fellow, and his general level of physical development is very high.

A Grave in a Trench.

I remember this was brought home to me by having baths at Amiens. There was one bathroom in the hotel, and it contained a bath, but no hot water ran into it. So I told my batman to get hot water brought there in the mornings. The bathroom was on the first floor of the hotel, across on the other side of the courtyard from where I slept. The assistant cook, a man six feet odd high, and weighing about thirteen stone, a merry, jovial great giant, used to heat water for me and put it into an enormous bronze tub, which held a whole bathful; and he and my batman used to carry this upstairs; but if I happened to come along at the same time, this great man used to bend down and pick me up with his free hand and set me on his shoulder, and so to the bathroom.

One morning, about a year later, he told me he was going to leave. I asked him if he had got the "sack," or if he were leaving of his own free will. "Neither," said he. "I'm called up; I'm of age." This great, enormous man had only then reached the age of seventeen years. It amazed me. I remember a sad thing happened. When he left I gave him fifty francs and one hundred "Gold Flake" cigarettes. He had to go through Paris to get to his regiment, and when he arrived at the Gare du Nord they searched him, and found the cigarettes, took them from him, and fined him two hundred and fifty francs. It was a sad gift.

About this time I painted de Maratray—philosopher, musician, correspondent and clown.

Fane had gone, and Captain Maude was A.P.M. Amiens. Maude was a good A.P.M. His police were well looked after and adored him. He never wanted an officer or man from the trenches to get into trouble, but did his best to get them out of it when they were in it. Often have I been sitting at dinner with him at the "Hôtel de la Paix" and one of his police would come in and say, "A young officer is at the 'Godbert,' sir. He's had too much to drink, and is behaving very badly." Maude would curse loudly at his dinner being spoilt, but would always leave at once, and would calm down whatever young firebrand it was, find out where he had to go, and have him seen off by lorry or train to his destination. All this meant much more trouble for Maude than to have him arrested, and much less trouble for the culprit; but he always put them on their honour never to do it again; and many are the letters I have seen thanking him for being "a sport," and promising never "to do it again"; and asking would he dine with them the next time they got a night off? That was Maude's idea: he could not do too much for the men from the trenches, and they appreciated it. Maude was loved all through the North of France, except by a few rival A.P.M.'s. One could easily judge what his character was like from his favourite song:—

"*Mulligatawny soup,*
A mackerel or a sole,
A Banbury and a Bath bun,

And a tuppenny sausage roll.
A little glass of sherry,
Just a tiny touch of cham,
A roly-poly pudding
And Jam! Jam!! JAM!!!"

A lot of nice people used to come to Amiens at that period; Colonel Woodcock and Colonel Belfield, the "Spot King," and Ernest Courage, "Jorrocks," in particular. It all became one large party at night for dinner. Maude was very popular with all the French officials, and great goodwill existed between the French and the British, and Marcelle's black eyes smiled at us from behind the desk, with its books, fruit, cheese and bottles; smiled so well that had she been different she might have out-pointed Marguerite as "Queen of the British Troops in Picardy." But no, her book-keeping and an occasional smile were enough for Marcelle, and she did them both exceedingly well.

Poor Marcelle! Afterwards I was told that when the Huns began to bomb Amiens badly she completely broke down and cried and sobbed at her desk. She was sent away down South, to Bordeaux, I think, and we never saw her again. It was sad. She was a sweet child, with her great dark eyes, and the little curl on her forehead, and her keen sense of the ridiculous.

The song of that time was:—

"Dear face that holds so sweet a smile for me.

Were it not mine, how 'Blotto' I should be."

But one night Carroll Carstairs of the Grenadier Guards breezed into Amiens, bringing with him a new American song which became very popular. The chorus ran something like this:—

"When Uncle Sam comes
He brings his Infantry;
He brings Artillery;
He brings his Cavalry.
Then, by God, we'll all go to Germany!
God help Kaiser Bill!
God help Kaiser Bill!
God help Kaiser Bill!
"For when Uncle Sam comes...." (Repeat)

The Deserter.

One day Maude asked me to go to the belfry, the old sixteenth-century prison of Amiens, a beautiful building outside, but inside it was very black and awe-inspiring. The cells, away up in the tower, with their stone beds and straw, rats and smaller animals, made one's flesh creep. I am sorry I never painted the old fat lady who kept the keys in the entrance hall, a black place, lit by an oil lamp which hung over the stone fireplace. I put off painting her and her hall then for some reason, and later she was killed by a shell at the door during the

The Great Mine. La Boisselle.

bombardment. Here in the belfry the deserters were put, in an endeavour to make them say who they were, and Maude asked me to go this day because he had an interesting case.

A young man in a captain's tunic had been found in a brothel, and his papers were very incomplete. He had no leave warrant. They found he had been living at the "Hôtel de la Paix" for about a week. He had come to Amiens on a motor-bicycle, which he left in the street. They telephoned to the "Captain's" regiment and found the "Captain" was with his unit, but a tunic had been stolen from him at Calais. They also found a motor-bicycle had been stolen from Calais, and that it corresponded in number with the one found in the street.

We were given a candle, and climbed the black stairs to his cell. The youth was in a bad state, sobbing. Maude told him how sorry he was for him, and asked him not to be a fool, but to tell him the truth, and he would have him out of that place at once. He agreed, and told a long story, or rather—another long story. This was his third day and his third story, and it turned out there was not a word of truth in this one either.

He was one of the best-looking young men I ever saw, tall, clean-cut and smart-looking. The next day Maude found out that most of his tears were due to the fact that he was very badly diseased, and of course, without any treatment, was getting worse daily. Maude could not stand this, so he sent him to the hospital for treatment, from which the youth promptly escaped, and was not found again for ten days. They knew some one must have been hiding him, probably a woman; which proved right. In ten days he was found, plus forty pounds, which the lady had given him.

Maude gave him one more twenty-four hours' chance in the belfry; but it was no good, only more lies. So he was sent to Le Havre, where I believe no deserter has ever lasted more than forty-eight hours without telling the truth and nothing but the truth. I presumed that after that he was shot. The only thing I learnt for certain, was that he was a Colonial private. Some time later I used to go very often to a little restaurant in Paris, and became friends with one of the head waiters. He said a customer had come in, giving the name of Lord X——, and had engaged a table for dinner. He evidently had some doubt about Lord X——, and asked me if I would know him if I saw him. I said, "Certainly," as the name given was that of the son of one of the best-known Earls in England. In he came for dinner, a very good-looking man, wearing the Légion d'Honneur. Lord X——, the deserter of the belfry!

The great mine at La Boisselle was a wonderful sight. One morning I was wandering about the old battlefield, and I came across a great wilderness of white chalk—not a tuft of grass, not a flower, nothing but blazing chalk; apparently a hill of chalk dotted thickly all over with bits of shrapnel. I walked up it, and suddenly found myself on the lip of the crater. I felt myself in another world. This enormous hole, 320 yards round at the top, with sides so steep one could not climb down them, was the vast, terrific work of man. Imagine burrowing all that way down in the belly of the earth, with Hell going on overhead, burrowing and listening till they got right under the German trenches—hundreds and hundreds of yards of burrowing. And here remained the result of their work, on the earth at least, if not on humanity. The latter had disappeared; but the great chasm, with one

The Butte de Warlencourt.

mound in the centre at the bottom, and one skull placed on top of it, remained. They had cut little steps down one of its sides, and had cleared up all the human remains and buried them in this mound. That one mound, with the little skull on the top, at the bottom of this enormous chasm, was the greatest monument I have ever seen to the handiwork of man.

There was another fairly large mine here, just by the Bapaume Road, and there was a large mine at Beaumont-Hamel, and also the "Cough-drop" at High Wood. These were wonderful, but they could not compare in dignity and grandeur with the great mine of La Boisselle.

Working out on the Somme, in the evenings as the sun was going down, one heard constantly a drone of aeroplanes, which quickly grew louder and louder, and before one could think, two of these great birds would pass just over one's head, quite close to the ground. A couple of minutes later, Bang! bang! bang! bang! and the boom and crash of the guns. Presently you would see the two birds, high up, returning to their aerodrome. They had gone up to the Boche trenches, in the eye of the sun, machine-gunning them and dropping small bombs.

The Butte de Warlencourt looked very beautiful in the afternoon light that summer. Pale gold against the eastern sky, with the mangled remains of trees and houses, which was once Le Sars, on its left. But what must it have looked like when the Somme was covered with snow, and the white-garmented Tommies used to raid it at night? It must surely have been a ghostly sight then, in the winter of 1916.

About this time I went to Paris several week-ends at odd times and painted for the Canadians Generals Burstall, Watson and Lipsett, also Major O'Connor. Poor Lipsett was killed by a shell later. He was a thoughtful, clever, quiet man, and was greatly respected. Burstall was a great, bluff, big, hearty fellow, and Watson was a fine chap, a real "sport." O'Connor was A.D.C. to General Currie, and had been twice wounded.

Paris! What a city!
"Paree!
That's the place for me.
Just across the sea
From Dover!"

CHAPTER VII

WITH THE FLYING CORPS
(OCTOBER 1917)

ABOUT this time, the C.-in-C. was granted the Order of a
Knighthood of the Thistle. It was given to him by the King
during his visit to France in a château at Cassel. No one was present
when he received this honour. Just afterwards I did a little interior of
the room.

General Trenchard and Maurice Baring chose out two flying boys
for me to paint, and they sat to me at Cassel. One was 2nd Lieutenant
A. P. Rhys Davids, D.S.O., M.C., a great youth. He had brought down
a lot of Germans, including two cracks, Schaffer and Voss. The first
time I saw him was at the aerodrome at Estre Blanche. I watched him
land in his machine, just back from over the lines. Out he got, stuck
his hands in his pockets, and laughed and talked about the flight with
Hoidge and others of the patrol, and his Major, Bloomfield. A fine lad,
Rhys Davids, with a far-seeing, clear eye. He hated fighting, hated
flying, loved books and was terribly anxious for the war to be over, so
that he could get to Oxford. He had been captain of Eton the year
before, so he was an all-round chap, and must have been a magnificent
pilot. The 56th Squadron was very sad when he was reported missing,
and refused to believe for one moment that he had been killed till they
got the certain news. It was a great loss.

The other airman chosen was Captain Hoidge, M.C. and Bar—
"George" of Toronto. Hoidge had also brought down a lot of Germans.
His face was wonderfully fitted for a man-bird. His eyes were bird's
eyes. A good lad was Hoidge, and I became very fond of him
afterwards. I arranged with Maurice Baring and Major Bloomfield that
Hoidge was to come to Cassel one morning at 11 a.m. to sit to me.
The morning arrived and 11 o'clock and no Hoidge. Eleven-thirty,
12—no Hoidge. About 12:30 he strolled into the yard and I heard him
asking for me in a slow voice. I was raging with anger by this time.
He came upstairs and I told him there was no use doing anything

Lieut. A. P. F. Rhys Davids, D.S.O., M.C.

before lunch, and that we had better go down and get some food. We ate silently. I could see he was rather depressed. About halfway through our meal, he said: "I'm lucky to be here with you this morning!" "Why?" said I. "Oh," he said, "I made a damned fool of myself this morning. Let an old Boche get on my tail. Damned fool I was—with my experience. Never saw the blighter. I was following an old two-seater at the time. He put a bullet through the box by my head, and cut two of my stays. If old B. hadn't happened to come up and chased him off I was for it. Damned fool! But the morning wasn't wasted, afterwards I got two two-seaters." I said: "Do you realise you have killed four men this morning?" "No," he said, "but I winged two damned nice birds." Then we went upstairs and he sat like a lamb.

One evening, during the King's stay at Cassel, I was working in

Lieut. R. T. C. Hoidge, M.C.

my room about 7 o'clock, when a little scrap of paper was brought me on which was written, "I am dining downstairs.—M. B." I went downstairs and there was Maurice Baring, and, with luck for me, alone. We had a great dinner. He was in his best form; for after dinner we went up to my room and sat by the open window and talked and talked. Suddenly Maurice stopped, and said: "What's that noise?" "What noise?" said I. So we looked down into the courtyard—only about ten feet—and there was "Boom," who had been dining with the King, and Philip Sassoon. "What the devil are you two doing?" said "Boom." "We've both been shouting ourselves hoarse for ten minutes. It's the last damned time you dine with Orpen, Maurice!" It's true we never heard them—but then Maurice was talking.

One morning, when the wind was very fresh, I got a telephone message from Major Bloomfield telling me to come to the squadron at once and see some "crashes." It was a glorious morning, blue sky, with great white clouds sailing by. I got down to the squadron as quickly as I could. A whole lot of novices from England had been sent out on trials, and the Major expected "great fun" when they landed.

The fire was made big and a great line of blue smoke whirled down the aerodrome to give the direction of the wind. Presently they began to come back. Some landed beautifully—one in particular—and the Major said to me: "Come on, I must go and congratulate that chap," and started running for the machine. When we got closer, he stopped and said: "Damn it! it's Hoidge, I forgot he was out."

I remember one poor chap in particular. He circled the aerodrome twelve times, each time coming down for a landing and each time funking it at the last moment. At last he did land, two or three bumps, and then—apparently slowly—the machine's nose went to the ground and gracefully it turned turtle. "Come along," said the Major, and when we got to the machine the wretched pilot was getting out from under it. "You unspeakable creature," said the Major. "Don't let me see your face again for twenty-four hours." And away limped the "unspeakable creature," covered with oil and dirt. I must add that after lunch the Major went up to him and patted his back and said he hoped he felt none the worse. But the thing that amazed me was, that although the machine seemed to land so gently, the damage to it was terrific—propeller and all sorts of strong things smashed to bits.

Ping-pong was the great game at this squadron (56th), and I used to play with a lot of them, including Hoidge and McCudden, but I did not know the latter's name at that time. It was before he became famous.

One day I went there with Maurice Baring, and the Major was greatly excited because they had just finished making a little circular saw to cut firewood for the squadron for the winter. The Major had a great idea that, as the A.D.C. to "Boom" was lunching, after lunch there would be an "official" opening of the circular saw. It was agreed that all officers and men were to attend (no flying was possible that day) and that Maurice should make a speech, after which he was to cut the end of a cigar with the saw, then a box was made with a glass

The Return of a Patrol.

front in which the cigar was to be placed after the A.D.C. had smoked a little of it, and the box was to be hung in the mess of the squadron. It was all a great success. Maurice made a splendid speech. We all cheered, and then the cigar was cut (to bits nearly). Maurice smoked a little, and it was put safely in its box. Then Maurice was given the first log to cut. This was done, but Maurice was now worked up, so he took his cap off and cut this in halves. He was then proceeding to take off his tunic for the same purpose, but was carried away from the scene of execution by a cheering crowd. It was a great day. I remember Maurice saw me back to Cassel about 1 a.m., after much ping-pong and music. "I'll go back to the shack where the black-eyed Susans," etc., was the song of the moment then in the squadron.

Shortly after this Major Bloomfield was ordered home, promoted and, I think, sent to America. At this loss, a great gloom fell over the 56th Squadron. I never saw any squadron in France that was run nearly so well as the 56th under Bloomfield, nor any Major loved more by his boys.

CHAPTER VIII

CASSEL AND IN HOSPITAL
(NOVEMBER 1917)

ABOUT this time I went to Paris and met several Generals and Mr. Andrew Weir (now Lord Inverforth), and it was arranged that Aikman was to go home to the War Office and that I, perhaps, might have my brother out later to look after me. Aikman left, and I was very lonely. A better-hearted companion and a kinder man one could not meet, and regarding the intricacies of "King's Regulations" and such-like things, he was a past master.

After this, whenever I went to Paris, the great thing was to stop on the way at Clermont and lunch with "Hunchie." "Hunchie" kept the buffet at the station. He had a broken back and had been a chemist in Paris, but said he had come to the station at Clermont for excitement. It was so exciting that Maude proposed stopping there for a rest cure! But "Hunchie's" lunches were excellent. I remember one day on my way to Paris, I asked him at lunch if he had any Worcestershire Sauce; he had not. He asked me when I was coming back North again. I said the next day, which I did, and stopped for lunch. He had the sauce. He had been to Paris to get it. "Hunchie" was a wonder, so was Madame, and so was their dog "Black."

One spot in Paris, the Gare du Nord, will always mean a lot to the British Army on the Western Front. What sights one saw there!— masses of humanity, mostly British officers and men, each with their little "movement order": there they were in the heart of the Gay City. Yet that little slip of paper would, in a couple of hours, send them to Amiens, and a little later they would be at the front suffering Hell. Laboreur did a wonderful etching of an officer bidding farewell to his wife at the Gare du Nord. It gave the whole tragedy of the place—the blackness, smoke, smell and crush. There, any night during an air raid, one could not help thinking what would happen if the Boche got a bomb on the Gare, with its thousands of fighting men all jambed together under its glass roof in the semi-darkness. What a slaughter!

Changing Billets.

And yet through it all, if the old Gare could only speak, it could tell some strange and amusing tales of that time—tales that would make one laugh, but with the laughter there would be a catch in the throat and a swimming in the eyes. It is extraordinary how funny sometimes the most tragic things can be.

The weather had become very bad and cold, and I worked on all impossible out-of-door days in my room in the "Hôtel de la Paix," which was known as the "Bar." My only rule was that the "Bar" was not open till 6.30 p.m. At times it nearly rivalled "Charlie's Bar." At what hour the "Bar" closed I was not always certain, as, no matter who was there, at about 10:30 I used to undress and go to bed, and so accustomed did I get to the clink of glasses and the squirt of the syphons that I slept calmly through it all. Among the regular attendants when in Amiens were Captain Maude, "Major" Hogg, Colonel MacDowall of the 42nd G.H., Colonel Woodcock, Colonel Belfield (the Spot King), Captain Ernest Courage (Jorrocks), Captains Hale and Inge (then of the Press), Bedelo (Italian correspondent), and Captain Brickman—a merry lot, taking them all round, and that room heard some good stories; some may have been not quite nice, but none were as dirty or disreputable as the room itself, with its smell of mud, paint, drink, smoke, and the fumes from the famous "Flamme Bleue" stove. The last man to leave the bar had to open the window. This was a firm rule. It sometimes took the last man a long time to do it, but it was always done.

By this period of the war nearly every French girl could speak some English, and great was their anger if one could not understand them. I remember a very nice girl, who worked at the "Hôtel de la Paix," came to me one day and said solemnly, "My grandfadder he kill him." "Gracious!" I said, "whom did he kill?" "He kill him," was the furious reply. Apparently the poor grandfather, living under German rule at Landrecies, had committed suicide.

I went back to Cassel and began to itch, mildly at first, and I was not in the least put out. My brother came to France, and I went to Boulogne to meet him. His boat was to arrive at 6.15 p.m., but did not get in till just 10 p.m. They had been away down the Channel avoiding something. Driving back to Cassel we had a fine sight of bombing and searchlights. Hardly a night passed at this period that the Boche did not have a "go" at St. Omer. One night, just then, they dropped three torpedoes in Cassel as we were having dinner, but Suzanne, the "Peach," at her desk, never fluttered an eyelid. I believe afterwards, during the summer of 1918, when things were quite nasty at Cassel, she never showed any signs of being nervous: just sat at her desk, made out the bills, and occasionally made some lad happy by a look and a smile.

On some evenings we used to give great entertainments in the kitchen of the "Sauvage." I would stand the drinks, and Howlett (my chauffeur) played the mouth-organ, and Green (my batman) step-

The Receiving-room: 42nd Stationary Hospital.

danced. It was an amusing sight watching the expressions of those old, fat Flemish workwomen of the hotel.

The itching got worse, so one wet, black evening I went to see the M.O., took off my clothes in a dirty, cold, dark room, and he examined me carefully with the aid of an oil lamp. "You've got lice," he said. "Really?" said I. "Have you got a servant?" "Yes," said I. "Well, go back and give him Hell, and tell him to examine your clothes." I asked him about my foot, which had a hole in it about the size of a sixpence. "That's nothing," said he. "Keep it clean." So back I went, down the black cobbled street, called up my faithful boys, Howlett and Green, and told them I was lousy. I took my clothes off, and they examined them with electric torches and candles and oil lamps. Not a thing could they find. "Do you mind my looking at you, sir?" said Howlett. So he had one look. Said he, "If it were lice got you into that state, you'd be crawling with them."

I stood the pain and itching another couple of days, and sent for the M.O. to come to me. As there was more light in my room, he came and had a look. "Ah!" said he, "I thought last time it might have been that: you've got scabies. You must leave here for X—— in the morning, and have all your bed-clothes sent round to me before you leave."

In the morning I broke the news gently to Madame that I was a "dirty dog," and that my bed must go for a bit to be purged, and went round to the A.P.M. to say good-bye. When I told him where I was being sent, he said, "That place! Don't you do it. I was waiting there the other day to see someone, and I counted ten bugs on the wall." That put the wind up me, so I wrote to the M.O. and said I had an important meeting at Amiens that evening at 6 p.m., and that I would report at the X— — hospital immediately after that. He seemed rather hurt at my getting out of his reach, but he let me go (as I mentioned having to see the C.-in-C. on the way. It was wonderful what the mention of the C.-in-C. did for one!). He gave me my slip for the hospital:

"Herewith Major Orpen, suffering from scabies. Please...."

and with this I departed for Amiens, where I reported to the Colonel of the X— — Hospital. Over a whisky-and-soda I gave him the "slip," and he looked at my arm and said, "Yes, scabies," and I was put into the isolation ward and treated for this disease. How more people did not die in that hospital beats me. I personally never got any sleep, and left in a fortnight nearly dead. Lights were out at 10 p.m. This sounds good, but there were about eight of us in the ward. I had to have my foot treated every three hours. The man in the next bed to mine was treated for something every two hours; and nearly all the other beds were treated three or four times during the night. For all these treatments the lights blazed about twenty times each night, and some of the treatments were very noisy. At 6.30 a.m., in the dark, the nurse came round, and anyone who was not dying was turned out of bed. Why, I know not: there was no heat in the place. If you were well enough you went off to a soaking sort of scullery and heated some water over a gas-jet and shaved. If you were not well enough, you sat in your dressing-gown on a chair. You were not allowed to sit on your bed. At 8 a.m. you were given an extraordinarily bad breakfast — porridge with no milk, tea with no sugar, bread with — most days — no butter. After breakfast you could go to bed again, but this was not allowed if you were going to be let out during the day, as I was most of the time. So there you sat again, freezing, till an orderly came and said your bath was ready, usually about 9.30 a.m.—three hours after you had left your bed. The bath was in an outhouse about fifty yards across the yard from the ward. In hail, rain or snow, you had got to go there. In it I was boiled in a bath, scrubbed all over with a nail-brush, and then smothered all over with sulphur—wet, greasy, stinking sulphur rubbed in all over me. I dressed by putting on a pair of pyjamas first. These more or less kept this grease from getting through to my other clothes, and I was allowed out to work—a sick, freezing, wet individual. But my room at the "Hôtel de la Paix" was warm, and I sat over my "Flamme Bleue" all the morning. After I had been treated with sulphur for "scabies" a couple of weeks, a hole came in my throat just like the one I had on my foot—a white hole with a black band round it, and all the flesh for about six inches beyond it a deep scarlet. One morning the boy who washed me said: "I beg your pardon, sir, but what are you being treated for?" "Scabies," said I. Said he: "Don't say I said so, sir, but show the M.O. that thing on your neck. You haven't got scabies, and this sulphur will kill you soon." So I waited for the M.O. till he did his rounds. When he came to me he said the usual, "Everything all right with you?" "No," said I. "I've got a scabie on my neck that is worrying me." So he had a look at it and said: "I don't think this treatment is doing you much good. I shall get you dismissed from the hospital to-day." So I was chucked out. I happened to have blood-poisoning, not scabies, and I have it still. During the time I was in hospital, I got four very amusing poems from a General at G.H.Q. They were the bright spots during those days. I am sorry they are too personal to print.

About this time an officer told me a good story about my friend, Carroll Carstairs. The Cambrai battle was on, and the Grenadier Guards were advancing through a village. Carroll was with a brother officer, and said suddenly, "Look at the shape of that church now! Isn't it magnificent?" Another shell shrieked and hit the structure, and he said, "Damn! the fools have spoilt it." I believe it was during this battle he earned the M.C.

My brother became very popular with those he met in France. Too popular, indeed, with the girls in the hotel at Amiens to please Maude

A Death among the Wounded in the Snow.

or myself. Maude and I used to complain about it. Maude would say, "William, here you and I have been slaving for months to make ourselves liked by these girls, and your blinking little brother comes along, and cuts us out in a few days. It's disgusting." It was true: Maude, the A.P.M., and I, "le petit Major," took a back seat. We worked hard to prevent it, my brother did nothing: he kept silent, laughed, and won. It was very sad, and we were much upset.

CHAPTER IX
WINTER (1917-1918)

CHRISTMAS came with much snow and ice. Maude and I went to dinner at Captain MacColl's mess in the Boulevard Belfort. Maude remarked once, "MacColl is the only intelligent Intelligence Officer I know." We had a great dinner, and at 10 p.m. Maude and I went, in a blinding snowstorm, to the police concert. I'll never forget the fug in that place: it reeked of sweat, drink, goose and fags. They were all very happy, these huge men; all singing the saddest songs they could think of, including, of course, "The Long, Long Trail." American police were there also. They had come to Amiens to learn their job. We left late, but we had promised to return to MacColl's mess, so started for there, but after we had fallen in the snow a few times, we gave the idea up and went to bed.

About this time I went to H.Q. Tanks, and painted the General and Hotblack, and had a most interesting time. General Elles was a great chap, full of "go," and a tremendous worker. Hotblack, mild and gentle, full of charm; one could hardly imagine he had all those D.S.O.'s, and wound stripes—Hotblack, who liked to go for a walk and sit down and read poetry. He said it took his mind off devising plans to kill people better than anything else.

Then there was the "Colonel" of the Tanks—"Napoleon," they called him. A great brain he had. Before the war he knew his Chelsea well, and the Café Royal and all the set who went there. And there was a dear young Highlander also, a most gentle, shy youth. He was very happy one day; he had a "topping" time. He was out with the Tanks, and he killed a German despatch-rider and rode home on his bicycle.

One morning when I was painting the General, he told me that my old "Colonel" from G.H.Q. was coming to lunch. I hadn't seen him since he sent the telegram, "When do you return?" When he arrived we were all in the hall, but he didn't take the slightest notice of me. Presently, we went in to lunch. He sat opposite to me, and about halfway through the meal, he said, "Hello, Orpen! I didn't see you

Some Members of the Allied Press Camp.

before." To which I replied, "You have the advantage over me, sir. I don't remember ever having seen you before." It was no good. We would never have made good friends.

I regret that one night, while I was staying at G.H.Q. Tanks, I got "blotto." It wasn't altogether my fault, people were so hospitable. It was a night when I dined with General Sir John Davidson, "the Poet," at G.H.Q. I left "Tanks" on a bitterly cold, wet evening, and called at the Canadian château at Hesdin. I found them all sitting round a big fire. It was tea-time. The Colonel, who saw I was cold, gave me a whisky-and-soda, which he repeated when I left. I then went on to the C.-in-C.'s château to see Major Sir Philip Sassoon, and found him in

Poilu and Tommy.

his hut outside the château. As soon as I sat down he rang his bell. The orderly came. "A whisky-and-soda for Major Orpen," said he. This came. When I had got through about half of it, his telephone rang. "Run upstairs, Orp," said he, "and see Allan (Colonel Fletcher), he's laid up in bed." So off I went and found his bedroom. As soon as I came in he rang his bell. His servant came. "Whisky-and-soda," said he. When I was about halfway through this, there were footsteps on the stairs. "That's the Chief coming," said the Colonel. "Gosh!" said

I, and I pushed my whisky-and-soda well under the bed. In came the C.-in-C. "Hello, little man!" said he, "you look cold; and they don't seem to be very hospitable to you here, either." He rang the bell. The orderly came. "Bring Major Orpen a whisky-and-soda," said he. That did it. He talked for about ten minutes, and left. And in came Philip with my half-finished drink, cursing. "I've been standing on those damned stairs with Orp's drink for the last half-hour waiting for the Chief to leave." So, of course, I had to finish it. And then the Colonel's. And I went off to General Davidson's, and he had a nice cocktail ready for me, and a good "bottle" for dinner—after which I do not remember anything. But it was a bit of bad luck, one thing happening after another like that.

When I went back to Amiens I saw a good bit of the Press. The "Major" had gone, and Captain Hale of the Black Watch had charge. A fine fellow, Hale, as brave as a lion. He told endless stories, which one could hardly ever understand, and he laughed at them so much himself that he usually forgot to finish them. Rudolf de Trafford was there, and old Inge, a much-travelled man; also Macintosh, a Parisian Scot. It was very peaceful; no one dreamt that shells were soon to come crashing through that old château. Ernest Courage, with his eyeglass fixed in his cap, used to come into Amiens and finish lunch with his usual toast, and then sing Vesta Tilly's great old song:—

"Jolly good luck to the girl who loves a soldier.
Girls, have you been there?
You know we military men
Always do our duty everywhere!
"Jolly good luck to the girl who loves a soldier.
Real fine boys are we!
Girls, if you want to love a soldier
You can all (diddley-dum) love me!"
and very well he did it.

General Seely asked Maude and myself to dine one night at the "Rhin." Prince Antoine of Bourbon was there—he was Seely's A.D.C. During dinner I arranged to go to the Canadian Cavalry H.Q. and paint Seely, which I did, and had a most interesting time. Munnings was painting Prince Antoine at this period, on horseback. He used to make

Bombing: Night.

the poor Prince sit all day, circumnavigating the château as the sun went round. I remember going out one morning and seeing the Prince sitting upon his horse, as good as gold. Munnings was chewing a straw when I came up to them. "Here," said he. "You're just the fellow I want. What colour is that reflected light under the horse's belly?" "Very warm yellow," said I. "There! I told you so," said he to the Prince. Apparently there had been some argument over the matter. Anyway, he mixed a full brush of warm yellow and laid it on. Just before lunch I came out again. There they were in another spot. "Hey!" said Munnings, "come here. What colour is the reflection now?" "Bright violet," said I. "There! what did I tell you?" said he to the

Prince; and he mixed a brush-load of bright violet, and laid it on.

As the sun was sinking I went out again, and there was the poor Prince, still in the saddle. Munnings had nearly as much paint on himself as on the canvas. He was very excited. I could see him gesticulating from a distance. When he saw me he called out: "Come here quickly before the light goes. What colour is the reflection on the horse's belly now?" "Bright green," said I. "It is," said he, "and the Prince won't believe me." And he quickly made a heap of bright green and plastered it over the bright yellow and bright violet reflections of the morning and midday. So ended the day's work, and the bright green remained in full view till the next sitting.

The day I arrived Munnings was much upset because he had no sable brushes. He was telling me about this, and said, "Do you mind my asking you three questions?" "Not at all," said I. "First," he said, "have you got a car?" "Yes," said I. "Second," said he, "have you got any sable brushes?" "Yes," said I. "Third," said he, "will you lend me some?" "Yes," said I, and handed him over all I had. When I was leaving I said to Munnings, "What about those sable brushes, Munnings?" He replied: "Don't you remember I asked you three questions?" "I do remember your asking me something," said I. "Well," said he, "the first question I asked was, 'Have you got a car?'" "What the hell has that got to do with my sable brushes?" said I. "A great lot," said he. "You can damn well drive to Paris and get some more for yourself. I haven't a car."

About a week later I painted the Prince. He was a most devoted A.D.C. to the General. It was very sad his getting killed afterwards.

CHAPTER X

LONDON (MARCH-JUNE 1918)

I WAS now ordered back to London—I forget what for, something about expenses, I think. Lord Beaverbrook had become my boss, and they were going to pay all my expenses. It was a nice thought, but they never did.

I went with my brother up to G.H.Q. on March 20th to get warrants from Major A. N. Lee, D.S.O., and went on to Boulogne, and there met Ian Strang, who dined with us at the "Morny." There was a raid on when we came out from dinner, and people wished us to take shelter; but we had dined very well. The next morning there was a thick mist low down, with a clear sky above. When I got on the boat I met General Seely, who introduced me to General Sir Arthur Currie, who said: "You used to billet at St. Pol, usedn't you?" "Yes, sir," said I. "Well," said he, "I have just come through it. They got seven fourteen-inch shells into it this morning." "Has the offensive started?" said I. "That's about it," said he.

London seemed very strange to me at first. I felt very out of things.

Nobody I met, except the soldiers, or those who had been to France like myself, seemed to have any thoughts in common with mine: they did not appear to want to think about the fighting man or of the colossal deeds that were being done daily and nightly on the several fronts. No, they all talked of their own war-work. Overworked they were, breaking up—some at munitions; some at shoemaking classes; others darning socks—and they were all suffering terribly from air raids. In fact, to put it in a few words, they were well in the middle of the world war; they were just the same as the fighting man in France or on some other front.

Then it was that the definite thought came to me: the fighting man, the Hero, will be forgotten; that the people of England who have not been "overseas" and seen them at work, would never realise what these men have been through—win or lose, they would never know.

Their constant talk was of the terrible things they at home were

Major-General the Rt. Hon. J. E. B. Seely, C.B., etc.

going through on air-raid nights. It hurt me—their complaining about their little chances of damage, when I knew that millions of men were running a big risk of being blown into eternity at any moment, day or night. It is true, my first visit home made me realise that the fighting man after the war would be ignored, and I knew the reason— "Jealousy." I had been given the chance of looking on, and I had seen and worshipped. But if I had not seen, I might have felt just the same as those who stayed at home. Jealousy is one of the strongest things the human mind has to struggle against. Even now, after joint victory, it is one of the things the Allied nations have to guard against, for it exists between them, but surely the bond of the dead, that great community: —

"The Chosen Few,
The very brave,
The very true,"

French, British, Belgian, Italian, Portuguese and American, surely they should be enough to hold us together in love and respect, without jealousy, or any envy, hatred or malice in our hearts!

It was decided that an exhibition of my stuff should be held, so photographs had to be taken of each little thing, a title given to each, and the whole bunch sent to G.H.Q. for Major Lee to censor, which he did, refusing to pass nearly all of them. But General MacDonough, however, squashed all that. Then one of my titles got me into trouble. My first "Colonel's" set had been waiting all the year to get something against me, and now they worked up a molehill to a mountain. I had to go constantly to the War Office, and I was talked to very severely. In fact, I was in black disgrace. My behaviour could not have been worse, according to Intelligence (F), or whatever they were then called at G.H.Q.

I was lunching with Maurice Baring at the "Ritz" one day, and he told me McCudden was in London. I said I would like him to sit. "Well, write and ask him," said Baring. "But," said I, "I don't know him." "Right," said Baring, "I'll write to him." The thing was arranged, and one morning I heard a cheery voice below and someone came bounding upstairs, and before I saw him he shouted: "Hello, Orps! Have you a ping-pong table here?" He was the little unknown boy at the 56th Squadron with whom I used to play ping-pong only a few months before. Now he was the great hero, Major McCudden, V.C., D.S.O., etc., and well he wore his honours, and, like all great people, sat like a lamb.

The news one got in those days was terrible — one could not realise it — it seemed utterly impossible. Péronne taken! Bapaume taken! The Huns were back over the old Somme battlefields; they had taken Pozières; the great American stores there had gone; they were back over the great mine of La Boisselle. Terrible! And the golden Virgin had fallen from the Cathedral tower, and one remembered the old

Major J. B. McCudden, V.C., D.S.O., etc.

prophecy, "When the Virgin of Albert falls from her tower the end of the war is at hand," and now she was down in the dirt of the street. Did it mean defeat? Amiens was being shelled, the Boche swarmed on the heights of Villers-Bretonneux, and they could see clearly that great landmark of Picardy, Amiens Cathedral.

The railroad from the North to Paris was smashed, and they very nearly destroyed the great railway bridge near Etaples—great masses of masonry were blown out of it—everything was bombed right back to the sea. Then the Huns turned South. On they rushed—Montdidier shelled, Clermont in danger, on they went to Soissons and Château Thierry. One Sunday news came to the War Office that Paris had been bombed all day. A few minutes later this was corrected to "Paris has

245

The Refugee.

been shelled all day." It was awful! unbelievable! Paris shelled! Where had the Huns got to? Was the prophecy true of the Virgin falling from her tower? Were the Allies beaten? All the towns in Germany were ringing their victory bells, and we had our backs to the sea. It was a black period.

The afternoon my exhibition opened, they sent a message for me to go to the War Office immediately. There a Colonel showed me a minute from Intelligence (F), G.H.Q. My former Colonel's followers had really put their backs into it this time. They got me fairly and squarely. The Daily Express (I think it was Lord Beaverbrook's little joke) published a supposed interview with me in which I laughed long and loud at "the Censor fellow." This, of course, I had never done, but there it was in print. Intelligence (F) saw it and sent it to the W.O. with the minute. I don't remember the exact words, but the gist of it was this: "That Major Orpen's behaviour had been such that they thought it undesirable that he should be allowed to set foot in France again under any circumstances until the war was terminated." I asked the Colonel what I could do. He said sternly: "Nothing." I asked him if I might have the minute for half an hour. He said: "No," and then "Yes," so I took it away to another and higher office. Here its career ended in the waste-paper basket. I went back to the Colonel, and said: "I regret, sir, I cannot return the minute, it has been destroyed." The expression on his face was priceless, and it gave me the only pleasure I had that day.

Shortly afterwards I lunched at a house—a large party, including two Generals. One sitting near me was telling a lady that he and the other General were going to G.H.Q. the next morning for two days. I said: "Sir, don't you want an extra batman with you?" He said: "Have you any business you want to go to France for?" "Yes, sir," said I, "I have a lot of my stuff moved to Boulogne from Amiens, and I want to see to it." He said: "All right, telephone to — — at the War House and he will have your warrant ready and will get your seat for to-morrow morning." Gee! I was excited when I left that lunch, and darted back to my studio and telephoned to the War Office. Everything was arranged. They even telephoned Intelligence (F) that my car was to meet me at Boulogne. That must have been a nasty knock for Intelligence (F), but my faithful Howlett was there with the car when I got off the boat. We went and had lunch at the "Morny," and I saw my stuff was quite safe at the "Windsor Hotel," then I motored off to St. Valery-sur-Somme and visited the Allied Press Château (Captain Rudolf de Trafford was now the Chief of the Allied Press, Captain Hale having gone back to his regiment, the Black Watch), and arranged with them that I could get a billet there if I could manage to break down the opposition at Intelligence (F). Then I motored back to the École Militaire at Montreuil, where I was to meet General Sir John

Davidson, who was giving me dinner and putting me up. After dinner he had to go and see the Chief at his château, and he asked me to go with him. The C.-in-C., as usual, was more than kind, and asked me to dinner the next night. Then I got a bright thought and I asked his A.D.C., Colonel Fletcher, if he would be so kind as to do me a real good turn. He said: "Certainly." So I explained that I wanted him to ring me up at "Bumpherie" (H.Q. Intelligence (F)) at 10 o'clock the next morning, and say the C.-in-C. wanted to know would I dine with him. At 9.15 a.m. the next morning I got down to the little wooden huts which were H.Q. Intelligence (F). There I saw, through the windows in the passage, the two Colonels and Major Lee talking. They saw me all right, but pretended not to, so I walked up and down till a few minutes after 10 a.m., when out came the Major. "Hello, Orpen! is that you? I didn't know you were here." I said cheerfully: "Oh yes, I've been here quite a long time. How are you, old bean? Lovely morning, isn't it?" He said: "Look here, a telephone message has just come through from the C.-in-C. He wants to know if you will dine with him to-night." I said: "A telephone message from the C.-in-C. to me! But why did you come out here?" He said: "To tell you, of course." "But," I said, "you didn't know I was here!" He said: "Answer 'Yes' or 'No.'" "Oh," I said, "answer 'Yes.' I want to fix up with him what date I am coming back to France to work."

That did the trick. Intelligence (F) saw they were beaten. No more opposition! Perfect harmony was established. I at once became "Orps." Drinks were offered, lunches, dinners—any old thing that could be done was "a pleasure."

The dinner at the Chief's was most interesting. Some American Generals were there, and I learnt a lot about how things were going on, and returned to London the next day, and started making arrangements to go back and work in France again.

About this time I received the following from France:—

"Dear Woppy, I am glad that you
Will soon be back at G.H.Q.,
With brushes, paint and turpentine,
And canvases fourteen by nine,
To paint the British soldier man

As often as you may and can.
The brave ally, the captive Boche,
And Monsieur Clemenceau and Foch;
But, on the whole, you'd better not
Paint lady spies before they're shot.
We're living in the Eastern zone,
Between the — —, the — —, the — —
(The orders of Sir Douglas Haig
Compel me, Woppy, to be vague.)
But you can find out where we are
And come there in a motor-car.
We hold a château on a hill
. . . . (Censored)
A pond with carp, a stream with brill,
And perch and trout await your skill.
A garden with umbrageous trees
Is here for you to take your ease.
And strawberries, both red and white,
Are there to soothe your appetite;
And, just the very thing for you,
Sweet landscape and a lovely view.
So pack your box and come along
And take a ticket for Boulogne.
The General is calling me.
Yours, till we meet again,
"M. B."

CHAPTER XI

BACK IN FRANCE
(JULY-SEPTEMBER 1918)

EARLY in July I returned to France. My brother had now left me, and was doing regular Army work, and I brought Dudley Forsyth over with me. We stayed in Boulogne a few days till our billets were fixed at St. Valery, and during this time I painted a portrait at "Bumpherie" of Lee, who had then become the boss of Intelligence (F) Section and was Colonel A. N. Lee, D.S.O. Things had changed. "The stream of goodwill, it would turn a mill" at "Bumpherie." "Dear old Orps"—nothing was too good for him. "Do you think you could put in a word for me to ——?" "If —— speaks of the matter to you, just mention my name." Oh yes, the Colonel was really my friend now, and all the underlings appealed to me—and a good friend he has been ever since. Dear old Tuppenny Lee; I hope he'll forgive me writing all this, but he was a bit tough on me that first year, and he knows it jolly well, but he has more than made up for it since by a long chalk. There was only one wrong note in the harmony at "Bumpherie" then, and that was a "Colonel" with a large head and weak legs. He never forgave me—he wasn't that sort of fellow.

St. Valery-sur-Somme is a very pleasant little town at the mouth of the river, and the Allied Press held a nice château with a lovely garden. When things were quiet they used to have musical evenings, when Captain Douglas would sing most charmingly, and Captain Holland would play the fool well. Poor Theo! The Boche were at it hard now, and they were bombing all round every night. One night my window and wooden shutters were blown in—four bombs came down quite close. The roar of their falling was terrific. I remember well, after the second had burst, finding myself trying to jamb my head under my bed, but there wasn't room. I was scared stiff.

Soon after this great things happened. The whole world changed— the air became more exhilarating, birds seemed to sing happier songs, and men walked with a lighter step. One great thing happened quickly

Lieut.-Colonel A. N. Lee, D.S.O., etc.

after another. Ludendorff's black day arrived, and the Boche were driven off the heights of Villers-Bretonneux, and they lost sight of Amiens Cathedral. One day news came that the French had attacked all along the line from Château Thierry to Soissons, and had taken four thousand prisoners! It was all wonderful! Any day on the roads then one passed thousands of field-grey prisoners—long lines of weary, beaten men. They had none of the arrogance of the early prisoners, who were all sure Germany would win, and showed their thoughts clearly. No, these men were beaten and knew it, and they had not the

Marshal Foch, O.M.

spirit left even to try and hide their feelings.

That great French song, "La Madelon de la Victoire," connecting the names of Foch and Clemenceau, was sung with joy, and yet, when sung, tears were never far away—tears of thankfulness! Many have I seen pour down the cheeks of great, strong, brave men at the sound of that song and the tramp of the sky-blue poilus coming along in the glare and dust.

Forsyth had a song which became very popular about this time. The chorus ran:—

"Mary Ann is after me,
Full of love she seems to be;
My mother says, it's clear to see
She wants me for her young man.
Father says, 'If that be true,
John, my boy, be thankful, do;
There's one bigger bloody fool in the world than you—
That's Mary Ann.'"

In August I went down South to paint Marshal Foch at Bon Bon. General Sir John Du Cane kindly put me up at the British Mission, which was quite close to the Marshal's château, and I had a most interesting week. The morning after I arrived, General Grant brought me over to the Marshal's H.Q., a nice old place. We were shown into a waiting-room, and in a couple of minutes General Weygand (Chief of Staff) came in, a quiet, gentle, good-looking little man. It was impossible to imagine him carrying the weight of responsibility he had at that time. He was perfectly calm, and most courteous, and after talking to General Grant for a few minutes, brought us in to the Marshal. And there was the great little man, deep in the study of his maps, very calm, very quiet. He would certainly sit. How long did I want him for? An hour and a half each day, for four or five days? Certainly. When did I wish to start? The next day? Certainly. He would sit from 7 a.m. to 8.30 a.m. for as many mornings as I wished. Might he smoke while he sat? Yes! Bon! Would I go and look out what room would suit me to work in? Any room I liked except the one I was in with the maps. I fixed up a little library to work in—a long, narrow, dark little place, but with a good light by the window. I got up very early the next morning and arrived there about 6.15 a.m., and as nobody seemed to be about, I walked in, and as the only way I knew how to get to the library was through the room with the maps, I opened its door, and there he was, deep in study. He got up, shook hands, and said he would be with me at 7 a.m. In he came at 7 a.m., very quietly, and sat like a lamb, except that his pipe upset him. It seemed that some of his English friends thought he was smoking too many cigars, and they had given him a pipe and tobacco, and asked him to try and smoke it instead. But up to that date the Marshal was not a star at pipe-smoking. He could light it all right, but after about two minutes it would begin to make strange gurgling noises, which grew louder and louder, till it went out. The next day I brought some feathers and cotton wool, and the Marshal looked on me as a sort of hero, because each time we rested I used to clean out the pipe and dry it.

During all the time he was sitting great battles were going on and the Germans were being driven back. News was brought to him about every ten minutes. If it was good, he would say "Bon!" If it was bad, he just made a strange noise by forcing air out through his lips. During that time the Americans were having their first big "do," and I remember he was very upset at the Boche getting out of the St. Mihiel pocket in the way they did, without being caught.

I remember one morning (the Marshal did not know I understood any French at all) a General came in and sat with him, and the Marshal, very quietly, gave him times, dates, places where battles would be fought up to the end of December 1918, naming the French, British and American Divisions, and so forth, which would be used in each. When I got back to the Mission, I wrote down some dates and places I remembered, but told no one, and, as far as I could judge, everything went exactly as he said it would till about the middle of October, when the Boche really got on the run. Then things went quicker than he expected.

It seemed amazing, the calmness of that old château at Bon Bon, yet wires from that old country house were conveying messages of blood and hell to millions of men. What must the little man have felt? The responsibility of it all—hidden in the brain behind those kind, thoughtful eyes. Apparently, his only worry was "Ma pipe." His face would wrinkle up in anger over that. That, and if anyone was late for a meal. Otherwise he appeared to me to be the most mentally calm and complete thing I had ever come across. I would have liked to have painted him standing by his great maps, thinking, thinking for hours and hours. Yes, the three memories I brought away from Bon Bon were maps, calmness, and a certainty that the Allies would be victorious.

While I was there General Grant brought me over to Vaux. What a hall! Surely the most beautiful thing of a private nature in existence, with its blue dome and black eagle at the top.

A German 'Plane Passing St. Denis.

I left one evening and stopped in Paris that night. There were two air raids, and in the morning I heard Big Bertha for the first time, and when we left about 10 o'clock, just past St. Denis, a Boche 'plane came over to see where the shells were falling.

There was a wonderful service in the Cathedral at Amiens one morning, the first since the bombardment, a thanksgiving for the deliverance of the city from shell-fire. The Boche had been driven further back and the old city was out of shell-range and at peace. It was a lovely morning with a strong breeze, a little sixteenth-century Virgin had been rescued from Albert Cathedral, and it was set up on a pedestal in the middle of the chancel. There was a guard of honour of

British and French A.P.M.'s Amiens.

Australians; birds were flying about above and singing; they had made the interior of the Cathedral their own. Bits of glass kept falling down, and the wind made strange whistling noises through the smashed and battered windows. It was all very impressive. General Rawlinson and his staff came over from Bertangles, a few natives of Amiens came into the town for it, otherwise the whole congregation was British. It was strange! Australian bugles blaring away inside those walls!

I painted Maude and Colonel du Tyl, the brave defenders of the interior of the city during the bombardment, in Maude's cellar in the "Hôtel de Ville." General Rogers (then Colonel Rogers) used to come in constantly — a charming man, very calm, with a great sense of humour, and as brave as a lion. His little brother was working under Maude. At that time his little brother was very silent—one could not get a word out of him. Maude used to call him "my little ray of sunshine." Now he is as cheerful a "Bean" as you could wish to find.

The day the Boche were driven out of Albert, General Rogers went there and brought back the story of the cat. When the Tommies got into the town, even through the din, they heard the wailing of a cat in agony, and they found her crucified on a door, so they naturally went to take her down, but as they were pulling the first nail out, it exploded a bomb and many were killed. It was a dirty trick! Yet they who did it may be sitting beside me now in the little Parisian café in which I write—it is full of Boche. It's a strange thought, almost beyond understanding.

The light in Maude's cellar was most interesting to paint, and I'm afraid I spent far too long at it, but Maude was a good companion. Things were changing now daily. Instead of feeling the sea just behind one's back, so to speak, each day, it was getting further and further away, and there were fresh fields to explore. I was due officially to leave for Italy, but I couldn't go. Why leave France when wonder after wonder was happening? Hardly a day passed that some glorious news did not come in. No, I couldn't tear myself away from Picardy and the North. I felt that I would feel more out of it in Italy than in London, and now I know I was right. I did not do much in the way of my own work, but I saw and felt things I would never have got down South— things which were felt so much that their impression increases rather than diminishes. It is difficult at times to realise what is happening. Somehow other things keep one from realisation at the moment, but afterwards these other things diminish in importance and the real impression becomes more clearly defined.

I painted General Lord Rawlinson at Bertangles, which was then his headquarters, a charming man with a face full of character. He paints himself, and was good enough to take great interest in the sketch I painted of him. He had a mirror put up so that he could see what I was doing. This wasn't altogether a help to me, because, at times, perhaps when I was painting the half-light on his nose, he would say: "What colours did you mix for that?" By the time I had tried to think out what colours I had mixed—most probably not having the slightest idea—I would have forgotten what part of the head I was painting and what brush I was using. But Bertangles in August was lovely, and the lunches in the tent, even though full of wasps, were excellent. Certainly H.Q. 4th Army was well run.

A little later the H.Q. 4th Army moved to the devastated country close to Villers Carbonelle on the Péronne side. It was a wonderful bit of camouflage work. This great H.Q. just looked like an undulating bit of country even when right up beside it. I remember standing in the middle of it one frosty moonlight night, and it was impossible to believe that there were hundreds of human beings all around me there in the middle of that abomination of desolation.

I also painted Brigadier-General Dame Vaughan Williams of the Q.M.W.A.A.C.'s at her H.Q., St. Valery—a strong-minded, gentle, earnest worker, much loved by those under her. She held a château in a large garden and held it well. The mess was excellent.

Some civilians had now come back to Amiens, and it was possible to get a room in the "Hôtel de la Paix," so I left St. Valery and came to live there. This hotel escaped better than any other house in Amiens from the shells and bombs. The glass was, of course, broken, and slates knocked off, but that was all, except where little bits had been knocked out of the walls by shrapnel. It was wonderful to be there and watch the town coming to life again week by week.

After a time the Allied Press came and patched up their château, or parts of it. Some of the correspondents slept there and some got billets outside. Shops began to open. The Daily Mail came once more, and gradually the streets filled with people, these streets, the pavements of which were now more hostile than ever. Even a few of the girls came and settled there—"early birds."

That sweet, natural woman, Sister Rose, had remained in Amiens all through the bombardment, and when the people began returning, she was asked one day: "Are not you pleased, Sister Rose, to have the people round you again?" To which she replied: "Yes, of course I am in some ways, but I loved the bombardment. I felt the whole city was mine, each street became very intimate, and I could walk through them and pray out loud to my God in peace. But now! why, if I prayed to

General Lord Rawlinson, Bart., G.C.B., etc.

my God in the streets of Amiens they would think me a damned lunatic!" I can understand her very human feeling at that time—people who had run away from the city in its agony returned when its tribulation was over, and claimed it as their own again when the calm of evening had come; while she, Sister Rose, had borne the burden and heat of the day. But this feeling soon left her, and she worked whole-heartedly once more to succour the poor in distress in the city she loved so well.

CHAPTER XII

AMIENS (OCTOBER 1918)

THE nights were very black, there being no lights in the streets at all.

A little later Maude left his billet on the Abbeville Road, and came to live with me in the "Hôtel de la Paix." One night we were dining there, and at about 8.45 p.m. a young Flying Officer left a friend and came and asked Maude if we would come to their table and have a drink with them. Maude said Yes, and the lad went back to his table. "Who is your friend?" said I. "I don't know," Maude replied. "They asked me for ten minutes' extension of time last night, and I gave it to them." Presently we went over to their table and they ordered a round of the deadly brandy of the hotel. Maude introduced me as Major Sir William Orpen, and I learnt that their names were Tom and Fred. After a couple of minutes Tom wanted to ask me something, and he started off this way: "By the way, Sir William— —" "A little less of your damned Sir William!" said I. "All right," said he, "don't get huffy about it, bloody old Bill." So naturally we all became friends, and we mounted the stairs to my room, and the bar was opened and Tom recited. Fred insisted on it. "But," said Tom, "you always cry, Fred, when I recite." "It doesn't matter, Tom," said Fred, "I like it." So Tom recited and Fred cried, and Maude and I looked on and wondered and drank "Spots." They left about 11 o'clock to drive back to the aerodrome in an old ambulance they had in the yard. At about 7 a.m. the next morning I was awakened by a violent knocking at my door, so I shouted: "Come in," and in came Tom and Fred. They both walked over and sat on my bed. "What on earth are you here at this hour of the morning for?" I asked. "That's just what we've come here to find out, bloody old Bill," said Tom. "Are you hurt, Bill?" "No," said I. "Why?" "No furniture broken, no damage done to the room, Bill?" "No," said I. "Why?" "Well, look here, Bill, it's like this," said Tom. "Fred and I are puzzled as to exactly what happened. Fred, tell him what happened to you, and then I'll tell him about myself."

Fred rubbed his chin and started: "Well, Bill, the first thing I remember was that I found myself walking along a country road, and I met a M.P. man. Said I: 'Can you please direct me to the Gare du Nord?' 'Straight on,' said he, 'and you'll find it on your left. It's about a twenty-minute walk.' So I went straight on, and sure enough I came to the Gare du Nord, and I came on here and found Tom juggling with the wheel of the old ambulance with its radiator against the wall." "Yes," said Tom, "and look here, bloody old Bill, I had spent half the night juggling with death with that wheel — thank goodness the engine wasn't going. Then Fred woke me up. What do you make of it all, Bill?" I couldn't make anything of it, so I dressed and we had breakfast and they went off to their aerodrome in the Somme mud.

After this we became great friends and we had many happy evenings, in some of which Tom looked for a "spot of bother," and Fred warned him "it was a bad show." On "good nights for the troops," which meant that the weather was impossible for bombing (they were night-bombers), they would come into Amiens for dinner. These nights were "not devoid of attraction," and on the "bad nights for the troops" I would often dine at the aerodrome and see the raiders off. It was uncanny, these great birds starting off into the blackness — to what?

Tom and Fred lived together in a little hut in the Somme mud, off the Péronne Road, which they called "Virtue Villa," and when I worked anywhere away up this old East-West Road, I never could resist visiting "Virtue Villa" on the way back. "Virtue Villa" with its blazing stove, its two bunks — Tom's below, Fred's upstairs — its photographs (especially the one of Fred with the M.C. smile), the biscuit-box seats and the good glasses of whisky — truly "Virtue Villa," with its Tom and Fred, was not "devoid of attraction" on a cold October evening, with the rain splashing on the water in the old Somme shell-holes.

They were a great couple and devoted to each other. One could not eat, drink or be merry without the other, yet they were completely different. Fred was a calm, thoughtful English boy, very much in love and longing to get married; but Tom was just a heap of fun, a man who had travelled to many corners of the earth, but at heart was still a romping school-boy.

Albert.

About this time George Hoidge's squadron came to a place near Albert, and I had the pleasure of seeing Colonel Bloomfield there again, still as hearty and full of fire as ever. He was going to sit, but things began to happen too quickly then, and I never got a chance of painting him.

Some weeks later, Hoidge came in and said: "I have bad news for you, Orps. Tom and Fred have gone West." It was bad news. Tom and Fred, two gallant hearts, dead! I was told afterwards how it happened. One of the last days of the fighting, Fred went out to test his machine with his mechanic. He taxied off down the aerodrome, which was a huge old Boche one that his squadron had moved forward to. As he was taxi-ing he hit a Boche booby trap, planted in the ground, and up went the machine and fell in flames. The mechanic was thrown clear, but not Fred. Poor Tom saw it all from the door of "Virtue Villa." Out he rushed straight into the flames to Fred. I feel sure Fred's spirit cried out when it saw Tom coming in to the flames: "You're looking for a spot of bother, Tom, but it's a good show, Tom, a good show!"

When the petrol burnt out and they got to them, they found Tom with his arms round Fred. Greater love hath no man. That is how Tom and Fred "went West." I hope they have found another "Virtue Villa" not "devoid of attraction" high up in the blue sky, where they were often together in this life. Let us admit they were a "good show"—in death they were not divided. Their Major wrote to me: "The Mess has never been the same since." The world itself will never be the same to those who loved Tom and Fred and their like who have "gone West."

Thinking of them reminds me of those good lines by Carroll Carstairs, written in hospital after he was so badly wounded:—

"I have friends among the dead,
Such a gallant company,
Lads whose laugh is scarcely sped
To the far country.
"Jolly fellows, it would seem
That they have not really gone—
Rather while I've stayed to dream
They have marched serenely on."

THE CHURCH, ZILLEBEKE, OCTOBER 1918

"Mud
Everywhere—
Nothing but mud.
The very air seems thick with it,
The few tufts of grass are all smeared with it—
Mud!

The Church a heap of it;
One look, and weep for it.
That's what they've made of it—
Mud!
Slimy and wet,
Churned and upset;
Here Bones that once mattered
With crosses lie scattered,
Broken and battered,
Covered in mud,
Here, where the Church's bell
Tolled when our heroes fell
In that mad start of hell—
Mud!
That's all that's left of it—mud!"

CHAPTER XIII

NEARING THE END
(OCTOBER 1918)

THE Boche were now nearly on the run. I remember one day I went out with General Stuart and Colonel Angus McDonnell — the General was the railway expert, and was out to ascertain what amount of damage the Boche had done to the lines, permanent way, etc. General Stuart was a quaint little man. He seldom spoke, but when he did it was very much to the point and full of dry humour. The Hon. Angus McDonnell, a true Irishman, was a most attractive person, full of charm. He'd kissed more than the Blarney Stone, and had received all the good effects, and we had some most interesting days together. On the particular one I mention, we went away beyond Cambrai to a place called Caudry, where the General inspected the station and the general damage to the metals and permanent way, after which we left and lunched by the side of a road which ran through fields. All was peace, not a sound from the guns — when suddenly shrapnel started bursting over these fields. No one was in sight; a few Englishmen on horseback galloped past, apparently for exercise. The Boche, I presume, couldn't see, but just let off on chance. It was better than leaving the shells there for us.

After lunch we motored down to St. Quentin, and on the way stopped and explored the great tunnel in the Canal du Nord. What a stronghold! It seemed impossible that the Boche could have been driven out of it. On the way down we travelled along a road pavé in the middle, with mud on each side and the usual rows of trees, then a dip down to the fields. These fields were full of dead Boche and horses. The road had evidently been under observation a very little while back, as the Labour Corps were hard at work filling in shell-holes, and the traffic was held up a lot. In one spot in the mud at the side of the road lay two British Tommies who had evidently just been killed. They had been laid out ready for something to take them away. Standing beside them were three French girls, all dressed up, silk

The Mad Woman of Douai.

stockings and crimped hair. There they were, standing over the dead
Tommies, asking if you would not like "a little love." What a place to
choose! Death all round, and they themselves might be blown into
eternity at any moment. Death and the dead had become as nothing to
the young generation. They had lived through four years of hell with
the enemy, and now they were free. Another day I went to Douai, and
there I saw the mad woman. Her son told us she had been quite well
until two days before the Boche left, then they had done such things
to her that she had lost her reason. There she sat, silent and motionless,
except for one thumb which constantly twitched. But if one of us in
uniform passed close to her, she would give a convulsive shudder. It

was sad, this woman with her beautiful, curly-headed son. Later she was moved to Amiens, where she had relatives. After about six months she became quite normal again, and does not remember anything about it. The last time I saw her she was cleaning the upstairs rooms at "Josephine's," the little oyster-shop off the Street of the Three Pebbles.

One night at the "Hôtel de la Paix" a weird thing happened. One often hears strange stories of the powers different men and women have over individuals of the opposite sex. As a rule, one hears, one smiles, or one is rather disgusted; but seldom do we admit to ourselves that these stories may be absolutely true—we nearly always smile and think we are clever, and say to ourselves: "Ah! there's something behind that." Rasputin, for instance, what was he? Had he power? We wonder a little and dismiss the thought.

On this night, at about 9 o'clock, the early diners had gone, but there were about thirty of us left who would testify to the truth of this tale. A man walked in and sat down at a large empty table. He was a French civilian, dressed in black, tall and slim, with an enormous brown beard—a "Landru." Marie Louise, one of the serving-girls, asked him what he required, and he said: "A glass of Porto." This she brought him, but as she was placing it on the table, he put out his hand and touched her arm, and let his fingers run very gently up and down it. He never spoke a word. She retired and returned with another glass of port, and sat down beside him and commenced to drink it; no word was uttered. Again he raised his hand, beckoned to another serving-girl; the same act was gone through, and she sat down with her port. This continued without a word of conversation until he had all the serving-girls, about eight of them, sitting round in silence. We all sat and looked on in amazement for a while, but after about ten minutes hunger got the better of us, and we started calling them for our food. They took not the slightest notice of us, but in the end we made so much noise that Monsieur Dyé, the manager of the hotel, came in. He was a hot-tempered man, who never treated the girls under him kindly, and when he saw and heard his customers shouting for food, and saw all his serving-girls sitting down drinking port, his face went black with rage, and he rushed over to their table and cursed them all roundly, but they took not the slightest notice. Then he turned on the

Field-Marshal Lord Plumer of Messines, G.C.B., etc.

man with the beard and ordered him out of the hotel. He never answered, but got up slowly, put on his hat and left. As soon as he rose from the table all the girls went back to their work as if nothing had happened, and we continued our dinner. It was a strange affair—not one of those girls remembered anything about it afterwards.

Again I went to Cassel, to paint General Plumer. I arrived there one evening, and had dinner with Major-General Sir Bryan Mahon, who was on his way to Lille. I woke up in the morning, got out of bed and collapsed on the floor. "'Flu!" After three days the M.O. said I must go to hospital. I said: "Hospital be damned! I'm going to paint to-morrow." So I wrote and told General Plumer I would work the next morning if he could spare the time to sit. He replied he could. So on a very cold morning I made my way rather giddily up the stone steps to the Casino and on to his little château. There I was met by the General's grand old batman. He stopped me and said: "Have you come to paint the Governor's portrait, sir?" "Yes," said I. "Well," said he, "let me have a look at you. You're feeling a bit cheap, ain't you? The Governor told me you've been having the 'flu'." "Yes," I said, "I'm not feeling up to much." "Well, now," said he, "the Governor is busy for the moment, but he told me to look after you and fix up what room you would like to work in, but first I want to get you a bit more up to scratch. Just come along and have a glass of port." So he brought me off and gave me an excellent glass. Then I chose the General's bedroom to work in, and we fixed everything up. Then he said: "Now I'll go and fetch the old man." Off he went and back he came, and with a wink, said: "He's coming," and in walked the General. A strange man with a small head, and a large, though not fat, body, and a great brain full of humour. He also was very calm, and made things very easy for me, but his batman was not so easy to please. When I got the General the way I wanted him, the batman leant over my shoulder, and said: "Is the Governor right now?" "Perfectly," I replied. "No, he ain't," said he, "not by a long chalk." And he went over to the General and started pulling out creases in his tunic and said: "'Ere, you just sit up proper—not all 'unched up the way you are. What would Her Ladyship say if I let you be painted that way?" At last we got him satisfied, and he departed. When the door was shut, the General said: "Well, that's over," and settled down in comfort.

After I had worked for about an hour and a half there was a knock at the door and in the batman came. He took no notice of the General, but laid his hand on my shoulder and said: "Look up at me." I obeyed. "Won't do," said he. "You wants keeping up to the mark," and retired, and came back with an enormous glass of port. When the sitting was finished, I went back to bed at the "Sauvage," very giddy and slightly muzzed.

The next morning the batman again arranged the General "to Her Ladyship's liking," and left. As soon as he had gone, the General said:

"We've got him on toast. He's worried to death because you haven't painted the gold leaves on my red tab. Don't do it till the very last thing." It worked splendidly. The old chap was really upset. Every hour he used to come in and tap me on the shoulder, point to the red tab, and say: "What about it? If you don't get them gold leaves proper, I'll get it from Her Ladyship." He was a great servant of the true old class, one of those who never lose their place, no matter how freely they are treated, and was ready to die for his master at any minute.

Soon after this the General and his staff moved forward, and Cassel became a dead little place as far as the Army was concerned. Things were going very quickly, and scarcely a day passed that one could not mark a new front line on one's map.

I went out to see the damage done to Bailleul. In a few days British artillery had flattened it out as badly as Ypres. One could hardly find out where the main Place had been. Now one could wander all over the Ypres salient. Was there ever a more ghastly place? Even the Somme was outdone. Mud, water, battered tanks, hundreds of them, battered pillboxes, everything battered and torn, with Ypres like a skeleton. The Menin Road, the Zonnebeke Road, what sights were there—mangled remains of superhuman effort!

I remember one day in the summer being down at Lord Beaverbrook's when news came in that Locre had fallen. I had no knowledge of Locre, but Lord Beaverbrook, I could see, felt that the loss of it was a very serious thing. So I went to see Locre—a ghastly place!—the fighting must have been terrific. Shell-holes full of dead Germans. Everything smashed to pulp. I should imagine, before Hell visited it, Locre must have been a very pretty little place. It is on a hill which looks down into a valley, with Mont Kemmel rising up the other side.

Suddenly my blood poisoning came on again badly, so I returned to Amiens on November 10. When we had just passed Doullens we got the news that the Kaiser had abdicated. Great excitement prevailed everywhere. The next day, at 11 a.m., I was working in my room and heard guns, so I went to the window and saw the shells bursting over the town, but I could not see the Boche 'plane. It must be very high, I thought. About ten minutes afterwards there was a sound of cheering,

Armistice Night. Amiens.

so I knew the fighting was over. I went again to the window and looked down into the courtyard. It was empty, except for one serving-girl, Marthe, who had her apron to her face and was sobbing bitterly. Presently, Marie-Louise came up to my room and told me the news, and we had a drink together in honour of the great event. Said I: "What has happened to poor Marthe? It is sad that she should be so upset on this great day. What is the matter?" "Ah!" said Marie-Louise, "it is the day that has upset her." "The day?" said I. "Yes," replied Marie-Louise, "you see, her husband will come out of the trenches now and

The Official Entry of the Kaiser.

will come back to her. C'est la Guerre!"

Later, Maude came in, and I asked him what on earth a Boche was doing over Amiens just at the moment the fighting ceased. "Oh," said Maude, "there wasn't any Boche, but the anti-aircraft chap got orders to fire off his guns for ten minutes when the Armistice was signed, but, as he had nothing but live shells, he thought he had better stop after two." But why he burst his shells right over the centre of the town was never explained.

Yet, on this day, looked forward to for years, I must admit that, studying people, I found something wrong—perhaps, like all great moments expected, something is sure to fall short of expectations. Peace was too great a thing to think about, the longing for it was too real, too intense. For four years the fighting men had thought of nothing except that great moment of achievement: now it had come, the great thing had ceased, the war was won and over. The fighting man—that marvellous thing that I had worshipped all the time I had been in France—had ceased actively to exist. I realised then, almost as much as I do now, that he was lost, forgotten. "Greater love hath no man"—they had given up their all for the sake of the people at home, gone through Hell, misery and terror of sudden death. Could one doubt that those at home would not reward them? Alas, yes! and the doubt has come true. It made me very depressed. The one thing these wonderful super-men gave me to think that evening was: "What shall we do? Will they do as they promised for us? I gave up all my life and work at home and came out here to kill and be killed. Here I am stranded—I cannot kill anyone any more, and nobody wants to kill me. What am I to do? Surely they will give me some job: I have done my bit, they can't just let me starve." "When you come back home again"—yes, that crossed their minds and mine for them. Wending my way home through the blackened streets that night, I met a Tommy who threatened to kill me because of his misery. I talked him down and brought him to my room, and told him I really believed he would have a great time in the future. I doubted what I said, but he believed me, and went off to his billet happy for that one night.

Could anyone forecast the tragedy that has happened to so many of these men since? That great human Field-Marshal, Lord Haig, the man who knows, works for them still, and asks—but who answers? Great God! it makes one think, remember, think and wonder, what impossibly thankless people human beings are. It is sad, but very, very true!

CHAPTER XIV

THE PEACE CONFERENCE

CAPTAIN Maude left Amiens and became Major Maude, D.S.O., A.P.M. Cologne. I missed him greatly, and it depressed me very much being left in that old town, but the doctors flatly refused to let me move, so I just had to grin and bear it.

I then got more ill and took to my bed. My recollections from that time to the middle of January are very hazy. People were very kind to me, and used to come and sit with me for hours, especially two Rifle Brigade boys—Stevens and Riviere—two of the best. Stevens had just come back from Brussels, where there had been great times, music and dancing. Apparently the great tune of that period was "Katie"; anyway Stevens could not get it out of his head. He never knew how near he was to sending me completely mad, by singing gently to himself as the winter afternoons drew in:—

"*K-K-K-Katie, beautiful Katie,*
You're the only g-g-girl that I adore,
When the ke-moon shines on the Ke-cowshed;
I'll be waiting at the Kitchie Kitchen door."

Long afterwards, during the Peace Conference, whenever I heard that tune in the "Majestic," my mind went back to the misery and semi-darkness in that dirty room in Amiens.

On New Year's Eve, Angus McDonnell came all the way from G.H.Q. and had me lifted out to dinner, so I must have been better then. General Sir John Cowans also came all the way from G.H.Q. to see how I was. Kindness is a wonderful thing.

The Allied Press disbanded, and I gave a dinner to the boys at the "Hôtel de la Paix." It was all arranged by my chauffeur, Gordon Howlett, and my batman, Green, and it was well done. Great were the songs and dances, and great was the amount of liquid put away. I was lifted downstairs and laid out beside the table, and the lads presented me with a magnificent silver ash-tray.

Towards the end of January, I was allowed out and about again,

General Sir J. S. Cowans, G.C.B., etc.

and I went up to G.H.Q. to paint the Q.M.G., who put me up in his château. I painted him, and also did some work down at "Bumpherie," including a drawing of Lieutenant Brooks, who took the most wonderful official photographs during the war, often at great personal risk. I remember a story that went round in 1917, in which there was not a word of truth, but it was amusing. A terrible-looking Tommy stopped Brooks in the Street of the Three Pebbles and said: "Say, guv'ner, when are you going to give me me photo?" "What photo? Who are you?" said Brooks. "Blimy," said the Tommy, "you don't

Field-Marshal Sir Henry H. Wilson, Bart., K.C.B., etc.

know me, and me the bloke as was killed going over the top for you!"

I now got a reminder that I was due in Paris to paint the Peace Conference. The whole thing had gone from my mind. I afterwards found the letter, which I apparently had received and read, dated December, telling me to go to Paris, but I was so sick I did not realise what it was about. I realised now right enough, so I packed my bag and breezed away to Paris, and found that great family gathering, the Peace Conference, and the life of the "Astoria" and the "Majestic" commenced for me.

The great family really was composed of a number of little families. Mine consisted of Lord Riddell, George Mair, Lieut.-Colonel Stroud Jackson, D.S.O., George Adam, Sidney Dark and Gordon

Knox, and great were the meetings at Foucquet's before lunch.

For the most part, my life consisted now of painting portraits at the "Astoria," or attending the Conference at the "Quai d'Orsay." During these I did little drawings of the delegates. For a seat I was usually perched up on a window-sill. It was very amusing to sit there and listen to Clemenceau—"Le Tigre"—putting the fear of death into the delegates of the smaller nations if they talked too long. Apparently, the smaller the nation he represented, the more the delegate felt it incumbent on himself to talk, but after a while, Clemenceau, with the grey gloves whirling about, would shout him down.

President Wilson occasionally rose and spoke of love and forgiveness. Lloyd George just went on working, his secretaries constantly rushing up to him, whispering and departing, only to return for more whispers. Mr. Balfour, whose personality made all the other delegates look common, would quietly sleep. The Marquis Siongi was the only other man who could hold his own at all with Mr. Balfour in dignity of appearance.

As a whole there was just a little mass of black frock-coated figures—"frocks" as we called them—sitting and moving about under the vast decoration of "Le Salon de l'Horloge." Some of the little people seemed excited, but for the most part they looked profoundly bored, yet they were changing the face of the map, slices were being cut off one country and dumped on to another. It was all very wonderful, but I admit that all these little "frocks" seemed to me very small personalities, in comparison with the fighting men I had come in contact with during the war.

They appeared to think so much—too much—of their own personal importance, searching all the time for popularity, each little one for himself—strange little things. President Wilson made a great hit in the Press with his smile. He was pleased at that, and after this he never failed to let you see all his back teeth. Lloyd George grew hair down his back, I presume from Mr. Asquith's lead. Paderewski—well, he was always a made-up job. In short, from my window-seat it was easy to see how self-important the majority of all these little black "frocks" thought themselves. It was all like an opéra bouffe, after the people I had seen, known and painted during the war; and these, as the days went by, seemed to be gradually becoming more and more forgotten. It seemed impossible, but it was true. The fighting man, alive, and those who fought and died—all the people who made the Peace Conference possible, were being forgotten, the "frocks" reigned supreme. One was almost forced to think that the "frocks" won the war. "I did this," "I did that," they all screamed, but the silent soldier man never said a word, yet he must have thought a lot.

I remember when the Peace Terms were handed to the Germans at the Trianon Palace, I tried my hardest to get a card to enable me to see it, but failed. This may not seem strange, but it really was, considering that about half the people who were present were there out of curiosity alone. They were just friends of the "frocks." This ceremony took place at 2.30 p.m. on that particular day. I happened to leave my room and go into the hall of the "Astoria" for something about 3 p.m. There I met Field-Marshal Sir Henry Wilson. I said: "How did you get back so soon, sir?" He said: "Back from where?" I said: "From the handing over of the Peace Terms." "Oh," he said, "I haven't been there. They wouldn't give me a pass, the little 'frocks' wouldn't give me one." "I've been trying for days, sir," I said. "They expect me to paint them, but they won't let me see them." "Look here, little man," he said. "I've been thinking as I was walking back here, and I'll give you a little piece of advice: 'Laugh at those who cry, and cry at those who laugh.' Just go back to your little room and think that over and you will feel better."

When I painted Sir Henry, he gave me his views on the brains and merits of many of the delegates, views full of wit and brilliant criticism, but when I had finished painting him I came under his kindly lash. He called me "a nasty little wasp," and he kept a "black book" for any of his lady friends who said the sketch was like him. In it their names were inscribed, and they were never to be spoken to again. With all his fun, Sir Henry was a deep thinker, and towered over the majority of the "frocks" by his personality, big outlook and clear vision.

General Botha was big, large and great in body and brain— elephantine! Everything on an immense scale, even to his sense of humour. He had no sign of pose, like most of the "frocks." He never

The Rt. Hon. Louis Botha, P.C., LL.D.

seemed to try to impress anyone. One could notice no change in his method or mode of conversation according to whom he was speaking. The great mind just went on and uttered what it thought, regardless of whom it uttered it to. In Mrs. Botha he had the ideal wife. Together they were like two school-children. "Louis" and "Mother," how well they knew each other, and how they loved their family and home! They were always talking of "home" and longing to get back to it. Alas! Louis only got back there for a very short time, and now "home" will never be the same for "Mother."

What arguments they used to have—fierce arguments which always ended the same way! "Louis" would make some remark which would absolutely pulverise "Mother's" side of the question, and as she was stammering to reply, he would say very gently: "It's all right, Mother, it's all right, you've won." And she would flash out with: "Don't you dare to say that to me, Louis! You always say that when you get the best of the argument."

She used to complain to me how terrible the General's love for bridge was, and how she used to be kept up so late. He would laugh and say: "But, Mother, you didn't get up till nine this morning. I was walking in the Bois at half-past six."

I remember one afternoon they came to my room and Mrs. Botha said: "Well, Louis, what kind of a morning had you?" He replied: "Not very good, Mother, not very good. You see, Mother, Clemenceau got very irritated with President Wilson, and Lloyd George the same with Orlando. No, it wasn't a very pleasant morning. Nearly everyone was irritable." Then "Mother" said: "I think it disgusting, Louis, that these men, settling the peace of the world, should allow their own little petty irritabilities to interfere with the great work." And Botha replied: "Ah! Mother, you must make allowances. Men are only human." "I don't make allowances," jerked in "Mother," "I think it's disgusting." "Don't say that, Mother," he replied. "I remember one time, long ago, when we made our little peace, you used to get very irritable at times, and I had to make a lot of allowances for you. You must try and make the same for these poor people now." "Mother" never even replied to this, but jumped from her chair and left the room, and the big man's face broadened into a smile. Yes, Botha was big—a giant among men.

Admiral Lord Wester Wemyss came along. He has a good head for a "Sea Dog." He brought the sea into the heart of Paris with him. A man of great charm, with a wonderful smile, which I did not paint.

I wrote and asked President Wilson to sit, and got a reply saying that as his time was fully occupied with the Peace Conference work, he regretted that he was unable to give any sittings.

I also wrote to Mr. Lansing and Colonel House, asking them. The Colonel rang up the same afternoon and said, "Certainly," would I name my day and hour? Which I did; and along he came, a charming man, very calm, very sure of himself, yet modest. During the sitting he asked me if I had painted the President. I replied: "No." He then

The Rt. Hon. A. J. Balfour. O.M.

asked me if I was going to do so, and I replied: "No," that the President had refused to sit. He said: "Refused?" I said: "Yes; he hasn't got the time." "What damned rot!" said the Colonel, "he's got a damned sight more time than I have. What day would you like him to come to sit?" I named a day, and the Colonel said: "Right! I'll see that he's here," and he did. Mr. Lansing was also very good about giving sittings, and we had a good time, as he loves paintings, and knows all the Art Galleries in Europe. He also paints himself in his spare time, and all through the Conference at the "Quai d'Orsay" he drew caricatures of the different delegates. President Wilson told me he had a large

President Woodrow Wilson.

collection of these.

When Lord Reading sat he had the "'flu," and did not talk, so I got nothing out of him except that he has a very fine head.

The Emir Feisul sat. He had a nice, calm, thoughtful face. Of course, his make-up in garments made one think of Ruth, or, rather, Boaz. He could not let me work for one minute without coming round to see what I was doing. This made the sittings a bit jerky. I was going to paint another portrait of him for his home, but we never hit off times when we were both free.

I asked Mr. Balfour to sit, and he asked me to lunch to arrange it. The subject was never mentioned, but the lunch in the Rue Nito was excellent, and it was a joy to listen to Mr. Balfour. One could also look down into President Wilson's garden, as Mr. Balfour's flat was on the second floor, and one could see over the armed defences and view the American Army on guard outside, with steel helmets and bayonets flashing in the sunlight.

Mr. Balfour did sit in the end. I remember he came to my room about 12.15 p.m. He was sound asleep by 12.35 p.m., but woke up sharp at 1 p.m., and left for lunch. What a head! It put all other heads out of the running. So refined, so calm, so strong, a fitting head for such a great personality.

Dr. E. J. Dillon very kindly asked me to dinner to meet Venezelos, and he arranged for him to sit, which he did at the "Mercèdes Hotel." He had a beautiful head, with far-seeing blue eyes, which had a distinctly Jewish look. It was difficult to paint him, as he had no idea of sitting at all. It was a pity, as he had a wonderful head to paint. His flesh was fresh and rosy like a young boy's.

Da Costa, of Portugal, came along: a bright little man, full of health and energy; and after him that quiet, thoughtful friendly person, Sir Robert Borden, of Canada; even then he looked rather tired and overworked.

General Sykes sat. What a strange head! A sort of mixture between Hall Caine and Shakespeare.

The day arrived when President Wilson was to sit. He was to come at 2 p.m., so I went back to the "Astoria" about 1.30. When I got to the door I found a large strange man ordering all the English motors to go one hundred yards down the Rue Vernet. No British car was allowed to stop closer. When I entered the "Astoria," one of the Security Officers told me that an American detective had been inquiring the direct route the President was to take to my room. I went on into another little room I had, where I kept my paints and things; and there I found two large men sitting in the only two chairs. They took no notice of me, and were quite silent, so I proceeded to get ready. Taking off my belt and tunic, and putting on my painting coat, I started to squeeze out colours, when suddenly in marched an enormous man. He looked all round the room and said in a deep voice: "Is Sir William Orpen here?" "Yes, I'm here," I said. He walked up to me and, towering over me, looked down and said in grave doubt: "Are you Sir William Orpen?" "Yep," I replied, in my best American accent. "Well," he said, "be pleased to dress yourself and proceed to the door and prepare to receive the President of the United States of America." That finished me—I had been worked up to desperate action. So I looked up as fully as I could in his face, and uttered one short, thoroughly English word, but one which has a lot to it. Immediately the two large men and the enormous one left the room in utter silence.

Shortly afterwards the President arrived, smiling as usual; but he was a good sort, and he laughed hard when I told him the story of the detectives. He was very genial and sat well, but even then he was very nervous and twitchy. He told endless stories, mostly harmless, and some witty. I only remember one. A king was informed that all the men in his State were obeying their wives; so he ordered them all before him on a certain day and spoke to them, saying he had heard the fact about their obeying their wives, and he wished to ascertain if it was so. So he commanded, "All men who obey their wives go to my left!" They all went to his left except one miserable little man, who remained where he was, alone. The king turned, and said to him: "Are you the only man in my State who does not obey his wife?" "No, sire," said the little man, "I obey my wife, sire." "Then why do you not go to my left as I commanded?" "Because, sire," said the little man, "my wife told me always to avoid a crush." It's a mild story, but it's the only one I remember. The only other thing I recollect about President Wilson is that he had a great admiration for Lord Robert Cecil.

General Sackville-West came, and we had some peaceful sittings. A very calm, very sad man, but he was kindness itself. Many are the acts for which I have to thank him.

Lord Beatty arrived in Paris. A lunch was given in his honour at the Embassy, after which he came back with me to the "Astoria," and sat. A forceful character! I may be wrong, but I imagine he did not love the "frocks."

George Adam gave a great dinner one night out at some little country place near Paris. Mr. Massey, of New Zealand, and Admiral Heaton Ellis were the two chief people present. Massey was a most pleasant big man, with kind, blue eyes—a simple, honest,

The Marquis Siongi.

straightforward person, large in body and big enough in brain to laugh at himself. He made me feel I was back painting the honest people in the war. He had none of the affectations of the "frocks."

I painted the Marquis Siongi in his flat in the Rue Bassano. There one worked in the calm of the East. People entered the room, people left, but I never heard a sound. The Marquis sat—never for one second did his expression give an inkling of what his brain was thinking about. He never moved; his eyelids never fluttered, and beside me all the time I worked, curled up on a sofa, was his daughter—surely one of the most beautiful women I have ever seen, soft and gentle, with her lovely little white feet. I loved it all. When I left that flat I could not help feeling I was going downstairs to a lower and more common world, a world where passions and desires were thrust upon one's eyes and ears, leaving no room for imagination or wonder. I never pass down the Rue Bassano now that I do not think of the Marquis and those lovely little white feet, the gentle manners and the calm of the East which pervaded those apartments.

General Smuts sat, a strong personality with great love for his own country, and a fearless blue eye. I would not like to be up against him, yet in certain ways he was a dreamer and poet in thought. He loved the people and hated the "frocks." He and I had a great night once at the servants' dance down in the ballroom of the "Majestic." I found him down there during the evening, and he said: "You've got sense, Orpen. There is life down here, but upstairs it's 'just death.'"

Mary was, of course, the "Belle of the Ball." No description of the Peace Conference could be complete without including Mary. One great man said that the most joyous sight he saw in Paris was Mary. Mary doled us out tea and cigarettes in the hall of the "Majestic"— doled them out with a smile of pure health. Mary came from Manchester, yet she made the Parisian girls look pale, pallid and washed out. Her rosy cheeks had a smile for everyone, men and women; one and all loved Mary. She really was the greatest personal success of the Peace Conference. How the people of Manchester must have missed her, and how lucky they are to have her back again!

Another delegate with no affectation was Mr. Barnes, a restful, thoughtful soul. He brought Mrs. Barnes in one afternoon, a charming, quiet lady. They should be painted together as an ideal English couple.

Another good Englishman, Lord Derby, our Ambassador, sat to me. Some day will be known all the good he has done in France. Loved by all, this joyous, bluff, big-hearted Englishman has done great things in keeping friendship and goodwill between the two nations through many anxious moments. One felt better after being at the Embassy and hearing his great laugh. He was not a bit like a "frock"; whether he loved them or not, I don't know. He was far too clever to let me know, but he was too kind-hearted to hurt anybody or anything, and he certainly loved the fighting man—French, English or American.

Mr. Hughes made a big mark at the Conference. He was as deaf as a post, but he had a cutting wit. Many are the good stories told about him, but they are not mine. Clemenceau and he used to have great jokes. Often I have seen them rocking with laughter together, Clemenceau's grey-gloved hands on Hughes' shoulders, leaning over him and shouting into his enormous deaf cars. He came to sit one day with The Times. He said: "Good morning." I asked him to sit in a chair. He sat, read The Times for about an hour and a half, murmured something that I did not catch, got up and left. The next day he rang up and asked if I wished for another sitting. I said: "No, sir," so that was my only personal meeting with Hughes; but I gather he was extremely cute and cunning, which is quite possible from the general make-up of his head.

That warrior, General Carton de Wiart, V.C., came to sit: a man who loved war. What a happy nature! He told me he never suffered any pain from all his wounds except once — mental pain — when he temporarily lost the sight of his other eye, and he thought he might be blind for life. A joyous man, so quiet, so calm, so utterly unaffected. What a lesson to the "frocks"!

Another man of great personal charm was Paul Hymans, of Belgium. He was greatly liked and respected by the British delegates.

CHAPTER XV

PARIS DURING THE PEACE CONFERENCE

SHORTLY after I arrived in Paris I found one could get "Luxury Tax Tickets." I had never heard of a Luxury Tax up North, but it was in force in Paris right enough. So I went to H.Q. Central Area, and inside the door whom should I meet but my one-time "Colonel" of G.H.Q. "Hello!" said he. "What are you doing in Paris?" "Painting the Peace Conference, sir," said I. "Well, what do you want here?" he asked. "I've come for some Luxury Tax Tickets, sir." "To what are you attached now?" he asked. "C.P.G.H.Q., sir," said I. "Well," he said, "if you are attached to G.H.Q. you must go there and get your Luxury Tax Tickets. You can't get them here." "Right, sir," said I. "Will you please sign an order for me to proceed to G.H.Q. to obtain Luxury Tax Tickets and return? and I will start right away, sir." "Well," he said, "perhaps, after all, I will allow you to have some here, as you are working in Paris." "Thank you very much indeed, sir," said I, clicking my heels and saluting. But it was no good, we never could become friends, as I said before.

One afternoon in the hall at the "Astoria" I saw a strange man—a paintable person—and I asked the Security Officers to get him to sit to me. He was a Polish messenger. He came along the next morning, sat down and smoked his silver pipe. I said: "Can you understand any English?" "Yes," said he, in a strong Irish accent, "I can a bit." "But," I said, "you talk it very well. Have you lived in Ireland?" "No," said he, "but I went to the States for about six months some fifteen years or more back, and that's where I picked up the wee bit I have." I began to think he must be de Valera or some other hero in disguise. Perhaps he was.

Field-Marshal Sir Henry Wilson asked me to dine at the "Majestic" one night. In the afternoon I got a telephone message that the place for the dinner had been changed from the "Majestic" to the Embassy. When I reached there I was received by Sir Henry (Lord and Lady

A Polish Messenger.

Derby were also present). He apologised to me for the room being a little cold. At dinner, which was perfect, he found fault and apologised for the food, for the wine, for the waiting—nothing was right. It was great fun. He kept it up all the evening. When saying good-bye to Their Excellencies, he said: "I can't tell you how sorry I am about everything being so bad to-night, but I'll ask you out to a restaurant another night and give you some decent food and drink."

About this time I painted Lord Riddell, who, with George Mair and others, was looking after the interests of the Press. Meetings were held twice a day and news was doled out by Riddell, such news as the P.M.

Lord Riddell.

saw fit that the Press should know. Great was the trouble when George Adam would suddenly burst into print with some news that had not been received through this particular official channel. Adam, having worked in Paris for years, knew endless channels for news that the others had no knowledge of.

Riddell was a great chap, full of energy, full of an immense burning desire for knowledge on every subject, too, in the world. One always found him asking questions, often about things that one would think it was impossible he should take any interest in. He must have a tremendous amount of knowledge stored up in that fine brain of his, for he never forgets, not even little things. He was most kind to us all and was hospitality itself. He personally was a very simple feeder, and he never drank any wine or spirits, but nothing was too good for those he entertained. A lovable man, well worthy of all the honours he has received. He had a great support in his secretary, Mrs. Read, a charming, gracious lady, who probably worked harder during those days than anyone else, except, perhaps, Sir Maurice Hankey.

One night I dined at "Ciro's" with George Adam and some others. I was late when I came in. Before we went into the dining-room, Adam told me to take notice of an English lady who was sitting a couple of tables away from ours. This I did, and I remembered having seen her constantly at the "Berkeley Hotel," London, years before. She was most peculiarly dressed in some sort of stuff that looked like curtains, tall and slim, with a refined, good-looking face, but a somewhat strange look in her eyes. She was with two men. Presently a lady joined the group from another table. Dancing began, and she left with one of the men, danced and came back again. I could not remember her name, so I asked Philippe, who told me she was an English duchess, but he could not remember what she duched over.

After dinner we went out and sat and watched the dancing and I forgot all about her. About eleven o'clock, during a lull between dances, she appeared before me. The moment she appeared two large waiters seized her by the back of the neck and ran her up the dance-hall and threw her out. A strange sight, surely! An English "duchess" being thrown out of a dance-hall in Paris.

Having been given a most excellent dinner by Adam, my feelings were roused at this peculiar treatment of the English aristocracy, so I went over to Philippe and asked him what he meant by this disgraceful behaviour to an English lady. He replied: "The men she was with left an hour ago." "But," said I, "I never saw her behave badly. Why didn't you ask her to leave?" "I did," said he, "but she just patted me on the back, and said, 'Don't let that worry you, old chap.'" Still, my feelings—thanks still to the dinner—were roused, so I went out into the hall to try and find her, as I had noticed she was wearing about twenty thousand pounds' worth of pearls round her neck. Not that I meant to take these, but I hated the thought of someone else doing so, and I wished to see her safely home, but she had gone—vanished! The only thing I learnt was that she was staying at the "Ritz." But when I inquired there they informed me that they were housing no English duchess.

A few days later I was passing the "Hôtel Chatham" and I saw her coming towards me, very well dressed, in white furs this time and the large globes of pearls still round her neck. She walked straight up to me: "I want you to do something for me," she said. I don't remember what I replied, but she said: "Don't be frightened—it's not immoral. I'm not that sort. I just want you to come along with me to 'The Hole in the Wall.'" "Where is it?" I asked. "I don't know," she said. "That's what I want you for. I want you to find 'The Hole in the Wall.'" "I'm sorry, Madam," I said, "I can't do it. I've got an engagement." She wiggled her finger in front of my nose, and said: "Ah, naughty, naughty boy!" and went on her way. I followed at a safe distance. Every man she met, no matter what class or nationality, she stopped, all the way down the boulevard, and asked them to find "The Hole in the Wall" for her.

None did, however, even though she was quite near it all the time, and the last I saw of her was when she disappeared down the steps of Olympia alone. Not quite the place for an English "duchess" to go alone, with twenty thousand pounds' worth of pearls in full view. I wonder who she was and where she is now? Perhaps in "The Hole in the Wall."

About this time I introduced Lord Riddell to Mrs. Glyn, and we had some very amusing out-of-door dinners at Laurent's. During dinner and afterwards, Mrs. Glyn would teach us many things about life, Nature and love: why women lost their lovers; why men did not keep their wives; the correct way to make love; the stupid ordinary methods of the male; what the female expected; what she ought to expect, and what she mostly got. It was all very pleasant, the modulated voice of Elinor under the trees and twinkling stars. Her elocution was certainly remarkable, and Lord Riddell's dinners excellent.

CHAPTER XVI

THE SIGNING OF THE PEACE

THE great day of the signing of the Peace was drawing near, and I worked hard to get the centre window in the Hall of Mirrors reserved for the artists. In the end, the French authorities sanctioned this. They also promised to do a lot more things which would have made the ceremony much more imposing, but these they did not do. It is a strange thought, but surely true, that the French as a nation seem to take, at present, little interest in pomp and ceremony. The meetings of the delegates at the "Quai d'Orsay," the handing over of the Peace Terms to our late enemies, were all rather rough-and-tumble affairs, and, in the end, the great signing of the Treaty had not as much dignity as a sale at Christie's. How different must the performance have been in 1870! One man, at least, was there who knew the difference—Lord Dunraven, who attended both ceremonies.

I drove out in the morning to Versailles with George Mair and Adam, and we all had lunch at the "Hôtel des Reservoirs." When we started to go to the Palace I found they had yellow Press tickets, by which they were admitted by the side gate nearest the hotel; but I had a white ticket, and had to enter by the main front gate. When I went round towards this gate I found that all the way down the square, and further along the road as far as the eye could see, the route was lined with people, about one hundred deep, with two rows of French cavalry in front. These people had all taken their places, and they would not let me through. I thought for sure I was going to miss the show, and the sweat of nerves broke out on me. By great luck I met a French Captain, to whom I, in my very broken French, explained my plight. He was most kind, took my card, made a way through the crowd, explained and showed my card to the military horsemen, and I was let through. Then the sweat began to run. I found myself about three-quarters of a mile away from the entrance to the Palace, all by myself in this human-sided avenue—thousands of people staring at me. I expected every minute to be arrested. Naturally, no one else entered

The Rt. Hon. the Earl of Derby, K.G., etc.

on foot. They all drove up in their cars. Guards at the gates scanned my dripping face, but not a word was uttered to me, no pass was asked for—nothing!

The marble staircase was most imposing, lined on each side by Municipal Guards, but the Hall of Mirrors was pandemonium, a mass of little humans, all trying to get to different places. In the end I got to the centre window. It was empty. I was the first artist to arrive, and very satisfied I was to have got there safely. Suddenly, up walked a French Colonel, who told me to get out. I showed him my card and told him this was the window reserved for artists. He explained that this had been changed, and that the next window was reserved for them, and led me off there. There I found all the French and American artists huddled together. As soon as the Colonel left, I crept back to the centre window. I was turned back again. This creeping to the centre window and being turned back continued till I spoke to M. Arnavon, who advised me to stop in the artists' window till just before the show started, and then to go to the middle window. Just before the beginning there was great excitement. A stream of secretaries came up the Hall, two carrying chairs, and with them two grubby-looking old men. The chairs were placed in the centre window, and the old chaps sat themselves down. They were country friends of Clemenceau's, and he had said that morning that they were to have the centre window, and that artists could go to—somewhere else. When the proceedings commenced I slipped in behind their chairs, and, except for a glare from "Le Tigre," I was left in peace.

Clemenceau rose and said a few words expressing a desire that the Germans would come forward and sign. Even while he was saying these few words the whole hall was in movement—nothing but little black figures rushing about and crushing each other. Then, amidst a mass of secretaries from the French Foreign Office, the two Germans, Hermann Müller and Doctor Bell, came nervously forward, signed, and were led back to their places. Some guns went off on the terrace—the windows rattled. Everyone looked rather nervous for a moment, and the show was over, except for the signatures of the Allies. These were written without any dignity. People talked and cracked jokes to each other across tables. Lloyd George found a friend on his way up to sign his name, and as he had a story to tell him, the whole show was held up for a bit, but after all, it may have been a good story. All the "frocks" did all their tricks to perfection. President Wilson showed his back teeth; Lloyd George waved his Asquithian mane; Clemenceau whirled his grey-gloved hands about like windmills; Lansing drew his pictures and Mr. Balfour slept. It was all over. The "frocks" had won the war. The "frocks" had signed the Peace! The Army was forgotten. Some dead and forgotten, others maimed and forgotten, others alive and well—but equally forgotten. Yet the sun shone outside my window and the fountains played, and the German Army—what was left of it—was a long, long way from Paris.

After seeing some of the great little black-coated ones leave, amidst great cheering, George Mair, Colonel Stroud Jackson and I went to the aerodrome and saw the Press photographs sent off to the waiting crowds in the British Isles. Then back to Paris. Paris was very calm, not the least excited. I remember Mair gave some of us dinner at Ciro's that night. When the band played the Marseillaise, we stood up on our chairs, held hands and sang and cheered, but no one else moved, so in the end we got down, feeling damned fools. It was all rather sad!

The next great show was the triumphal march through the Arc de Triomphe. It was fine! But it must be admitted that the Americans scored. They had picked men trained for months for this march, and along they came in close formation, wearing steel helmets. It was a fine sight!

But there were great moments when Foch passed, and when Haig passed at the head of his men, and the roars that came from the "Astoria" must have been heard a long way off. The "Astoria" was the hotel reserved by the Kaiser for his friends to witness his triumphal entry into Paris, so we had a good view. He chose well.

I remember during the war, when a "frock" visited some fighting zone, he was always very well looked after and entertained by whatever H.Q. he visited, and I was amazed on this day to find Field-Marshal Lord Haig and General Sir John Davidson lunching alone at the "Majestic." Lord Allenby was also lunching at another table and General Robertson at another. To me it was ununderstandable. These representatives of the dead and the living of the British Army, on the day of its glory, being allowed to lunch alone, much as they might have wished it.

As far as I remember, Lord Derby gave a dinner in their honour that evening, but I am certain the "frocks" did nothing. After all, why should they fuss themselves? The fighting was over. The Army was nothing—harmless! Why should they trouble about these men? Why upset themselves and their pleasures by remembering the little upturned hands on the duckboards, or the bodies lying in the water in the shell-holes, or the hell and bloody damnation of the four years and odd months of war, or the men and their commanders who pulled them through from a bloodier and worse damnation and set them up to dictate a peace for the world?

Signing the Peace Treaty.

The war was over, the Germans were a long, long way from the coast or Paris. The whole thing was finished. Why worry now to honour the representatives of the dead, or the maimed, or the blind, or the living that remained? Why? In Heaven's name, why not?

I remember one day, during the Peace Conference in the "Astoria," asking a great English General about the delegates and how things were getting on, and he said: "I wish the little 'frocks' would leave it to us—those who fight know best how to make peace. We would not talk so much, but we would get things settled more quickly and better." Surely that was the truth!

MORE FROM THE SAME SERIES

Most books from the 'Military History from Original Sources' series are edited and endorsed by Emmy Award winning film maker and military historian Bob Carruthers, producer of Discovery Channel's Line of Fire and Weapons of War and BBC's Both Sides of the Line. Long experience and strong editorial control gives the military history enthusiast the ability to buy with confidence. The series advisor is David McWhinnie, producer of the acclaimed Battlefield series for Discovery Channel. David and Bob have co-produced books and films with a wide variety of the UK's leading historians including Professor John Erickson and Dr David Chandler.
Where possible the books draw on rare primary sources to give the military enthusiast new insights into a fascinating subject.

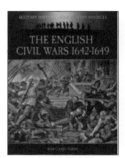
The English Civil Wars

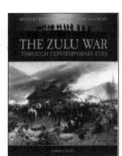
The Zulu Wars

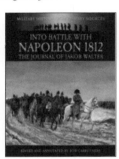
Into Battle with Napoleon 1812

Waterloo 1815

The Anglo-Saxon Chronicle

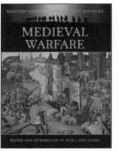
Medieval Warfare

Renaissance Warfare

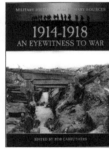
1914-1918

Sea Battles in the Age of Sail

Sun Tzu - The Art of War

Recollections of the Great War in the Air

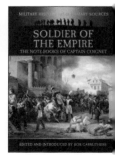
Soldier of the Empire

For more information visit www.pen-and-sword.co.uk